C0-AJQ-569

A Volume in
Research in Management
Education and Development

Rethinking Management Education for the
21st Century

Rethinking Management Education for the 21st Century

Edited by

Charles Wankel
St. John's University

and

Robert DeFillippi
Suffolk University

INFORMATION AGE PUBLISHING

80 Mason Street
Greenwich, Connecticut 06830

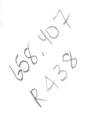

658.407
R438

Library of Congress Cataloging-in-Publication Data

Rethinking management education for the 21st century / edited by
Charles Wankel and Robert DeFillippi.
    p. cm. – (Research in management education and development)
Includes bibliographical references.
  ISBN 1-930608-21-7 – ISBN 1-930608-20-9 (Ppk.)
1. Management–Study and teaching. 2. Business education. I. Wankel,
Charles. II. DeFillippi, Bob. III. Series.
  HD30.4 .R482 2002
  658.4'07124–dc21
         2002008458

Copyright © 2002 Information Age Publishing

All rights reserved. No part of this publication may be reproduced, stored on a
retrieval system, or transmitted, in any form or by any means, electronic, mechani-
cal, photocopying, microfilming, recording or otherwise, without written permis-
sion from the publisher.

Printed in the United States of America

CONTENTS

Section III
Rethinking Management Education for Executives

Section IV
Critical Reflections on Management
Education for the 21st Century

LIST OF CONTRIBUTORS

William P. Anthony	Florida State University, Tallahassee, FL
Elena Antonacopoulou	University of Manchester, Manchester, United Kingdom
Kathy Lund Dean	Idaho State University, Pocatello, ID
Robert DeFillippi	Suffolk University, Boston, MA
Eric B. Dent	University of Maryland University College, Adelphi, MD
Gerald R. Ferris	Florida State University, Tallahassee, FL
Ellen Foster-Curtis	Pennsylvania State University, Malvern, PA
David C. Gilmore	University of North Carolina at Charlotte, Charlotte, NC
Veronica M. Godshalk	Pennsylvania State University, Malvern, PA
Michael G. Harvey	University of Oklahoma, Norman, OK
Robert W. Kolodinsky	James Madison University, Harrisonburg, VA
Anne M. McCarthy	University of Baltimore, Baltimore,MD
Thomas E. Moore	Babson College, Babson Park, MA
Nick Nissley	University of St. Thomas, Minneapolis, MN
Darryl Reed	York University, Toronto, ON, Canada
Sabine Seufert	University of St. Gallen, 9000 St. Gallen, Switzerland
Mary L. Tucker	Ohio University, Athens, OH
Charles Wankel	St. John's University, New York, NY

INTRODUCTION

AT THE OUTSET OF RESEARCH IN MANAGEMENT EDUCATION AND DEVELOPMENT

Charles Wankel and Robert DeFillippi, Editors

This book series focuses on compelling trends in theory and practice likely to influence twenty-first century management education. Each volume will examine an innovative management education and development theme from a variety of empirical and theory-based perspectives and provide insightful analyses and summary lessons learned relevant to both university-based and corporate-based management educators. The book series promotes the discovery and dissemination of innovative theories and best practices.

Anticipated themes of future volumes in the series include assessments of technological innovations in management education, such as those based in Internet technologies and other new media; creating virtual learning communities and advances in distance learning; global differences and trends in management education from a comparative perspective and comparative studies of management education across industries; corporate

Rethinking Management Education for the 21st Century
A Volume in: Research in Management Education and Development, pages ix–xv.
Copyright © 2002 by Information Age Publishing, Inc.
All rights of reproduction in any form reserved.
ISBN: 1-930608-21-7 (cloth), 1-930608-20-9 (paper)

universities and strategic approaches to management development; comparative studies of management curricula; and critical approaches to management education.

Our first volume examines a series of innovative and distinctive approaches to rethinking management education for the 21st century. We have assembled a distinguished international panel of leaders and scholars in management education whose contributions reflect diverse perspectives on management theory and practice. We have organized these perspectives under four themes, each of which contains multiple chapter contributions.

Theme one "Rethinking What We Teach" focuses on specific domains of management education and development. Gerald Ferris and his associates open with their observation that of all the interpersonal skills critical to managerial success, political skill is the most important and often neglected of managerial competencies. Political skill is seen as a unique form of social skill that managers—particularly top managers—must have to influence and control others to achieve organizational objectives. Political skill is conceptualized to include self and social astuteness, influence and control, networking and building social capital, and genuineness/sincerity. Their chapter describes various techniques and training methods for developing and shaping political skill. Particular emphasis is given to drama-based training and executive coaching. Other methods reviewed include assessing oneself through interest and personality inventories, holding critique/feedback sessions, videotaped role-playing with feedback, counseling, leadership training, behavioral modeling, mentoring, and developmental simulations. The authors recommend future research on cross-cultural issues and the political complexities involved in the success of overseas assignments. Such international studies may help determine what aspects of political skill are generalizable across cultures, and which aspects need to be situationally shaped and developed.

Nick Nissley examines how aesthetic epistemology (aesthetic ways of knowing), or arts-based learning, is informing the practice of management education. This chapter discusses arts-based learning in organizations—how artful ways of knowing are being practiced in organizations. His chapter includes a comprehensive literature review and examples of how arts-based learning is being practiced in management education—framed by the art forms of music (e.g., blues, jazz, and orchestra), drama (e.g., theater and cinema), literature (e.g., novels and poetry), visual arts (e.g., corporate art), dance, and storytelling. The growth in arts-based learning in management education is not confined to the United States. Many of the examples noted in this chapter are from the United Kingdom, Australia, and New Zealand. In addition, he explains how the heavily European-influenced theoretical base of organizational aesthetics continues to inform the practice of arts-based learning. As the sharing and documentation of arts-based learning practices continues, Nissley anticipates that arts-based learning will not be the domain of one national culture; but instead, arts-based learning will allow management educators to cross the boundaries of nations and cultures.

Anne McCarthy and associates conclude part one of our volume with their original insights on service learning, which they define as experiential learning in which students directly apply what they are learning in the classroom as they perform service work at a community agency. Service learning can help integrate the university with its community and, in the process, prepare students for productive careers, citizenship, and community involvement. In addition, service learning fulfills the need to link classroom theory to real world practice. The authors review the research literature on how service learning helps integrate theory application, skill acquisition and civic engagement. Their review suggests that service learning always involves an emphasis on intentional learning of theory and skills, and sometimes is designed to bring about a transformation of the service learning student and the recipient and/or community context of the service-learning project. In addition to these conceptual insights and commentary, the chapter offers valuable practical advice on how to incorporate service learning into management course teaching. Hence the chapter authors provide a balanced assessment of both service learning theory and its practice.

Part Two "Rethinking Management Education in Cyberspace" opens with a comparative assessment by Veronica Godshalk and Ellen Foster-Curtis of four different models of distance learning to deliver online MBA curricula to part-time students. They first examine the classical model of online delivery of the college's standard MBA curriculum. This model is illustrated through a case study of the online MBA at Regis University and the chapter authors' own experience at Pennsylvania State University. Next, the authors discuss the educational portal model, which uses a third party website to host a school's online curriculum. This model is examined through the experience of Drexel University in offering a technology based M.B.A. using Ecollege.com as the portal provider. Model three, the tailored training approach, allows the university to offer a specialized curriculum tailored to the needs of a specific corporate client or target market. This model is demonstrated through the case of the University of Tennessee's development of a Physician Executive M.B.A. program. Model four, the university-spin-off, involves the creation of an independent spun-off business venture to create and deliver online M.B.A. programs. This approach is examined in terms of ventures launched by Indiana University and Babson College. The chapter authors carefully review the faculty and curricular issues, technology requirements, and funding and institutional commitment requirements for each model and suggest conditions favoring use of one or another of them.

Sabine Seufert next examines eLearning models of web-based education and web education support services. Her chapter offers a breathtaking, panoramic view of six landscapes for eLearning business models and best practices emerging from both the corporate and academic sectors. These models include Ala Mater Virtualis or traditional university offering of online services, as illustrated by the Wharton Business School; the Virtual University or for-profit online university, illustrated by Phoenix University; the University Network or alliance of university online partners, illustrated by the Singapore-MIT Alliance; the Education Consortium of companies that pool their training resources, as illustrated by Cardean University; the E-Learning Providers model that offer educational portals and support learning communities, illustrated by eMind.com; and the Corporate University that is part of a private corporation, illustrated by Motorola University. Seufert compares these models in terms of their degree of virtuality and degree of cooperation among participants. She also identifies key success factors for each model and concludes with a forecast of major trends impacting eLearning development and their implications for both management education institutions and individual management educators.

Part three "Rethinking Management Education for Executives" opens with Eric Dent's thought-provoking critique of doctoral education and innovative suggestions for developing doctoral programs more attuned to the learning requirements of executive managers seeking doctoral education. Dent's assessment of the current state of doctoral education in the US suggests a strong mismatch with the needs of contemporary business executives for coping with a turbulent business environment, developing critical and multidisciplinary problem solving skills, and managing a complex array of geographically dispersed virtual relationships. Dent next examines how the Doctor of Management Program at University of Maryland University College (where Dent is Executive Director for Doctoral Programs) addresses each of these concerns. The chapter then examines four other doctoral programs (George Washington U., Case Western Reserve U., Cranfield U., and Union Institute), which are focusing upon doctoral education for management executives. Dent argues persuasively why most doctoral programs would benefit greatly from a wholesale introspection and rethinking of the goals and strategies of their programs.

Tom Moore examines competition within the market for executive education and observes how three sets of rivals have enjoyed distinctive market place perceptions. Universities are the "thought leaders," consulting firms enjoy the advantage of scalability and global reach, and corporate universities are best suited for aligning executive education with the strategic goals of client organizations. However, a fourth set of competitors, namely the for-profit online education ventures created by universities and their business schools are beginning to reshape the competitive landscape. Moore, executive director for Babson College's for-profit online executive education, provides an insider's perspective on the emerging market for online executive education and the competitive responses by a variety of American universities (Babson, Cornell, Duke, NYU, Temple and UMUC) offering online executive education programs. Moore concludes that the creation of for-profit online executive education subsidiaries maintains and projects to a larger population the university's thought leadership through the power of the web. Moreover, online executive education offerings increase the global reach, technology, and cycle time of university programs and thus enhance their competitive position in relation to consulting firms and corporate universities.

Part four "Critical Reflections on Management Education for the 21st Century" opens with Elena Antonacopoulou's penetrating critique of commercialization, digitization and corporatization trends in management education. She examines how these trends promote a view of management education as a commodity. The rise of corporate universities (emphasized in both parts two and part three of this volume) is viewed as furthering each of these trends in management education. Moreover, she views these trends as confusing training with learning. She also observes that training does not always imply learning because the expectations of the individual from training are often subordinated to the expectations of the organization. In place of training, Antonacopoulou advocates an ideology of education based on the Greek concept of paideia, or the cultivation of each individual's natural, in-born potential in every domain of social activity. She forcefully advocates that management education should stand for the development/nurturing of managers who accept responsibility for the decisions they make and the impact of those decisions on the public good.

Darryl Reed closes our volume by examining how the processes of globalization and their effects should be incorporated into management education. Reed compares Habermasian critical theory with mainstream management education approaches to positive analysis (social sciences), normative analysis (ethics, political philosophy) and strategic analysis (management, public policy) of international business practices and processes. Reed's pedagogical conclusions from these analyses include the need for business ethics courses to move beyond individualistic ethical theory and incorporate normative political theory (including issues of international relations) as tools for addressing issues of fairness in international business practices. He insists that management educators and management education students need to evaluate the legitimacy and fairness of the political and economic institutions and policies that determine how business is conducted and regulated. In order for students to carry out such analyses Reed recommends critical perspectives be introduced across the entire management education curriculum as part of a comparative approach that includes both a critical micro and macro level understanding of how to affect socially responsible change in a global economy.

In reflecting on this volume, we are cognizant of several underlying values that account for the diverse views and perspectives represented by the chapter contributors. It is not the intention of *Research in Management Edu-*

cation and Development to promote a unified canonical view of its subject matter. Rather, we seek to reflect the diversity and at times conflicting perspectives that knowledgeable corporate and university based management educators hold on a given subject. Hence, in the present volume, you will need to decide for yourself whether you are more sympathetic to the positive analysis of corporate universities suggested in separate chapters by Sabine Seufert and Tom Moore, or whether you are more heedful of the critical analysis of corporate universities articulated in the chapter by Elena Antonacopoulou. Similarly, you may choose between Darryl Reed's call for a more politically critical perspective in management education or Eric Dent's advocacy of a more pragmatic and action-oriented approach to doctoral education. This volume and future volumes will provide both positive and normative analyses of management education issues.

Another value reflected in the current volume is our belief in a holistic approach to management education. Part one of this volume thus attends to the needs for political calculation and savvy (Ferris et. al), aesthetic inspiration (Nissley), and social action (McCarthy et al.). These are not mutually exclusive choices but rather supplementary facets of a more holistic view of management education, and we sincerely hope you will find value in all three perspectives and devise means to integrate them into your management education practice.

A third value reflected in this volume is our embrace of technological innovation as a tool to enhance management education. The present volume explicitly addresses the role that web-based technology can play in promoting improved doctoral education (Dent), executive education (Moore), MBA education (Godshalk and Foster-Curtis) and international education (Seufert). It is our hope that future volumes will address other technological innovations, such as computer simulation and virtual reality in promoting superior management education.

A fourth value reflected in this volume is our commitment to internationalizing management education theory and practice. As American educators with extensive international teaching portfolios, we have grown to appreciate the diversity of perspectives on management education that are not rooted in the US. As a result, this volume includes distinctive contributions from Cypriote (Antonacopoulou), Swiss (Seufert) and Canadian (Reed) contributors, whose perspectives at least partly reflect their internationally diverse roots. We plan to further expand the international boundaries of our contributors in future volumes in the hope of broadening our horizons and yours on management education.

A fifth value reflected in this volume is our commitment to both theory and practice. We have demanded that all our chapter contributors address both the theoretical foundations of their management domain and its practical implications. Although some chapters may have a somewhat greater emphasis on either theory or practice, we firmly believe that both are important and each adds value to the other.

Lastly, this volume acknowledges but possibly under-represents the value of both academicians and practitioners in providing useful perspectives on management education and development. Although our contributors include an Executive Director for Doctoral Programs (Eric Dent) and a second executive director for Executive Education (Tom Moore), the contributors to our first volume are primarily academicians with outstanding international reputations within their fields of management practice. However, these academics have also practiced what they preach in applying their ideas as educators and consultants. We would like in future volumes to include contributions from outstanding corporate education and corporate training executives and practitioners and to open a greater management education dialog with for-profit vendors of management education innovations.

This volume is a beginning. We have attempted to be as explicit as possible about our underlying values and their expression in the contents and contributors. And, as we rethink management education for the 21st century, we hope to share our journey with you in future volumes of this book series.

SECTION I

RETHINKING WHAT WE TEACH

CHAPTER 1

DEVELOPMENT OF POLITICAL SKILL

Gerald R. Ferris, William P. Anthony, Robert W. Kolodinsky, David C. Gilmore, and Michael G. Harvey

Continuous improvement in skills is required if managers are to be effective in today's highly complex and dynamic environmental conditions. Given that interpersonal skills become more critical as managers move up the hierarchy in organizations, perhaps the most important competency required in mobilizing workers to produce peak performance is political skill. Political skill is seen as a unique form of social skill that managers—particularly top managers—must have to influence and control others to achieve organizational objectives. Politically skilled managers are astute in understanding social situations, genuine and sincere in their interpersonal interactions, effectively influence others to follow their lead, and adeptly build social capital. While some individuals seem to naturally have such skill, most of us have to develop it. This chapter describes various techniques and training methods for developing and shaping one's political skill. Particular emphasis is given to two rising stars in the training world, drama-based training and executive coaching.

Rethinking Management Education for the 21st Century
A Volume in: Research in Management Education and Development, pages 3–25.
Copyright © 2002 by Information Age Publishing, Inc.
All rights of reproduction in any form reserved.
ISBN: 1-930608-21-7 (cloth), 1-930608-20-9 (paper)

For nearly a century, behavioral scientists have been interested in understanding interpersonal influence and effectiveness as it transpires in both general social situations as well as in organizational settings. In 1912, Dale Carnegie offered his first course on "effective speaking and human relations," and later went on to publish his best-selling book *How to Win Friends and Influence People* (Carnegie, 1936), which was at one time second only to the Bible in nonfiction books sold in the United States (*New York Times,* 1955). As early as 1920, Thorndike coined the term "social intelligence" to refer to the ability to understand others and act appropriately in social situations (e.g., Thorndike, 1920). Subsequently, scholars have developed other influential social skill-related constructs including practical intelligence, emotional intelligence, and interpersonal intelligence, which are now widely viewed as important extensions beyond the previously narrow focus on cognitive mental ability as the primary key to success in life. In fact, some scholars now believe that interpersonal effectiveness is a primary determinant of an individual's success in organizational settings. For example, Fry and Pasmore (1981) stated that "how well an executive manages relationships with others politically and interpersonally is a primary determinant of his or her success" (p. 277).

This focus on interpersonal effectiveness is particularly relevant in organizational settings as we have tried to increase our understanding of phenomena such as leadership, interpersonal influence, and career success. However, while research in these areas has increased dramatically during the past several decades, much is still unknown, particularly in how interpersonal effectiveness actually transpires (e.g., House & Aditya, 1997). Indeed, one of the foremost authorities in the area of interpersonal influence suggested that for all we have learned about forms of influence, we know next to nothing about the components of interpersonal " *style*" (Jones, 1990). While various writers have addressed interpersonal style issues under such rubrics as *political skill, savvy,* and *street smarts, political skill* is the one construct that has emerged as the sole social competence component developed to explicitly address social influence skills in work settings (e.g., Ferris, Perrewé, Anthony, & Gilmore, 2000; Perrewé, Ferris, Frink, & Anthony, 2000).

Whereas political skill is believed to be partly dispositional, we also view it as a competency that can substantially be shaped or developed. However, to date, no systematic efforts have been made to propose the precise ways to go about developing political skill. The purpose of this chapter is to address this need, and we do so by discussing the different dimensions or facets of political skill and the most appropriate training and development methods for shaping and developing each. Furthermore, we carefully examine executive coaching as a development technique ideally suited to shaping political skill.

POLITICAL SKILL IN ORGANIZATIONS

A perspective shared by many organizational scientists is that organizations are inherently political arenas (Mintzberg, 1985). Furthermore, there is evidence that organizations are changing so as to place a premium on social interaction, orchestration of individual efforts toward team outcomes, and so forth. In this regard, it is assumed that performance, effectiveness, and career success are determined only in part by cognitive mental ability and hard work, but as much or even more by social astuteness, positioning, and savvy. Indeed, many scholars in this area have argued that the way to get ahead in organizations is to build social and political competence (e.g., DeLuca, 1992; Mintzberg, 1983; Pfeffer, 1981). For example, Mainiero (1994) argued that political skill is a vital component contributing to women's career advancement, and Jackall (1988) implicitly made reference to political skill in his discussion of the importance of style in managerial effectiveness.

The research of Ferris and his colleagues (Ferris, Russ, & Fandt, 1989; Ferris, Bhawuk, Fedor, & Judge, 1995) has focused on the demonstration of political behavior in organizations. However, they noted that a serious omission has been the failure to examine the political skill of the actor or influencer, leaving us ill-informed about why political behavior is or is not successful (Ferris, Fedor, & King, 1994). It is not enough to study the particular influence tactics or political behaviors that reflect the "what" of influence; that is, what types of influence tactics are being used. We also need to critically examine the political skill of the influencer in order to understand the style used to carry out influence attempts; that is, the "how" of influence. Among other issues, political skill allows influencers to effectively manage attributions of intentionality and to disguise self-serving opportunistic motives (Ferris et al., 1995) historically regarded as the ultimate objectives of influence attempts (e.g., Jones, 1990).

By design, our initial conceptualization contends that the political skill construct is not totally dissimilar from other previously outlined interpersonal effectiveness constructs. Instead, we view political skill as similar in some ways to related conceptualizations of social, emotional, and practical intelligence, and to other notions of interpersonal style (e.g., "savvy" and "street smarts," e.g., Sternberg, 1997). For example, Komitzki and John (1993) identified several qualities underlying the concept of social intelligence including understanding people, being warm and caring, being open to new experiences, knowing social rules, and having social adaptability. Goleman (1995) related emotional intelligence to abilities such as effectively controlling impulse, delaying gratification, regulating moods, and the ability to empathize with others. Attempting to identify strategies of effective managers/organizational politicians, Jackall (1988) reported the following actor characteristics:

1. mastery of public faces; enabling situationally appropriate behavior;
2. ability to read and conform to social situations; enabling self and social adaptation; and
3. self control of emotion, expression, etc. to convey proper image (pp. 46-47).

However, Jackall (1988) suggested that, more than just descriptive characteristics, it is style that truly differentiates effective and ineffective managers.

Another related area of study is social skill. Argyle (1969) suggested that social skill is reflected in the effective exercise of persuasion, explanation, and other influence mechanisms that reveal the ability to control others. Furthermore, Meichenbaum, Butler, and Gruson (1981) noted that social skill reflects the capacity and knowledge of both what to do and when to display certain behaviors, in addition to possessing behavioral control and flexibility. Kilduff and Day (1994) found that social astuteness of managers contributed significantly to their career success. The program of research at the Center for Creative Leadership on "management derailment" has identified lack of social or interpersonal skills as one of the leading causes of this problem (Van Velsor & Leslie, 1995). Additionally, Baron and Markman (2000) argued that social understanding and influence skills, combined with network-building or social capital enhancement, were fundamental to the success of entrepreneurs.

Our analysis of the related literature, along with our own notions, indicate that the political skill construct intersects the domains of social, emotional, and practical intelligence, self-monitoring, personality characteristics, interpersonal skills, intuition, and style, essentially incorporating small pieces of each, as applied to behavior in the workplace (e.g., Ferris, Perrewé, et al., 2000). Thus, we view political skill as an interpersonal style construct, which combines interpersonal perceptiveness or social astuteness with the capacity to adjust one's behavior to different and changing situational demands in a manner that inspires trust, confidence, and genuineness, and effectively influences and controls the responses of others.

We would suggest that people high in political skill not only know precisely what to do in different social situations, but exactly how to do it with a sincere, engaging manner that disguises any ulterior motives and inspires believability, trust, and confidence, and renders the influence attempt successful. This does not simply involve the demonstration of particular behaviors that might be regarded as contributing to effective interpersonal interactions. Instead, political skill allows people to create synergy among discrete behaviors that transcend the simple sum of the parts to realize a set of interpersonal dynamics and effective execution that enables individuals to reach higher levels of personal and career success (Ferris, Perrewé, et al., 2000). Consequently, we view effective political skill as a source of sustained personal competitive advantage which is rare, adds value, is difficult to imitate, and cannot be substituted (Barney, 1991). In addition, political skill has been suggested to build resistance and protection in individuals, and essentially serve as an antidote to the dysfunctional consequences of stress, particularly for managers and executives (Perrewé et al., 2000).

DIMENSIONS OF POLITICAL SKILL

Implicit in our discussion above is the acknowledgment that political skill is a multidimensional construct, made up of several distinctive yet somewhat related components. Indeed, recent efforts to psychometrically establish and validate the political skill construct have confirmed that it reflects the four underlying dimensions of self and social astuteness, interpersonal influence/control, network-building, and genuineness/sincerity (Ferris, Kolodinsky, Hochwarter, & Frink, 2001).

Self and Social Astuteness

This political skill dimension has a strong relationship with the literatures in self-monitoring (e.g., Snyder & Gangestad, 1986), interpersonal perception (e.g., Jones, 1990), social intelligence (e.g., Thorndike, 1920), practical intelligence (e.g., Sternberg, 1997), self-presentation (e.g., Leary, 1995), emotional stability (e.g., Barrick & Mount, 1991), and emotional intelligence (e.g., George, 2000; Goleman, 1995). Individuals possessing political skill are astute observers of others and are keenly attuned to diverse social situations. They comprehend social interactions easily and accurately interpret their behavior, as well as that of others, in social settings. They are keenly aware of their surroundings, have strong powers of discernment, and can shrewdly adapt their behavior to individuals as well as groups. They are often seen as ingenious, even clever, in dealing with others. While not necessarily seen as social chameleons, highly politically skilled people nonetheless are quite capable of appropriately adapting their behavior to each social situation and to changing situational demands. In summary, politically skilled people have an accurate understanding of social situations, as well as the interpersonal interactions that take place in these settings.

Interpersonal Influence/Control

While this political skill dimension is related to many content areas, perhaps its strongest ties are to the various literatures on influence and impression management (e.g., Giacalone & Rosenfeld, 1989), power and power tactics (e.g., French & Raven, 1959), and leadership (e.g., Yukl, 1998). Politically skilled people have a strong and convincing personal style that tends to exert a powerful influence on those around them. They appear to others as being socially skilled, and they use such skill to control their environments. Politically skilled individuals are adept at recognizing and using the appropriate influence tactics for a given situation. Masters of the quid pro quo, they are often highly skilled negotiators and dealmakers, and adept at conflict management. Although these individuals are not always overtly political, they are seen as competent leaders who play the political game fairly and effortlessly. This facile political style is seen as a positive, rather than negative, force within the organization. In summary, people who are highly politically skilled are influential and are able to effortlessly control important socio-organizational situations.

Network Building/Social Capital

Related literatures for this political dimension can be found in structural and relational embeddedness (e.g., Granovetter, 1973), social capital theory (e.g., Nahapiet & Ghoshal, 1998), and in work on human capital (e.g., Loury, 1977). Individuals with strong political skills are adept at developing and using diverse networks of people. The literature supports this notion (e.g., Baron & Markman, 2000). For example, Luthans, Hodgetts, and Rosenkrantz (1988), in their examination of successful managers, found networking to be, by far, the most dominant activity on which these managers spent time. In their study, networking activities included behaviors of interacting with outsiders and socializing/politicking, or the use of social and political skills to get ahead. People in these networks tend to hold assets seen as valuable and necessary for successful organizational functioning. By the sheer force of their typically charismatic personalities, politically skilled people tend to easily develop friendships and build strong, beneficial alliances and coalitions. Politically skilled individuals enjoy a favorable social identity among those in their network, resulting in significant and tangible benefits, such as gaining favorable reactions to one's ideas, enhanced access to important information, and increased cooperation and trust (e.g., Baron & Markman, 2000). They know when to call on others for favors, and are perceived as willing to reciprocate in kind. In addition, they inspire commitment and personal obligation from those around them. In short, politically skilled people are perceived as having high levels of social capital.

Genuineness/Sincerity

Lending credibility to the efficacy of this political skill dimension are the related literatures on interpersonal trust (e.g., Boon & Holmes, 1991), emotional intelligence (e.g., George, 2000; Goleman, 1995), impression management (e.g., Giacolone & Rosenfeld, 1989), self-monitoring (e.g., Snyder & Gangestad, 1986), and self-presentation (e.g., Leary, 1995). Those possessing political skill appear to others as having high integrity, authenticity, and sincerity. They are, or appear to be, honest, open, and forthright. Because their actions are never seen as manipulative or coercive, politically skilled employees inspire trust and confidence in and from those around them. Their tactics are often seen as subtle and their motives do not appear self-serving. Rather, people around them believe their motives are pure and honest. They are quite capable of disguising ulterior motives when deemed necessary. Others would not describe them as hypocritical. Instead, they appear to others as being straight shooters who are exactly what they claim to be. In sum, highly politically skilled people appear to others to be congruent, sincere, and genuine.

The description of political skill and its dimensions might appear to suggest that this is inherently a purely dispositional construct, with politically skillful people believed to be born, not made. We do not believe that to be entirely the case. Certainly, we regard political skill as being partly dispositional whereby some are naturally predisposed to reflect facility in this area. But, we also believe that there is much about political skill that can be acquired by individuals through careful shaping and development. Precisely how this shaping and development takes place is the focus of the remainder of this chapter.

SHAPING AND DEVELOPMENT OF POLITICAL SKILL

While our formal education teaches us specific content-related knowledge and skills, it does a poor job in helping individuals learn the skills needed to interact effectively with others. Even corporate training programs focused specifically on developing interpersonal skills often fall short in part because the learning environment is not entirely safe, thus discouraging risk-taking (Fry & Pasmore, 1981). Transfer of training, defined as "the effective and continuing application of newly acquired skills on the job" (May & Kahnweiler, 2000, p. 353), continues to be a critically important issue for organizations (e.g., Broad, 1997). This is especially true since organizations have come to realize that inadequate transfer of training can result in largely wasted training investments, particularly in "soft skills" management training areas such as interpersonal communications and negotiating (e.g., Broad & Newstrom, 1992; Georges, 1996). According to a widely respected transfer of training framework (Baldwin & Ford, 1988), effective transfer must take into account such factors as trainee characteristics, training design, work environment, and learning retention. If learning retention and increased behavioral flexibility are to occur, one must design and implement training that provides a good match between trainee characteristics and the environment in which they work. Our recommendations for developing political skill are made with this transfer of training framework in mind.

By its very nature, political skill appears to represent the type of competencies that defy conventional classroom training and education. Therefore, we believe that more traditional content-oriented training methods will play a secondary role in favor of more active, experiential, involvement-related, and process-oriented techniques. Ferris, Perrewé, et al. (2000) made an initial, but only limited, effort to discuss the ways we might try to develop political skill. In the remainder of this chapter, we make a more focused and detailed effort to articulate the training and development methods that need to be employed to most effectively build, shape, and enhance political skill.

An initial consideration here is to attempt to establish as specific a focus as possible to the target skills or competencies to be developed. In so doing, we believe it is best to focus on the behaviors and skills that are reflected in the four different dimensions or components of political skill, and on the accompanying training and development methods most appropriate for building such competencies. As later shown, many of these exercises and activities concurrently aid in the development of more than one political skill dimension. The first technique to be reviewed, drama-based training, is particularly useful in developing each of the four dimensions. Then, various techniques targeted for specific political skill dimensions are covered next. Next, executive coaching is suggested to "bring it all together" as a premier method for developing outstanding political skill in top managers.

Drama-Based Training

In a *New York Times* article more than a decade ago, Drake (1987) reported that a new type of training for managers and executives was taking place and involved taking acting classes. This early interest has turned into an industry, with many hundreds of companies turning to a drama-based alternative form of training to educate and train both employees and managers (St. George, Schwager, & Canavan, 2000). According to St. George et al. (2000), today's training, more than ever before, needs to be compelling, realistic, practical, relevant, and lasting. In addition, training should encourage risk-taking and facilitate improved awareness and behavioral flexibility. They suggest a new paradigm for organizational training, drama-based training, as a "contextual training model that includes lifelike simulations for participants to practice managing complex human interactions in a safe and controlled learning environment" (p. 15). In drama-based training, the focus is on the delivery of behaviors in a convincing way, through emotion regulation and control, nonverbal cues, tone of voice inflexion, and so forth. Given that "people skills" have become more critical to personal and organizational success than ever before, training to build such skills needs to be more absorbing for participants, and thus implies a search for techniques that go beyond the limitations of conventional training methods (St. George et al., 2000).

Such efforts and building skill through dramaturgical approaches seem to possess the requisite power and rea-lism to build and shape political skill through embedding the trainee in a realistic role that simulates the day-to-day social interactions one encounters at work. St. George et al. (2000) offer various levels of drama-based training contingent upon the goals of the training. For example, if increased awareness about a particular work-related issue (e.g., sexual harassment; unethical work practices) is the goal, low-impact drama-based training with scripted scenes or vignettes supporting the training content can be used to reach large audiences in relatively short periods of time. As with low-impact training, moderate-impact drama-based training helps increase awareness but also involves audience participation (e.g., asking questions; small-group work) in order to explore each audience members' own thoughts, emotions, and motivations pertaining to the training content. Perhaps the most effective form of drama-based training is high-impact training, a program that is staged by trainers (not actors, as in the low- and moderate-impact forms) and real organizational members themselves. High-impact drama-based training is highly customized, targeted, improvisational, context-focused, and flexible, geared to helping real organizational members learn new skills in an experiential manner. In this type of training, trainees become actively involved in the training content, "not as a role-play but in his or her professional capacity, participating directly as a factfinder and potential agent of change" (St. George et al., 2000, p. 18).

High-impact drama-based training is particularly effective for developing interpersonal skills, especially political skill. Like the other drama forms, it is very effective in increasing awareness that aids self and social astuteness. Unlike the other forms, it involves the trainees as active participants in real work issues and in their same occupational capacities. Its content can also be targeted explicitly for developing specific political skill dimensions. For example, to help develop the astuteness, influence, and genuineness dimensions, vignettes can be scripted to help engage participants in a drama involving various ways to influence a peer to work late one evening. Cues would be subtly suggested that the peer (an experienced trainer in this case) does not want to work late, but would do so if an adequate *quid pro quo* offer would be extended. However, the peer might continue to give subtle cues (e.g., "I was thinking about going to a ballgame" or "Tonight's not the best night for me to work late"), but waits for the trainee to make such an offer.

At any stage during the drama, the "reality" can be frozen and questions asked of the trainee about current thought processes, alternatives considered, and emotions felt. Without giving answers but rather encouraging deeper thinking and alternative ways of behaving, the drama can then continue until the trainer believes that the trainee has been stretched in previously unconsidered ways. When trainees finally realize in this vignette that they have to "give something to get something," and do so in a genuine way, the influence transaction more easily transpires. Similar vignettes can be scripted to focus on building networks (e.g., developing a high-powered team for an ad hoc project that requires after-hours work) or improving one's genuineness or sincerity (e.g., dealing with a co-worker's loss of a close family member).

A drama example provided by St. George et al. (2000) "revealed to the participant that it was not *what* she was saying but *how* she was delivering the message that was making all the difference" (p. 18, italics in original). As stated earlier, the knowledge of influence tactics is not enough to effectively carry out influence attempts. Drama is particularly effective at training participants' alternative *styles of delivery* to affect change. As such, drama-based training, especially the high-impact variety, is particularly helpful in developing political skill.

In addition to drama-based training and coaching (described later), other useful techniques can be effectively used to develop political skill. In this next section, various techniques are offered as targeted interventions for developing each of the individual components of political skill.

Developing Self and Social Astuteness

Effective techniques to develop self and social astuteness must provide participants with feedback about their social interactions, including their level of awareness in social situations, about how well they understand such situations, and about multiple behavioral response alternatives. In addition to drama-based training and coaching, there are a number of other training and developmental methods that can enhance self and social astuteness. These include interest and personality inventories, critique/feedback sessions, videotaped role-playing with feedback, and counseling.

Interest and Personality Inventories
The Meyers-Briggs Type Indicator (MBTI; Consulting Psychologists Press, 2000), the Keirsey Temperament Sorter (Keirsey, 1997), the NEO-PI

R (Big Five) personality inventory (Costa & McCrae, 1992), and other similar personality and interest self-diagnostic inventories help an individual understand their own personality makeup and traits, particularly as they are compared to others with differentiated personality types. They typically are easy and quick to take, offering nearly immediate feedback to the participant. For example, the Keirsey Temperament Sorter is on-line and free, with immediate scoring and explanations for all temperament types. Such diagnostic tools can help sort out, for example, differences in such traits as extraversion, desire for social interaction, need for power, decision-making style, and other factors related to political skill. These are especially helpful if they are accompanied by group discussion that allows individuals to explore and get feedback from others.

Critique/Feedback Sessions

Critique or feedback sessions can range from 360-degree feedback and evaluation sessions to one-on-one sessions with the individual's boss. If such interactions are positive, constructive, and developmental as opposed to negative and personal, they can be very effective in assisting individuals in understanding their strengths and weaknesses, as well as in diagnosing improvement areas needed for enhancing interpersonal effectiveness. Moreover, these sessions can significantly aid in increasing one's awareness of, for example, behaviors that are seen as too assertive or, alternatively, too meek for certain situations. As such, the sessions themselves become a source of valuable data to both the providers and receivers of the feedback. Much real-world learning about how to deal with others can take place in such sessions, since they are often rich in emotionally-charged content for all participants. In addition, if politically skilled individuals are participating, they represent an opportunity to model appropriate behaviors and skills to the other participants.

Videotaped Role-Playing with Feedback

Another method to develop social awareness and to ultimately learn more astute ways of interacting with others is to videotape role-play sessions, ideally with real organizational members who have various levels of social astuteness. As individuals' role play difficult interpersonal dilemmas faced on the job, they obtain a better understanding of the skills needed to be effective. These skills are made even more salient when the role-play is videotaped and played back for class critique. For example, one of your authors regularly uses a role-play simulation whereby a manager has to counsel a young subordinate who is frequently absent. The subordinate is a very good employee and is a single mother with small children who are frequently ill. The feedback is especially useful if there are single mothers in the critique group who can lend their perspective. The point of the role play is to teach problem- solving and interpersonal skills to assist the subordinate in developing viable solutions to her absenteeism problem. An important byproduct of such role-play sessions is that individuals become more aware of both their own social behavior and of various responses from those with whom they are interacting. Stopping the video-tape and providing feedback at critical junctures allows participants to assess other behavioral response alternatives that they can draw upon in the future.

Counseling

One of the most effective ways to develop awareness and behavioral flex-ibility is to become involved with regular counseling sessions with a coun-seling professional. Such sessions can be one-on-one with a counselor or in a group format. Group counseling can be facilitated by one or more pro-fessional counselors, and ideally with other individuals dealing with similar issues. One advantage of counseling when compared to some of the other activities and exercises mentioned is that the confidential nature of such sessions provides participants with a safer environment in which they can more easily share troubling issues. Effective counseling usually takes place only after many sessions, but often results in very effective ways of dealing with self and others.

Developing Interpersonal Influence/Control

Perhaps more here than for the other three dimensions, developing skills to influence and ultimately control the behaviors of others (as man-agers need to effectively do) will require experience in multiple training methods in order for greater understanding of each unique situation and behavioral flexibility to occur. Some of the same techniques used for the self and social astuteness dimension are effective for this component as well, and include critique/feedback sessions, and videotaped role-play with feedback. In addition to those techniques already mentioned, other partic-ularly effective techniques for increasing one's influence skills include leadership training, behavioral modeling, mentoring, and developmental simulations.

Leadership Training

Sometimes called human relations training, leadership-training experi-ences have been popular since the 1950s. Many business schools and con-sulting organizations offer a variety of these programs, often firmly grounded in established leadership theories (Yukl, 1998). Such programs typically involve such activities as case analysis, role-playing, problem solv-ing, and communication exercises. The idea is to concentrate on the skills needed by an effective leader: communication, empathy, goal setting, coaching, and other issues related to influencing others. Ultimately, the most effective leaders have followers who willingly and enthusiastically work to help achieve the vision, goals, and priorities set by the leader. Helping develop managers into leaders is a primary focus of such programs, in which learning how to effectively influence others is a primary goal.

Behavioral Modeling

Based on Bandura's (1986) social learning theory and often included as part of overall leadership training, behavioral modeling is perhaps the primary interpersonal skills training technique used in business today (May & Kahnweiler, 2000; Russ-Eft, 1997), and its efficacy for training effectiveness has been widely validated (e.g., Burke & Day, 1986; Harrison, 1992). In behavioral modeling, experts demonstrate the proper way to exercise particular skills, typically in a role-play format. Once the new skills are modeled, effective transfer of training to obtain optimal skill acquisition, generalization, and maintenance will typically occur only with repeated practice by participants (May & Kahnweiler, 2000). Because behavioral repetition is an important key to permanently increasing one's behavioral flexibility, the most effective behavioral modeling programs require participants to practice the newly learned skills. We suggest that the best way to practice influencing others is to use the new skills in any social setting in which an influence situation occurs, regardless of whether it is in the workplace or not.

Behavioral modeling methods can be effectively used in combination with drama-based training techniques in developing powerful political skill development programs. The following example is illustrative of ways in which these techniques can be combined to develop influence skills. Initially, trainers might explain the definition of political skill to the trainees, with particular emphasis on the four dimensions. Then the trainers (or actors) could act out a vignette concerning how a common problem is handled poorly (i.e., with little or no political skill) and then handled effectively (i.e., with high political skill). For example, there's a subordinate (played by a trainer) who is perceived to have excellent potential, but has yet to live up to that potential by performance review time. A supervisor (played by a trainer) with low political skill might come on too strong by focusing solely on that poor performance and by asserting his/her authority with threats (e.g., insisting that such performance will not be tolerated for much longer). Discussion can follow the "negative" role play.

Then, a role-play for the same situation is performed with a trainer playing a highly politically skilled "supervisor." In this more "positive" role play, the supervisor can demonstrate expert use of two or more of the political skill dimensions. For example, an astute supervisor might first ask the subordinate's views on the subordinate's own performance. In many cases, the subordinate will already know that he/she are performing poorly, and will express a desire to do better, perhaps even offering solutions for improved performance. After hearing the subordinate's views, the supervisor can then adapt his/her approach to each subordinate. For example, for subordinates who appear to be devastated by their own poor performance, the trainer can model good political skill by offering feedback on subordinates' comments (i.e., to show that he/she was listening intently), and by telling subordinates to not be too hard on themselves. With this new information (i.e., that the subordinate is devastated already), supervisors can choose to use a more soft-handed influence approach (e.g., use of reason versus assertiveness) in advising subordinates on ways to improve performance. Moreover, supervisors might refer a potential mentor from their social network in order to help subordinates work on areas that need strengthening. Throughout the role play, trainees are encouraged to take notes and ask questions. After the role-plays are finished with the actors (i.e., trainers), trainees can then be matched with other trainees and practice the newly learned skills with real issues facing them in their organizations.

Mentoring

Assigning individuals to work with skilled mentors is another important way to develop influence skills. Individuals can observe professionals in real work situations as they exercise influence in meetings with subordinates and peers. Language, facial expressions, body posture, and gestures will convey messages to observers as to how influence is best exercised. The keys are to be sure that individuals are assigned to talented and understanding mentors who have plenty of social influence interactions, and are given plenty of opportunities to discuss various social influence interactions encountered. Hence, effective mentors not only model effective influence behaviors so that proteges learn by observation, but also take time to discuss various social interactions so that proteges can more fully understand how and why mentors acted in such a manner.

Developmental Simulations

Placing individuals in work-related situations where they must exercise influence in a simulation activity can be very effective learning experiences, especially if followed by a discussion and critique by peers. For example, suppose that one must deal with a very smart but very disagreeable computer programmer. While the firm depends very heavily on this individuals' superior work, his sour attitude negatively affects everyone around him. What influence tactics and strategies could be used to change this person's attitude? Simulations encourage individuals to come up with various influence strategies and communication methods to attempt to change disagreeable situations.

Developing and Managing Networks/Social Capital

Building and managing networks are critical for effective political skill. Knowing the "right" people (i.e., people who can assist in meeting goals and objectives) is critical in acquiring resources, gaining access, and otherwise exercising influence. This involves more than just helping educate people in how to build connections, allegiances, and contacts, it also focuses on how such social capital can be leveraged to develop coalitions when support needs to be mobilized. More than simply *quid pro quo* favor doing, building a network also involves building skills in inspiring people to support and/or follow you.

There are numerous ways to develop skills to build and maintain a valued social network. Some of the previously mentioned techniques for other political skill dimensions are certainly applicable here. Drama-based training and critique/feedback sessions, for example, can be extremely useful in providing pertinent feedback to trainees about the ways to develop social capital. For example, drama vignettes or feedback sessions can be focused entirely on how various organizational members developed, or failed to develop, relationships with people holding valued resources. Session participants who know each other in a work-related context can be particularly helpful in recommending alternative ways for objects to build valued networks.

Team training activities are especially useful in giving individuals practice in developing a network, particularly if such activities last at least a few days and if they involve valued outcomes that require networking to mobilize complementary human resources. Counseling with a professional who is skilled in helping clients improve social relations can be particularly useful in helping those individuals who are extremely meek or frightened to take some chances in expanding their social contacts. For those who "come on too strong" in a manner where extreme extraversion eventually wears out its welcome with others, counseling can probe for causes of such behavior and encourage individuals to consider being more parsimonious in their outbursts.

Leadership training and behavioral modeling are both particularly helpful in encouraging individuals to take risks and try new behaviors in social contexts. For example, skilled actors or trainers can model effective ways of negotiating with others in ways that provide for synergistic, "win-win" outcomes that lead to future dealings with valued partners. For those who continually fall short regarding the confidence to convince more senior or more successful people to be part of their network, "what have I got to lose" programs could be developed and practice sessions arranged to encourage risk-taking.

Mentors can be particularly helpful in teaching protégés networking skills. Politically skilled mentors will already possess valued networks that can directly benefit proteges. Recalling the various ways in which the network was built will enable mentors to disseminate valuable information to mentees. Hopefully, this will also result in giving proteges the needed confidence to try building their own network in similar ways.

Other useful common sense ideas for building social capital include volunteering, being generous with favors, doing good work, getting the job done on time, and getting others excited to work with you. All of these activities will enable individuals to be viewed as effective, and will allow the collection of social debt when support from others is needed. Also, form allegiances and coalitions with other effective people by demonstrating that you understand their work and can help them to do a better job. Additionally, do not burn bridges, but rather work to maintain contacts with people that perhaps are not currently needed; they may become very much needed in the future. All these things will help develop a resource-rich network that will ultimately aid them in various work and nonwork endeavors.

Developing Increased Genuineness/Sincerity

The fourth dimension found to underlie political skill is genuineness or sincerity. In many respects, this is the real essence of what makes political skill work because it involves being able to execute the influence attempt in a manner that makes it actually not appear to be an influence attempt. The fundamental error people make that leads to influence attempts failing is that they over-do it, come on too strong, are perceived to be manipulative, and so forth, all of which makes others (e.g., targets) question their motives, feel like they are being manipulated, and react negatively.

Certainly, part of the development and shaping of political skill involves effective communication skills that are inspirational and influential. Towler and Dipboye (2001) recently investigated the nature of charismatic communication training. They found that people receiving charismatic communication training employed more animated gestures, more analogies and stories, and were perceived by others as more effective communicators than those receiving only presentation training. Communication training is also useful here since it emphasizes empathy, non-verbal cues tone of voice, and so forth. Some individuals may believe that this is not appropriate training since it could be viewed as deceptive. It may imply being "two faced" (i.e., acting one way but believing another). Our intent is not to imply this, but rather to suggest that using political skill should not be done in a manipulative or deceitful manner. We believe that the most effective influence attempts are made in a truthful, empathic, genuine manner, because they inspire trust and confidence for the long-term. Of course, any influence attempt is an effort to "get one's way," and it may involve some tacit levels of deception, but we do not suggest training on misrepresenting the truth or in how to be dishonest without appearing to be so. Honoring commitments, promises, and allegiances are essential activities in building social capital.

Disguising ulterior motives and inspiring trust and confidence while being, or appearing to be, sincere and genuine calls for sophisticated training and development approaches. While many other techniques have been mentioned above, drama-based training and behavioral modeling are probably most ideal for demonstrating, for example, alternative ways of showing sincerity or insincerity. Actors could role play various levels of sincerity for different situations along a continuum from extremely insincere, cold, and blunt to a softer, gentler, more caring manner. A death in the family of a co-worker would likely require different body language and affect than someone winning the lottery. Such genuineness variations could be modeled by actors and then later practiced by trainees. Videotaping these sessions would be especially helpful for those missing some segments or as refresher exercises for participants.

BRINGING IT ALL TOGETHER: THE ROLE OF EXECUTIVE COACHING IN POLITICAL SKILL DEVELOPMENT

As one moves up the hierarchy, technical expertise becomes less of an issue, and political skill becomes increasingly important for successful managers as the scope of their jobs become broader. At executive levels, political and strategic skills are critical to success. Possessing the vision to see new strategic opportunities, and the political savvy to muster the support and obtain scarce organizational resources for a new concept, largely determine success at this level. Therefore, as one progresses up the hierarchy in organizations, political skill becomes increasingly important while technical "know how" becomes less so. The real irony is that many promotion decisions are predicated upon an individual's technical performance, with little concern for how a person may deal with the political challenges he or she might face.

Additionally, research also suggests that many managers become derailed by over-reliance on technical strengths to the expense of interpersonal, social, or "softer skills." McCall, Lombardo, and Morrison (1988) outlined ten fatal flaws that lead to executive derailment. More than half of the fatal flaws deal with issues such as insensitivity to others, being perceived as arrogant, failing to delegate, being overly ambitious, inability to adapt to a boss, and overdependence on someone. Only one of the ten flaws focused on failure to make the business work. Political savvy and interpersonal issues appear to be far more troublesome for managers to master than technical issues. When managers and executives find themselves in jobs that require high levels of political skill, they often turn to executive coaches for assistance.

Kilburg (2000) defined executive coaching as a "helping relationship formed between a client who has managerial authority and responsibility in an organization and a consultant who uses a wide variety of behavioral techniques and methods to assist the client to achieve a mutually identified set of goals..." (p. 65-67). The executive coaching process usually begins with some assessment done by the coach. The assessment might include interviews with people with whom the executive works (e.g., peers, subordinates, and boss), 360-degree feedback instruments, and/or psychological instruments (Kiel, Rimmer, Williams, & Doyle, 1996). Based upon this assessment, the coach aggregates the information, provides feedback to the executive, and then jointly the two determine what issues are facing the executive. Once the executive has determined his/her needs, then desirable changes can be contemplated.

The focus of executive coaching is usually on job-related themes such as being more strategic and learning to delegate to subordinates, managing upward influence, managing conflict, emotional competence, influencing others without formal authority, how to coach and develop subordinates, and building coalitions. Witherspoon and White (1996) noted that the focus of executive coaching is on executive suite skills such as "political savvy, strategic agility, and vision and purpose " (p.127). Clearly, the political aspect of these themes is obvious, positioning political skill as a key focus of executive coaching. Indeed, Ferris, Perrewé, et al. (2000) suggested that executive coaches working with managers on skill deficiencies and development today reported most of their time was spent on the development of social and political skill.

Executive coaching is a process that is on going, and depends heavily upon the relationship between the two parties. Ideally, executive coaching is done at the executive's workplace, involves a few hours to a few days per month, and likely continues for months or years. For example, Kiel et al. (1996) suggested one day per month during the first year, and a half day per month during the second year of a coaching relationship. Diedrich (1996) recommended that executive coaching should be done for a contractual period of at least 12 months, and advises that coaching assignments of less than 6 months' duration be avoided. There do not appear to be any quick fixes when developing subtle changes in political skill and behavior.

Executive coaching is not therapy, but relies heavily upon a partnership between the coach and executive. The coach helps the executive identify issues that will likely affect performance in the executive role, works with the executive to develop new behaviors, and provides ongoing feedback to develop the subtle changes in behavior that can enhance the executive's effectiveness. As Witherspoon and White (1996) noted, "coaching is more personal and individualized than other forms of organized learning..." (p.127). For example, how does an executive deal with a superior who is micromanaging him or her? The executive and the coach might explore alternative strategies that the executive might use to alter a more powerful superior's behavior in this politically sensitive situation.

After considering various alternatives and evaluating likely consequences, the executive can choose a way to approach this situation. Then the coach would likely suggest that the executive and coach role-play a meeting between the executive and the coach acting as the micromanaging superior. At the conclusion of the role-play (which could be video-taped), the coach provides feedback on what was said, how it was said, and the impact of the meeting. By such behavioral rehearsal/feedback, the executive can experiment with new behaviors, get feedback from the coach, and learn to alter behavior in subtle ways that can dramatically change the impact upon others. There is no guarantee that the executive will alter the superior's behavior, but the approach is likely to be better thought out since the behavior has been rehearsed and feedback has been provided by an independent observer before the "real" interaction occurs.

While some people acquire political skill earlier in their careers, either by trial and error or by observation, there is no doubt that possession of such political skill is critical to success at executive levels in organizations, and can have a big impact on organizational effectiveness. The potential fallout from a failed executive inside an organization is huge, and executive coaching or other one-on-one development is an attractive alternative to "cleaning up the mess" afterwards. The unique problems that each executive is facing commonly necessitate such an intense and individually tailored approach as offered by executive coaching. Kilburg (2000) noted that executive coaching increases psychological and social awareness and understanding, increases tolerance for ambiguity, increases tolerance and range of emotional responses, and increases flexibility in and ability to develop and maintain effective interpersonal relationships. These areas are central to our conceptualization of political skill.

In summary, executive coaching is a premier way to help executives develop political skill. A skilled executive coach well versed in both the content dimensions of political skill and in wide-ranging training techniques can help executives build strong but flexible political skill in a relatively short time. In particular, a skilled coach can immediately help an executive become more aware of politically charged environments, and a more astute observer of political situations and people. Over time and with practice, executives can refine novice skills into a well-integrated skill inventory and smooth functioning style that will help them more effectively deal with a wide range of situations.

CONCLUSION

Inherent in the responsibilities associated with becoming a manager is the necessity to interact with and influence others. As one moves up the organizational ladder, the day-to-day tasks become less focused on technical issues and more on interpersonal and human resources issues. As such, managers need to effectively influence and control the actions of their subordinates—hence, they need political skill. Political skill is made up of four primary dimensions, including self and social astuteness, influence and control, networking and building social capital, and genuineness/sincerity. While some individuals naturally seem to have facility in this area, we believe that most need to learn and practice ways to become more interpersonally effective.

This chapter highlights various ways political skill and its dimensions can be developed. Drama-based training, with its emphasis on involving participants emotionally, is particularly effective in demonstrating various ways political skill can be developed and practiced. Executive coaching is perhaps the premier one-on-one technique for helping top managers recognize political situations and then idiosyncratically and effectively deal with them. Other effective methods for understanding and building political skill include assessing oneself through interest and personality inventories, holding critique/feedback sessions, videotaped role-playing with feedback, counseling, leadership training, behavioral modeling, mentoring, and developmental simulations.

Future work should consider the increased importance of cross-cultural issues and the complexities involved in the success of overseas assignments, which necessitates perhaps more than ever the need to be politically skilled. This will help us to determine what aspects of political skill might be generalizable across cultures, and which aspects need to be situationally shaped and developed.

Political skill is becoming increasingly recognized as a critical competency, essential for job and career success of managers and executives. Therefore, political skill needs to be incorporated into the broader repertoire of key management competencies and management education needs for the 21st century.

REFERENCES

Argyle, M. (1969). *Social interaction*. Chicago: Aldine.

Baldwin, T.T., & Ford, K.J. (1988). Transfer of training: A review and directions for future research. *Personnel Psychology, 43*, 63-105.

Bandura, A. (1986). *Social foundations of thought and action: A social cognitive theory.* Englewood Cliffs, NJ: Prentice-Hall.

Barney, J. (1991). Firm resources and sustained competitive advantage. *Journal of Management, 17*(1), 99-120.

Baron, R.A., & Markman, G.D. (2000). Beyond social capital: How social skills can enhance entrepreneurs' success. *Academy of Management Executive, 14,* 106-116.

Barrick, M.R., & Mount, M.K. (1991). The big five personality dimensions and job performance: A meta-analysis. *Personnel Psychology, 44,* 1-26.

Boon, S.D., & Holmes, J.G. (1991). They dynamics of interpersonal trust: Resolving uncertainty in the face of risk. In R.A. Hinde & J. Grobel (Eds.), *Cooperation and prosocial behavior,* 190-211. Cambridge: Cambridge University Press.

Broad, M.L. (1997). Transfer concepts and research overview: Challenges for organizational performance. In M.L. Broad (Ed.), *Transferring learning to the workplace,* 1-18. Alexandria, VA: American Society for Training and Development.

Broad, M.L., & Newstrom, J.W. (1992). *Transfer of learning: Action-packed strategies to ensure high payoff from training investments.* Reading, MA: Addison-Wesley.

Burke, M.J., & Day, R.R. (1986). A cumulative study of the effectiveness of managerial training. *Journal of Applied Psychology, 71,* 232-246.

Carnegie, D. (1936). *How to win friends and influence people.* New York: Simon and Schuster.

Cascio, W.F. (1995). Whither industrial and organizational psychology in a changing world of work. *American Psychologist, 50,* 928-939.

Costa, P. T., Jr., & McCrae, R. R. (1992). *NEO PI-R: Professional manual.* Odessa, FL: Psychological Assessment Resources.

DeLuca, J.M. (1992). *Political savvy: Systematic approaches to leadership behind the scenes.* Horsham, PA: LRP Publications.

Diedrich, R. C. (1996). An iterative approach to executive coaching. *Consulting Psychology Journal: Practice and Research, 48*(2), 61-66.

Drake, G. (1987). Acting lessons for the political world. *New York Times,* (February 10), 22.

Egan, G. (1994). *Working the shadow side.* San Francisco: Jossey-Bass.

Ferris, G.R., Bhawuk, D.P.S., Fedor, D.B., & Judge, T.A. (1995). Organizational politics and citizenship: Attributions of intentionality and construct definition. In M.J. Martinko (Ed.), *Advances in attribution theory: An organizational perspective,* 231-252. Delray Beach, FL: St. Lucie Press.

Ferris, G.R., Fedor, D.B., & King, T.R. (1994). A political conceptualization of managerial behavior. *Human Resource Management Review, 4:* 1-34.

Ferris, G.R., Kolodinsky, R., Hochwarter, W.A., & Frink, D.D. (2001). *Conceptualization, measurement, and validation of the political skill construct.* Paper presented at the Academy of Management, 61st Annual National Meeting, Washington, D.C.

Ferris, G.R., Perrewé, P.L., Anthony, W.P., & Gilmore, D.C. (2000). Political skill at work. *Organizational Dynamics, 28,* 25-37.

Ferris, G.R., Russ, G.S., & Fandt, P.M. (1989). Politics in organizations. In R. A. Giacalone & P. Rosenfeld (Eds.), *Impression management in the organization,* 143-170. Hillsdale, NJ: Lawrence Erlbaum.

French, J., & Raven, B. (1959). The bases of social power. In D. Cartwright (Ed.), *Studies in social power.* Ann Arbor, MI: Institute for Social Research.

Fry, R., & Pasmore, W. (1983). Strengthening management education. In S. Srivastva (Ed.), *The executive mind: New insights on managerial thought and action,* 269-298. San Francisco: Jossey-Bass.

George, J.M. (2000). Emotions and leadership: The role of emotional intelligence. *Human Relations, 53*(8), 1027-1056.

Georges, J.C. (1996). The myth of soft-skills training. *Training, 33,* 48-54.

Giacalone, R.A., & Rosenfeld, P. (1989). *Impression management in the organization.* Hillsdale, NJ: Lawrence Erlbaum Associates.

Goffman, E. (1959). *The presentation of self in everyday life.* Garden City, NY: Doubleday.

Goleman, D. (1995). *Emotional intelligence.* New York: Bantam Books.

Granovetter, M.S. (1973). The strength of weak ties. *American Journal of Sociology, 78,* 1360-1380.

Harrison, J.K. (1992). Individual and combined effects of behavior modeling and the cultural assimilator in cross-cultural management training. *Journal of Applied Psychology, 77,* 952-962.

Hochschild, A.R. (1990). *The managed heart: Commercialization of human feeling.* Berkeley, CA: University of California Press.

House, R.J., & Aditya, R.N. (1997). The social scientific study of leadership: Quo Vadis? *Journal of Management, 23,* 409-473.

Jackall, R. (1988). *Moral mazes: The world of corporate managers.* New York: Oxford University Press.

Jones, E.E. (1990). *Interpersonal perception.* New York: W.H. Freeman.

Keirsey, D.W. (1997). *Keirsey temperament sorter II.* Prometheus Nemesis Book Company.

Kiel, F., Rimmer, E. Williams, K., & Doyle, M. (1996). Coaching at the top. *Consulting Psychology Journal: Practice and Research, 48*(2), 67-77.

Kilburg, R.R. (2000). *Executive coaching: Developing managerial wisdom in a world of chaos.* Washington: American Psychological Association.

Kilduff, M., & Day, D.V. (1994). Do chameleons get ahead? The effects of self-monitoring on managerial careers. *Academy of Management Journal, 37,* 1047-1060.

Kosmitzki, C. & John, O.P. (1993). The implicit use of explicit conceptions of social intelligence. *Personality and Individual Differences, 15,* 11-23.

Leary, M.R. (1995). *Self-presentation: Impression management and interpersonal behavior.* Boulder, CO: Westview Press.

Loury, G.C. (1977). A dynamic theory of racial income differences. In P.S. Wallace & A.M. LaMonde (Eds.), *Women, minorities and employment discrimination,* 153-186. Lexington, MA: Lexington Books.

Luthans, F., Hodgetts, R.M., & Rosenkrantz, S.A. (1988). *Real managers.* Cambridge, MA: Ballinger.

Mainiero, L.A. (1994). On breaking the glass ceiling: The political seasoning of powerful women executives. *Organizational Dynamics, 22,* 5-20.

May, G.L., & Kahnweiler, W.M. (2000). The effect of a mastery practice design on learning and transfer in behavior modeling training. *Personnel Psychology, 53,* 353-373.

McCall, M. W., Lombardo, M.M., & Morrison, A.M. (1988). *The lessons of experience: How successful executives develop on the job.* New York: Lexington Books.

Meichenbaum, D., Butler, L., & Gruson, L. (1981). Toward a conceptual model of social competence. In J.D. Wine & D. Smye (Eds.), *Social competence,* 36-60. New York: Guilford Press.

Mintzberg, H. (1983). *Power in and around organizations.* Englewood Cliffs, NJ: Prentice-Hall.

Mintzberg, H. (1985). The organization as a political arena. *Journal of Management Studies, 22,* 133-154.

Myers, I.B. (1998). *Introduction to type: A guide to understanding your results on the Myers-Briggs Type Indicator* (6th ed.). Revised by L.K. Kirby & K.D. Myers. Palo Alto, CA: Consulting Psychologists Press.

Nahapiet, J., & Ghoshal, S. (1998). Social capital, intellectual capital, and the organizational advantage. *Academy of Management Review, 23,* 242-266.

New York Times. (1955). Dale Carnegie, author, is dead. November 2.

Perrewé , P.L., Ferris, G.R., Frink, D.D., & Anthony, W.P. (2000). Political skill: An antidote for workplace stressors. *Academy of Management Executive, 14,* 115-123.

Pfeffer, J. (1981). Management as symbolic action: The creation and maintenance of organizational paradigms. In L.L. Cummings & B.M. Staw (Eds.), *Research in organizational behavior, 3,* 1-52. Greenwich, CT: JAI Press.

Russ-Eft, D. (1997). Behavioral modeling. In L.J. Bassi & D. Russ-Eft (Eds.), *What works: Training and development practices,* 105-149. Alexandria, VA: American Society for Training and Development.

Snyder, M., & Gangestad, S. (1986). On the nature of self-monitoring: Matters of assessment, matters of validity. *Journal of Personality and Social Psychology, 51,* 125-139.

Spencer, L.M., & Spencer, S.M. (1993). *Competence at work: Models for superior performance.* New York: John Wiley and Sons.

St. George, J., Schwager, S., & Canavan, F. (2000). A guide to drama-based training. *National Productivity Review,* (Autumn), 15-19.

Sternberg, R.J. (1997). Managerial intelligence: Why IQ isn't enough. *Journal of Management, 23,* 475-493.

Thorndike, E.L. (1920). Intelligence and its uses. *Harper's Magazine, 140,* 227-235.

Towler, A., & Dipboye, R.L. (2001). *Effects of charismatic communication training on motivation, behavior, and attitudes.* Paper presented at the 16th Annual Conference of the Society for Industrial and Organizational Psychology, San Diego.

Van Velsor, E. & Leslie, J.B. (1995). Why executives derail: Perspectives across time and cultures. *Academy of Management Executive, 9*(4), 62-72.

Witherspoon, R., & White, R.P. (1996). Executive coaching: A continuum of roles. *Consulting Psychology Journal: Practice and Research, 48*(2), 124-133.

Yukl, G. 1998. *Leadership in organizations* (4th ed.). Upper Saddle River, NJ: Prentice Hall.

CHAPTER 2

ARTS-BASED LEARNING IN MANAGEMENT EDUCATION

Nick Nissley

This chapter seeks to describe an emerging phenomenon in management education—how aesthetic epistemology (aesthetic ways of knowing), or arts-based learning is informing the practice of management education. It provides a literature review and examples of how arts-based learning is being practiced in management education—framed by the art forms of music (e.g., blues, jazz, and orchestra), drama (e.g., theater and cinema), literature (e.g., novels and poetry), visual arts (e.g., corporate art), dance, and storytelling.

This chapter serves to recognize those management educators who are rethinking the traditional logico-rational paradigm (way of knowing) that presently frames much of management education. Ironically, from within the arts community, artists such as Cimino (1995) and Cleveland (2000), and arts organizations such as the US-based Arts & Business Council (2001), the Center for the Study of Art & Community (2001), the Center for the Social Application of the Arts (2001), and the UK-based Arts & Business (2001) are engaging in a similar exploration. The chapter does not seek to suggest that aesthetic epistemology (aesthetic ways of knowing) or arts-based learning can, or should, replace any of the more conven-

Rethinking Management Education for the 21st Century
A Volume in: Research in Management Education and Development, pages 27–61.
Copyright © 2002 by Information Age Publishing, Inc.
All rights of reproduction in any form reserved.
ISBN: 1-930608-21-7 (cloth), 1-930608-20-9 (paper)

tional practices of management education. Mindful of multiple ways of knowing, this chapter seeks to identify arts-based learning as a valuable adjunct to the current dominant pedagogy of management education.

In this chapter, the term "arts-based learning" is used to broadly refer to ways that "the arts" are being introduced into management education. Elsewhere the term "aesthetic epistemology" (Nissley, 1999a) has been used to refer to aesthetic ways of knowing. And, similarly, others have sought to describe this phenomenon that is here referred to as arts-based learning, calling it: "aesthetic modes of knowing" (Reimer & Smith, 1992, p. 23), "arts based training" (Arts & Business, 2001), "art as a way of knowing" (Greene, 1995), "aesthetic experiential learning" (Merritt, 1995), "expressive arts consulting and education" (California Institute of Integral Studies, 2001), "arts-based educational programming," or "creative learning" (Vaill, 1996).

AESTHETIC EPISTEMOLOGY AND MANAGEMENT EDUCATION

In the broader context of organizational studies, Barrett (2000, p. 229), recognizing the short comings of the dominant logico-rational paradigm, asks, "If rational ways of knowing are inadequate, are there any alternatives?" Similarly, and more specific to the field of management education, Alvarez & Merchán (1992) assert that the act of management requires the use of several types of knowledge. This chapter is an examination of one type of "other" knowledge—aesthetic epistemology and its application in management education.

Outside of the mainstream organizational studies literature, in the field of organizational folklore, there has been a call to examine the aesthetic dimension of organizational life. In a special section of *Western Folklore* ("Works of Art, Art as Work, and the Arts of Working: Implications for Improving Organizational Life"), Jones (1984) introduces four essays that address the aesthetic dimension of organizational life, from the organizational folklore perspective. He posits, "A model of art, therefore, would seem defensible in studying organizations, offering a metaphor which, analogically, can help us understand and improve organizational life" (p. 176). Elsewhere, within the interdisciplinary field of organizational studies, organizational aesthetics is an emerging sub-specialty (e.g., Strati, 1992, 1999; Linstead & Höpfl, 2000). Generally speaking, organizational aesthetics provides us with an aesthetic way of understanding organizational life. This chapter more specifically discusses arts-based learning in organizations— how artful ways of knowing are being practiced in organizations. While a recent issue of the Society for Organization Learning's journal, *Reflections* (2001), was dedicated to "The Arts in Business and Society," it provided a more limited understanding of arts-based learning in organizations.

Many disciplines have recognized the value of encouraging the use of aesthetic epistemology in examination of their respective disciplines. Consider the following breadth of examples: *geology* (Shea, 2000; Pestrong, 1968; Yasso, 1972; Williams, 1976; McKee, 1979; Melhorn & Kaplan, 1982; Leveson, 1988), *geography* (Porteous, 1986; Sandberg & Marsh, 1988; Kennedy, Sell, & Zube, 1988), *medicine* (Hansen, Porter, & Kemp, 2000; Ratzan & Carmichael, 1991), *nursing* (Valiga & Bruderle, 1997), and *law* (Robbins, 1990).

Within the discipline of management, there are examples of the use of aesthetic epistemology to frame understanding within the sub-disciplines of: *accounting* (Chua & Degeling, 1993), *business ethics* (Brady, 1986; Kennedy & Lawton, 1992; McAdams & Koppensteiner, 1992; Shaw, 1992; Gilbert, 1997; Garaventa, 1998; Gerde, Shepard, & Goldsby, 1996; Giacalone & Jurkiewicz, 2001; Williams, 1997), *intellectual capital* (Rivette & Kline, 1999), *marketing* (Schmitt & Simonson, 1997), *consumer behavior* (Pink, 1998), *product design* (Gelernter, 1999), *customer service* (Höpfl, 1995), *leadership* (Palus & Horth, 1996, 1998, 2001), *manufacturing* (Thomas, 1994, pp. 246-250), *conflict management* (Rothman, 1997, pp. xi-xvi), *organization design* (Hatch, 1999), *organization development* (Bowden & Craven, 2001; Ramsey, 1996, 1997), and *career management* (Butler & Waldroop, 1999; Albion, 2001; Whyte, 2001). Even the specialty field of financial management has engaged aesthetic epistemology as a way of knowing about: *money* (Standish, 2000), *markets* (Tamarkin, Krantz, & Labarre, 1999), *business valuation* (Link & Boger, 1999), and *political economy* (Huey & Okrent, 1999).

Yet, our understanding of aesthetic ways of knowing in the field of management education has been examined only little outside of metaphorical conceptualizations of "the art of good teaching" in management education (*Journal of Management Education*, Special Issue: The Art of Good Teaching, 1997) and Bilimoria's (1999) pondering, of "what if management schools focused on helping students gain facility in harnessing aesthetic and evocative aspects to the same degree as developing technical and administrative knowledge and skills" (p. 466). Few people beyond Vaill (e.g., 1989, 1996, 1998)[1] have tried to answer Björkegren's (1993) poignant question: "What can organization and management theory learn from art?" Ironically, however, arts-based learning journals, such as the *Journal of Aesthetic Education* (1996) have dedicated special issues to explore the relationship between arts and leadership—seeking to examine art's relationship with organization and management theory. This chapter seeks to describe, through a literature review and examples, how aesthetic epistemology (aesthetic ways of knowing), or arts-based learning is informing the theory and practice of management education—or, *what management education can learn from art.*

This chapter is organized around two main approaches to arts-based learning. One is an approach concerning the metaphorical conceptualization of "the art of management" as related to management education. The other approach moves beyond this view of art as an organizing metaphor to also consider how managers are engaging with the arts, and not just thinking about them. Within this approach, examples of both *art-perceiving* (e.g., watching a play, reading a novel, viewing a corporate art collection) and *art-making* (company-sponsored and self-initiated) are provided within the practice of management education. This chapter focuses on the company-sponsored type (e.g., formal management education) versus the self-initiated or self-directed type of arts-based learning noted in Taninecz (1996). Taninecz describes a growing number of "executives who satisfy a need far removed from the mental and physical constraints of corporate corridors," noting "these white-collar sculptors, painters, and poets—in addition to satisfying a need to express themselves—believe that creative pursuits can enhance leadership capabilities and management acumen" (p. 111).

THE ART OF MANAGEMENT EDUCATION— METAPHORICALLY SPEAKING

As already mentioned, this chapter does not restrict this examination to the metaphorical conceptualization of "the art of management." Instead, this chapter views "the art of management" as an organizing metaphor *and* a means for managers to engage with the arts and not just think about them. White (1996) reminds us that both the metaphorical and literal conceptualizations exist:

> Many sources in management theory refer to the 'art' of management. This usage of the term may be metaphorical, but if there is a literal dimension—a dimension defined by purely aesthetic considerations—then it may be argued that if there is an art to management, and if in general the purpose of art is to create objects of beauty, then it would follow that whatever is managed, if managed well, must be in some sense beautiful. (p. 204)

First, consider the following examples of the "art of" metaphor that can readily be found in the titles of books that seek to educate managers (see Appendix A). However, this is not a recent phenomenon. Recall, Chester Barnard (1940) viewed management as "a matter of art rather than a science" (p. 325). Second, and similarly, article titles, such as the following, seek to metaphorically remind us of the role of the use of the metaphorical conceptualization of "the art of management" in management education: "Learning from a Masterpiece" (Cohen & Jurkovic, 1997); "The Dance Steps Get Trickier All The Time" (Stewart, 1997); "Crafting Strategy" (Mintzberg, 1987); "Advertising: The Poetry of Becoming" (Levitt, 1993); and "Leadership as a Performing Art" (Quigley, 1998). Third, consider examples from management books that do not use the "art of" metaphor in the title, but instead use the arts to illustrate a specific point. James

O'Toole's (1995) book, *Leading Change: Overcoming the Ideology of Comfort and the Tyranny of Custom*, is an example of organizational literature that embeds the art metaphor in the content versus the title. On the cover of O'Toole's book is James Ensor's painting, *Christ's Entry into Brussels in 1889*. O'Toole describes Ensor's painting:

> The subject matter is a crowded street scene, the nineteenth-century equivalent of a New York ticker-tape parade to honor the return of a conquering hero. The celebrating crowd is frenzied, the myriad participants all joyously doing their own wild and crazed things. There is a band with a drummer in the foreground, but nobody is marching to his beat. This is a chaotic party—colorful, glorious, raucous, and, Ensor hints, decidedly democratic. Indeed, Ensor depicts the *demos* in all its self-interested diversity and variety, in this parade of the people, by the people, and for the people, there is no discernible beginning or end to the rowdy mass of humanity filling the streets of the Belgian capital." (pp. 1-2)

After involving the reader in the painting, O'Toole notes:

> Then it hits you: Where is Christ in all this confusion? You double-check the title to see if you read it correctly. Yes, you did; but shouldn't he be in the forefront, *leading* the parade? Shouldn't he be the focus of the painting? ... After much searching, the Redeemer is finally located in the background, a little to the left of center, almost lost in a throng of revelers that threatens to engulf him. (p. 2)

In Ensor's painting, Christ is not placed at the center of attention, as the tradition of western art has done for nearly two millennia. Instead, the Christ who visits Brussels in Ensor's painting must compete against the distractions of modernity, while no one pays attention to the messiah. O'Toole uses Ensor's *Christ's Entry into Brussels in 1889* because of the powerfulness of the visual metaphor. He summarizes the positioning of Christ and the painting's relevance to our understanding to organizations, noting,

> And that condition turns out to be a pretty fair assessment of the starting place of all would-be agents of change in modern societies and organizations. The painting thus raises a question that has remained paramount to this day: Is leadership possible in modern, complex systems, or is "democratic leadership" simply an oxymoron? (p. 3)

THE ART OF MANAGEMENT EDUCATION— MOVING BEYOND METAPHOR

As already noted, the "art of" metaphor can readily be found in the titles of books and articles that seek to educate managers, as well as embedded in the context of those books—to illustrate a point. Here we turn our attention to examples of how arts-based learning is being used in the education and development of managers at work. We will examine examples of how arts-based learning in management education is being expressed in a variety of places, including: books for managers—seeking to develop their aesthetic competencies (e.g., Dobson, 1999; Palus & Horth, 2002), management/leadership development curriculum (e.g., Di Ciantis, 1995), artist-in-residence programs (e.g., Harris, 1999; Manning, 1998; Peiken, 2000; Arts/Industry, 2001; Arts & Business, 2001; Poetry Places, 2001), as well as management professional associations (e.g., Taylor, 2000, 2001).

This section provides a literature review and examples of how arts-based learning is being practiced in the management education classroom—framed by the art forms of music (e.g., blues, jazz, and orchestra), drama (e.g., theater and cinema), literature (e.g., novels and poetry), visual arts (e.g., corporate art), dance, and storytelling. Next, we'll begin by examining how the musical arts are being engaged in management education.

Musical Arts

Disciplines beyond management and organizational studies—as varied as geology (e.g., McKenzie, 1988; Plummer, 1988) and nursing (Valiga & Bruderle, 1997) have begun to explore their relationship with music. There are also a growing number of references in the management and organizational studies literature that explore the music-organization relationship, such as Pogacnik's (1999) connection between music and listening, Hawkins' (1998) connection between music and dialogue, and Jones & Shibley's (1999) discussion of the "practice culture" of musicians and the "performance culture" of organizations—asserting that each has a lot to learn from the other. Examples of how the musical arts are being engaged by management education include the musical arts of jazz, orchestra, and blues, as well as other musical forms—including drumming circles to chamber music (Sicca, 2000). Guidebooks for trainers and management educators incorporating music in training have found their way to the bookstores (e.g., Brant & Harvey, 2001). While management educators have been studying musical groups (e.g., orchestras, chamber music and jazz groups)—seeking to understand their group processes and dynamics (e.g., Murnighan & Conlon, 1991; Weick, Gilfillan, & Keith, 1978), this section reports how management educators are using music to engage managers—not merely how management scholars are seeking to understand musical groups.

Jazz

The jazz metaphor has been extensively covered in the organization and management studies literature (e.g., *Organization Science* (1998)—special issue on jazz improvisation and organizing). Consider the following examples. Weick (1990, 1998), Barrett (1998, 2000), and Hatch (1997, 1998, 1999) engage an understanding of jazz improvisation to better our understanding of organizational improvisation. Perry (1996) extends this understanding of improvisation to learning and strategy. Similarly, Bastien & Hostagier (1988, 1992) use the jazz performance metaphor to better understand the process of organizational innovation and cooperation.

Practitioners have joined academic theorists, seeking to make sense of jazz as a metaphor for organizational life. For example, Jazz Impact (2001) engages organizations with jazz music—as an arts-based learning approach to management education. Michael Gold founded Jazz Impact in 1997 after doing a workshop with Lucent Technologies. Gold, who has a doctorate in music history, formerly headed the jazz department at Vassar College. He left academia to perform arts-based learning in organizations— teaching managers about improvisation and collaboration (Tellijohn, 2001).

Orchestra

Mirvis (1998) asks us to consider other musical metaphors (e.g., orchestral, rock-and-roll, country-western, grunge and rap) that may be useful in developing our understanding of organizational life. Mintzberg (1998) and Atik (1994), for example, examine the orchestra conductor as a metaphor for organizational leadership. Similar to "Jazz Impact," mentioned above, practitioners have joined academic theorists, seeking to make sense of the orchestra as a metaphor for organizational life. For example, the musicians of Orpheus (2001), the conductor-less orchestra, have entered conversations with business organizations who seek to learn how the Orpheus orchestra's way of creating music may serve as a model for their own organization (Seifter, 2001; Lieber, 2000; Traub, 1996; Lubins, 1999). Harvey Seifter, the Executive Director of the Orpheus Chamber Orchestra, and Peter Economy (2001) have co-authored a book about the "Orpheus Process"—how the Orpheus model of organizing may help other organizations re-create this model of collaborative leadership.

In addition, "The Music Paradigm" (2001) brings business organizations together with orchestra musicians, as the business organization seeks to learn different ways to "look at" organizational life. After participating in a "Music Paradigm" experience (conducted by Stamford (Connecticut) Symphony Orchestra conductor, Roger Nierenberg), Paul Charron, Chairman and CEO of Liz Claibourne called it an extremely effective learning experience, noting "I think we gained new valuable insights by our ability to look at the concepts of leadership, communication, and collaboration through the lens of a different medium" (Gershman, 2000). Gershman describes another example of how "Music Paradigm" has been engaged by a corporation for executive development and help in furthering their most critical strategic objectives—the merger of Bank of America and Nations Bank in 1998.

The process that "Music Paradigm" uses can best be described as an interactive demonstration of leadership skills (e.g., communication, listening, teamwork). Participants from the business are seated in the middle of a real live symphony orchestra, where they can closely observe the musicians. The conductor and musicians perform a number of role playing demonstrations, followed by discussion with participants and musicians about what happened during the demonstration. Thus, the orchestra serves as a laboratory for studying organizational dynamics (Sciolino, 2001).

Blues

Beyond the orchestra pit, yet similar to "The Music Paradigm," "Face the Music" (2001), a hybrid of organization development consultants' and blues musicians' work with organizations—actually creating blues music and exploring the "down-side" of organizational life (Muoio, 2000). Mitch Ditkoff (Face the Music, n.d.), founder of "Face the Music," explains how they use blues music as a means of arts-based learning in organizations:

> Most people who work in a corporation are usually experiencing some form of the "blues"—a mixed bag of complaints, gripes, and grumbles that become a kind of low-grade virus on the job ... At the turn of the century, when field workers and share croppers had the blues, their response was basic and soulful. They sang it. And, that quite simply, was the beginning of their change process. In fact, that's how all change begins. By somebody "telling it like it is"—from the heart—in a way that can be heard. In most corporations, however, there are very few opportunities for people to do this.

"Face the Music" facilitates managers in writing and singing the blues—about workplace life—so, change may be realized.

Country

Most of the literature that relates country music to organizational studies (e.g., Conrad, 1988—which examines country music work songs as a hegemonic form) is from the "worker" perspective. This could provide the manager with an "other" perspective (an other voice) from which one could examine the practice of management. However, little academic study or practitioner work has been done in the arena of country music and management education.

Percussive

Similar to "Face the Music," who use blues music as an arts-based learning approach to management education, *Fast Company* (Pratt, 2000) has noted a growing interest in using drumming and other percussive instruments as another musical approach to arts-based learning in organizations. A number of musicians are bridging the worlds of music and organization, consulting to corporate clients. These include: "One World Music" (2000), "Village Music Circles" (2000), "UpBeat Drum Circles" (2001), and "African Percussion" (2001). These consulting musicians assist organizations with team building, collaboration, creativity, and diversity training—through making a connection to musical concepts such as rhythm and tempo.

Opera

Rothman's (1997) text on organizational conflict uses a musical metaphor—opera, as an example of arts-based learning, noting: "In opera, singers recite long and sometimes tedious narratives of everyday tensions, strife and conflict. Such narration (the recitative) works its way toward a more passionate expression and culmination in the aria" (p. xii). Rothman (p. xv) then creates an acronym (ARIA), which serves as an applied framework for approaching conflict (A=antagonism, R=resonance, I=invention, A=action).

Other Examples

Examples beyond the formal musical structures of jazz, orchestra, blues, and opera, including musical analogies and "workplace songs" are mentioned below. Consider, for example, Shafritz's (1999, pp. 64-65) *Shakespeare on Management*, identifies musical analogies from Shakespeare's writings—allowing the reader to 'tune-in to the Bard'—for wise business counsel.

Also, consider Channon's (1992) description of General Motors of Canada which introduced its new vision and values by asking each manufacturing unit to create a parade float representing one of the company's key values. The floats were part of a parade, central to an entire day of culture-building ritual. The day concluded with the "GM Acceleration Song," revised to incorporate the new values created by the leadership team. This is an example of how "workplace songs" (Nissley, 2000) are used as a means of arts-based learning in educating managers—in this case, educating managers about the company's values through creative visioning.

Finally, consider that this past year (2000), at the Academy of Management's Annual Meeting (which is dominated by the logico-rational paradigm), one could find a jazz pianist teaching management educators about improvisation and the relation to leadership as well as a researcher who presented her partially completed dissertation, including three folk songs she wrote and sung—describing her own and other managers' experiences of loss and transition during an organizational redesign (Brearley, 2000).

Drama Arts (Theater and Cinema)

The use of drama, including stage performance (theater) and screen performance (cinema) as means of management education is growing beyond the metaphorical (e.g., Pitcher, 1996; Vaill, 1989). This is evidenced by the emerging acceptance of drama within the practice of formal management education within academia as well as the growth of consultants engaging in theater-based training within businesses. Similarly, many references exist discussing the use of film as a general resource for management education.

In general, Brookfield & Preskill (1999) discuss how "dramatizing discussion" (p. 122) can be used as an art-based learning pedagogy to invite students to report their conversations through some sort of dramatic art (e.g., comedic skit). Specific to management education, consider how organizational members create dramas during a future search conference (Weisbord, 1992; Weisbord & Janoff, 1995). A future search conference functions as an organization development intervention, designed to articulate strategic vision for an organization. Weisbord and Janoff (1995) describe the section of the future search design that asks participants to focus on the desired future, imagining that they have made their dreams come true. Participants are asked to create and present scenarios. These creative presentations often take the form of a drama. Similarly, consider how Skandia Corporation is using drama as a means of knowledge creation (von Krogh, Ichijo, & Nonaka, 2000, p. 96). After engaging in a strategy development process, the team of managers was asked to encapsulate their insights in the form of a "future drama." that could be performed by professional actors. This allowed their insights to be shared with a larger audience of Skandia managers. Professional actors, to an audience of approximately 125 managers, performed the "future drama." This is an example of how an arts-based learning approach was used for management education in the strategic planning process. More critically, Ferris (2001) provides an example of how Augusto Boal's ideas from *Theater of the Oppressed* were used in a teambuilding intervention in a software company. Also, Pine & Gilmore (1999) provide an intriguing example of how theater-based understanding is used in experience marketing. On a larger scale, Julia Rowntree (2001) as Director of the London International Festival of Theatre (LIFT) Business Arts Forum has created a forum for managers and business workers to engage with the arts. Rather than offering an arts-based learning service to a single organization, Rowntree has created a shared learning process between private, public, volunteer, NGO organizations *and* the LIFT performers. She created the LIFT Business Arts Forum—"a linked series of seminars and performances in the festival that brings together people from the arts and private and public sectors to develop insights into how the world works" (p. 77). She was motivated by a discovery that business managers "hungered to embark on different kinds of conversation beyond the boundaries of their own organizations. They had a desire to engage with the arts in a search for new language and new metaphors" (p. 77).

Consider the following examples from stage performance (theater) and screen performance (cinema), which show how these two dramatic forms are being engaged as a means of arts-based learning in management education.

Theater

Within the halls of academia, at the 1998 Annual Meeting of the Academy of Management, Steven Taylor (2000) presented straight fiction—a play, *Capitalist Pigs*. Taylor followed this up with another play, *Soft Targets*, presented at the 2001 Annual Meeting of the Academy of Management. Similarly, Barry Oshry (2001) has recently written and had performed a three-act play that theatrically presents his ideas about power and organizational systems (Power and Systems, 2001). In addition, popular business literature is emerging, such as these books dedicated to what Shakespearean drama may teach us about management: Whitney & Packer (2000), Shafritz (1999), Augustine & Adelman (1999), Corrigan (1999), and Burnham, Augustine, & Adelman (2001). Finally, there is a growing number of consultants engaging in theater-based training (e.g., Sittenfeld, 1999; Performance of a Lifetime, 2001; Harvard Management Update, 1999; Houden, 1997), including scripted stage performances (e.g., Theatre at Work, 2001; Drama Works, 2001) as well as unscripted improvisational theater (e.g., On Your Feet, 2001; Pacific Playback, 2001; Barton, 2000). Within work organizations we are witnessing the development of "organizational theater," which Schreyögg (2001) defines as tailor-made plays staged for a specific organization, often dramatizing critical problems of work life. He notes that in 1997, over 2000 organizational theater performances were conducted in France, and 200 in German organizations. Even the venerable Globe Theatre has teamed up with Cranfield University's School of Management (Praxis: The Centre for Developing Personal Effectiveness, 2001), creating an arts-based learning collaboration.

In addition, academic review of scripted stage performances (e.g., Davies & Hancock, 1993) and unscripted improvisational theater (e.g., Moshavi, 2001; Crossan, White, Lane, & Klus, 1996; Yanow, 2001) are also occurring. More specifically, consider the following: Garaventa (1998) examines drama as a tool for teaching managers about business ethics, Moshavi (2001) describes how improvisational theater techniques can be used in management education, and Czarniawska-Joerges & Jacobsson (1995) use the specific dramatistic metaphor of *commedia dell'arte* to interpret organizational life in a Swedish organization. Management educators in academia have even sought to improve their teaching by improving their theatrical skills (Greenberg & Miller, 1991).

Cinema

Many references exist which discuss the use of film as a general resource for management education (e.g., Carley, 1999), as well as addressing specific areas, such as organizational behavior and management theories and concepts (Champoux, 1999a; 2000a; 2000b), business ethics (Gerde, Shepard, & Goldsby, 1996; Giacalone & Jurkiewicz, 2001; Williams, 1997) and leadership (Wolff & Clemens, 1999). Champoux (1999b) has even considered the specific genre of animated films as a teaching resource for the management educator. The Hartwick Humanities in Management Institute (n.d.) at Hartwick College (USA) provides university faculty with over twenty film cases and more than fifty literature cases. Similarly, the management educator can find practical assistance on how to integrate movies into management training by visiting *moviesforbusiness.com* (2001). One can even pick up the popular business magazine *Inc.* (Buchanan & Hofman, 2000) and read about the growing awareness that movies may serve as a pedagogy for leadership development. From the practitioner perspective, Palus & Horth (2002), from the Center for Creative Leadership (CCL), have created a technique for leaders to explore scenarios—to navigate through complexity toward a preferred future. The technique, framed by the movie metaphor, they call "movie making." This arts-based learning approach to management education involves participants in producing a wall-sized collage of images and words, then telling an imaginative story of where an organization might be headed.

Literary Arts

Beyond the current management education fad of "Shakespeare on ..." (e.g., Whitney & Packer, 2000; Shafritz, 1999; Augustine & Adelman, 1999; Corrigan, 1999; Burnham, Augustine, & Adelman, 2001), there has been a serious growth of fiction as a popular genre of literary art within the organizational studies and management education classroom (e.g., Burden & Mock, 1988; DeMott, 1989; Alvarez & Merchán, 1992; Czarniawska-Joerges & Guillet de Monthoux, 1994; Nelson, 1995; Phillips, 1995; Brawer, 1998; Knights & Wilmott, 1999; Mayer & Clemens, 1999). Jackson (2001) asserts there is a "new literary genre [of] business books"—in an article where he questions the use of literary art for management education's sake. Some specialized attention has been focused on the use of fiction in teaching ethics in management education (e.g., Kennedy & Lawton, 1992; McAdams & Koppensteiner, 1992; Shaw, 1992). Czarniawska (1999) even proposes the fiction literature genre of the detective story as helpful in understanding management work, and similarly Parker, Higgins, Lightfoot, & Smith (2001) propose that science fiction may enrich our understanding of organizational life. In addition to detective stories and science fiction, the comic genre is also being used in management education (e.g., Telescope Comics, 2001).

Poetry has also become a popular genre of literary art in the management education classroom (e.g., Mangan, 1996; Bilmoria, 1999; Ebers, 1985; Whyte, 1994, 2001; Windle, 1994; Autry, 1994, 1996). From a practice perspective, Palus & Horth (2002) describe a group of engineering managers at a coal-fired power generating station, who created Japanese haiku poetry as a means of expressing their experiences.

Many of these "border crossers" (e.g., Czarniawska-Joerges & Guillet de Monthoux, 1994; Czarniawska, 1999; Knights & Wilmott, 1999; Brawer, 1998) who are engaging fiction as a genre of literary art within the management education classroom suggest that the novel provides a vehicle for bringing the subject matter to life in a way that can make it easier for students to explore the experience of managing and organizing. For these people, the novel is often used in place of the narrow, technical and disembodied representation of management found in most textbooks.

Of course, for the management educator, there is a general problem of credibility in using arts-based learning as an aid to understanding management and the organization of work. More specifically, novels, classified as fiction, are placed at the opposite end of the spectrum from management textbooks. Yet, even in the focused area of "downsizing," one can find management professors' syllabi with readings from the world of fiction, such as, *Human Resources: A Corporate Nightmare* (Kemske, 1995) and *The Ax* (Westlake, 1998).

There even exist resources to assist the management educator who wants to integrate literary art (and cinema art) into his/her classroom. For example, The Hartwick Humanities in Management Institute at Hartwick College (USA), mentioned above, provides university faculty with cases (22 film cases and 57 literature cases) to enhance management and leadership education. This aesthetic way of knowing is described by Hartwick as: "Transforming great texts and films into unforgettable management and leadership lessons" (Hartwick Humanities in Management Institute, n.d.). Also, consider the example of Ken Adelman, who co-authored *Shakespeare in Charge*, with Norm Augustine (1999), the ex-Chairman and CEO of Lockheed Martin, who manages a management education business, "Movers and Shakespeares" that focuses exclusively on the wisdom of the Bard to inform managers (Carvajel, 1999; Forbesfyi, 2000; McNatt, 1998).

Visual Arts

Corporate Art

Corporate art, referring to art found within collections held by corporations and exhibited in the workplace environment (Martorella, 1990, p. 4), can be a site of management education (Nissley, 1999b). Marjory Jacobson (1993) wrote *Art for Work: The New Renaissance in Corporate Collecting.* Jacobson, an art historian, examined 40 corporate art collections, exploring the relationship between business and art. This in-depth study leads her to a recognition of corporate art as "a highly sophisticated management tool" used by organizations that are "experimenting with novel ways to educate ... the workforce" (back page of cover jacket). She also suggests that the 40 innovative corporate art programs that she studied "are often highly sophisticated management tools ... a kind of educational stock with a high-yield cultural return" (pp. 8-9).

Consider the following two interview comments from organizational executives, expressing their ideas about the functional value of corporate art. It is obvious why corporate art is a means of arts-based learning in organizations, and a potentially valuable means of management education. First, in an interview with art historian Marjory Jacobson (1993), Donald Marron, chairman of Paine Webber Group, Inc., reflected on the function of corporate art: " ... you are around it twenty-four hours a day, and it serves not only as a communication device but is the background that sets a certain sensibility" (p. 58). He continues, "Contemporary art reflects contemporary trends. What you want is for everyone who works for you to be as much in touch with the issues of the day as possible" (p. 59). Second, Dr. Thomas Bechtler, CEO of Hesta AG, Zug describes the functional value of corporate art, also during an interview with Marjory Jacobson (1993): "A work of art is always a condensation of the complex reality. So, art can be a means through which one learns to perceive an intricate situation through a simplified image" (p. 170). Finn & Jedlicka (1998) have also contributed to the development of the relationship between business leaders and the arts, offering a history of the growth of business-arts alliances during the past three decades.

Art Museums

Similar to corporate art, Nissley (2001) describes how an art museum (The Toledo (Ohio) Art Museum) is using their art collection as a means of engaging managers with organizational life issues. This program, which was designed to bring the museum into the workplace, is called *Art & the Workplace,* and is made possible by the Lila Wallace-Reader's Digest Fund's Museum Collections Accessibility Initiative (DeVitta, 1999). The *Art & the Workplace* program is a partnership between the Toledo Museum of Art and local businesses, where workers and managers from these area businesses visit the museum and learn about the museum's collection. However, they do not merely learn about the collection, as traditionally framed by the art educator or art historian. Instead, they also learn about *their* workplace and organizational life issues—through analogically mediated inquiry (AMI); a process similar to that described by Barry (1994). This program is an example of arts-based learning in management education—and, an answer to Björkegren's (1993) question, *"What can organization and management theory learn from art?"*

Learning Interventions
The general training and development literature has recently spoken to the potential value of visual art in facilitating learning in organizations (e.g., Simmons, 1999; Cohen & Jurkovic, 1997), building on some older references that spoke to "picture power" (Morgan, 1993, pp. 215-234). Consider the following five examples.

First, Marjory Parker (1990) describes an application of arts-based learning intervention in the workplace. She focuses on a process of arts-based learning of the organization's vision and values, at Europe's largest producer of aluminum, Norway's Hydro Aluminum Karmøy Fabrikker. In *Creating Shared Vision: The Story of a Pioneer Approach to Organizational Revitalization,* Parker, the organizational consultant who helped them through the strategic visioning process, describes why pictures really are worth a thousand words. The final vision statement was co-created by nearly every employee, over a two-year period. It was not a piece of writing at all, but an extraordinary mural of a flourishing garden, in which every plant and element embodied rich metaphorical meaning.

Second, Sims & Doyle (1995) describe an arts-based learning technique, called cognitive sculpting, a "technique for helping managers to talk through and develop their view of difficult and complex issues, which are given expression by arranging a collection of objects, some of them symbolically rich, in an arrangement or sculpture" (Sims & Doyle, 1995, p. 117).

And third, Nissley & Jusela (2001) describe a similar arts-based learning technique and its use by managers in a knowledge creation process. Similar to the cognitive sculpting technique and the process described by Nissley & Jusela, Barry (1996) provides an example of his work with Kinetic Family Drawing technique to better understand management and organizational life.

Fourth, De Ciantis (1995) also describes a training technique (Touchstone), employed at the Center for Creative Leadership (CCL), that uses art to help people develop as leaders. It is based upon an exploration of artistic modes of inquiry. Di Ciantis (1995) describes it:

> ... the touchstone exercise, asks participants to think about their experiences in the program and, using a variety of materials, create an object that will remind them of what they most want to focus on in their workplaces. They

then write about its meaning in a "learning journal," and if they wish, verbally share the story with the whole participant group. (p. 1)

The program has even included an outcomes assessment that found the program to have a positive impact, and that the aesthetic-based epistemology contributes to that impact (Young & Dixon, 1995). This learning exercise incorporates visual art, including sculpting, and drama performance. This technique is used by CCL in a program, "Leading Creatively," that defines a set of "aesthetic competencies" for leadership. Palus & Horth (1998, 2002) note that their work in the "Leading Creatively" program has led them to find two sets of competencies necessary to lead creatively: rational skills and the often neglected aesthetic competencies. Palus & Horth (1998) designed the Leading Creatively (LC) program:

> ... to help people in organizations discover their aesthetic competencies and learn to apply them to complex challenges in their work ... We do this by engaging participants in art-intensive experiences designed, over the course of a week, to help them perceive and make sense of a particular challenge each faces as a leader, and to help them uncover and strengthen innate aesthetic competencies. (p. 6)

Fifth, Root Learning (2001), an Ohio-based consulting business, has developed a learning technology they refer to as "learning maps." Learning maps are pictorial representations of organizational life and issues, created jointly by Root Learning artists and the contracting organization. They serve as a means of focusing and stimulating dialogue, drawing upon the participant's aesthetic ways of knowing.

Learning Maps are an example of how organizations are beginning to use pictorial representations of organizational life to facilitate management education. There is an emerging specialty within facilitation, referred to as "visual practitioners"—facilitators who capture ideas and synthesize conversations on large paper, creating a colorful mural from words and images. There are diverse styles, and practitioners have coined many names to identify and differentiate their work: graphic recording, graphic facilitation, reflective graphics, mindscaping, visual thinking, information architects, visual synthesis, graphic translation, group graphics, and ideation specialists (see the International Forum of Visual Practitioners Web Site: http://www.hnl-consulting.com/ifvp.html).

Movement Art/Dance

Movement art/dance is the least represented of the arts in management education. The dance metaphor is more common than the actual use of dance as an aesthetic way of knowing. For example, consider the following three management titles that make use of the dance metaphor: 1) *The Dance of Change: The Challenges of Sustaining Momentum in Learning Organizations* (Senge, Kleiner, Roberts, Ross, Roth, & Smith, 1999), 2) *Dance Lessons: Six Steps to Great Partnerships in Business and Life* (Bell & Shea, 1998), and 3) *The Dance Steps Get Trickier All the Time*—referring to the sense of rhythm required to manage knowledge intensive companies (Stewart, 1997). In addition, some texts, such as Rothman's (1997, p. xi) book, use dance as an aesthetic way of knowing to describe organizational phenomena. Rothman specifically uses dance as a means to describe conflict, in the following story:

> Several years ago I helped run a conflict resolution workshop in the Caucasus region of the former Soviet Union, a region with one of the world's highest densities of different, and contending, ethnic groups. About fifteen of these groups were represented at the workshop. Each night the participants would gather for vodka and more relaxed conversation, which often included stories of military brawn and bravado told by a Chechen political functionary named Shamil. One night the vodka was flowing a little more freely than usual, and this 6'5", three-hundred-pound Chechen announced, "Now, I will dance!" The group became still as Shamil began his traditional Chechen dance. Soon he was virtually flying through the air, slapping his huge hands against his knees and feet. The passion of his dance, of his identity, seemed to levitate him off the ground. Six months later when Russian troops stormed into Chechnya expecting a lightning-fast victory, I thought, "Boris Yeltsin would know there is no way this war will end quickly and easily if he had experienced that Chechen dance."

In addition, Saner (2000, pp. 171-175) discusses business negotiation and the flow of movement between disputants, referring to it as the "negotiation dance." Similarly, Albion (2001) uses the ballet metaphor to provide career management insight—offering three tips for using the discipline of ballet to relaunch a fulfilling career.

Examples of the actual use of dance as an aesthetic way of knowing are not as prevalent as use of the dance metaphor. Yet, The Stuart Pimsler Dance and Theater Company in Minneapolis, Minnesota, offers a glimpse of how dance and management education may become partners. While The Stuart Pimsler Dance and Theater Company does not exclusively work with managers, they work with healthcare professionals in their *Caring for the Caregiver Workshop*, using movement (dance) as a medium for participants to explore ways to express the feelings associated with their profession (Pimsler, 1996, pp. 19-22). Also, management consultant Barry Oshry has experimented with the dance metaphor *and* the actual use of dance to explore power in organizational systems in his work "The Terrible Dance of Power" (2001).

Storytelling

There has been an explosive growth in management scholars' interest in organizational discourse and narrative (e.g., Grant, Keenoy, & Oswick, 1998; Czarniawska, 1998), and more specifically, an interest in management storytelling. For years, management scholars have explored storytelling, covering a breadth of management topics, including: managerial communication (e.g., Armstrong, 1992), problem solving (e.g., Mitroff & Kilmann, 1975), organizational culture (e.g., Jones, 1991; Wilkins, 1984), organizational structure (Browning, 1991), strategy (e.g., Barry & Elmes, 1997; Shaw, Brown, & Bromiley, 1998), and organization development (e.g., Boje, Fedor, & Rowland, 1982; Boje, 1991a).

Recently, there has emerged a more practical and focused exploration of the use of stories in management/leadership and organization development. The following are examples of books written for managers—so they may more effectively use storytelling in: coaching (Parkin, 2001), training (Koppett, 2001; Parkin, 1998), influencing (Simmons, 2001), knowledge management (Denning, 2001), and simply becoming a better leader (Gargiulo, 2001). As management scholars and educators have begun to see organizations as occurring in and through stories—or as Boje (1991b) asserts, organizations are a big conversation, an on-going storytelling event—the "art of storytelling" will remain center stage in management education.

CONCLUSION

Today, there are examples emerging that show how organizations are moving beyond the one-shot use of arts-based learning, to beginning to integrate many art forms into an arts-based learning approach to management education, as well as embedding arts-based learning in their culture (e.g., Harris (1999); Manning (1998); Peiken (2000); Arts/Industry (2001); Arts & Business (2001); Poetry Places (2001)—descriptions of artist-in-residence programs in the US and in the UK). Also, consider, The St. Paul Companies, an insurance products company, based in St. Paul, Minnesota, that formed a unique partnership with COMPAS (1999), a Minnesota community arts organization—to create the "Diversity Education and the Arts" initiative. This initiative has begun to integrate many art forms into an arts-based learning approach to diversity education for managers. The company's "Arts and Diversity Committee's" mission states that the Committee "uses the broad spectrum of artistic expression to promote awareness about diversity issues." This unique program combines opportunities for leadership development with development of awareness about diversity issues—through the means of arts-based learning.

The examples provided in this chapter suggest that the use of aesthetic ways of knowing or arts-based learning has begun to grow, since Barnard (1940, p. xiv) called for managers to engage the aesthetic dimension of organizational life. Today there exists a growing *theory* base within the interdisciplinary field of organizational studies—the growing sub-specialty of organizational aesthetics (e.g., Strati, 1999, 1992; Linstead & Höpfl, 2000). In addition, there is growing recognition of the *practice* of arts-based learning in organizations—the actual *doing* of arts-based learning in management education. Today, there is also a growing recognition for the need to adequately train arts-based learning practitioners. In the US, the California Institute of Integral Studies has recently announced a post-baccalaureate certificate program in "Expressive Arts Consulting and Education" (California Institute of Integral Studies, 2001), and in Europe, Arts & Business's Creative Forum has been presenting training for the arts-based trainer since 1998 (Arts & Business, 2001).

It should be noted that the growth in arts-based learning in management education is not confined to the United States. Many of the examples noted in this chapter are from the United Kingdom (e.g., Sims & Doyle, 1994; Praxis: The Centre for Developing Personal Effectiveness, 2001), as well as Australia (e.g., Brearley, 2000), and New Zealand (e.g., Barry, 1994, 1996). In addition, the heavily European-influenced (e.g., Strati, Gagliardi, Linstead, Höpfl) theoretical base of organizational aesthetics continues to inform the practice of arts-based learning. In 2000, the European Institute for Advanced Studies in Management held a Workshop on Organising Aesthetics in Siena, Italy, organized by Strati and Guillet de Monthoux. And, in 2001 the Critical Management Studies Conference, held in Manchester, England, sponsored a stream in "Art and Aesthetics in Management and Organisation." Thus, this does not appear to be a US-centered phenomenon, with examples found throughout Europe and Australia/New Zealand. As sharing and documentation of arts-based learning practices continues, we will likely find that arts-based learning is not the domain of one national culture; but instead, we will find that arts-based learning allows us to cross the boundaries of nations and cultures.

The value of aesthetic ways of knowing has been asserted in a 1997 *Chronicle of Higher Education* article, where art historian Barbara Stafford asserted the importance of developing visual competence, especially now, where we're moving from a script-based to an image-based marketplace. And, similarly, Ramírez (1996) warns us of our over-dependence on discursive symbol systems (versus presentational symbol systems) as a growing problem. In fact, the Academy of Management created an "aesthetic submissions" category at the 2000 Annual Meeting in Toronto—allowing for the aesthetic representation of organizational and managerial life.

Why is this phenomenon of arts-based learning emerging? Marcuse (1977) suggests of arts-based learning, that the images and languages in works of art make "perceptible, visible, and audible that which is no longer, or not yet, perceived, said, and heard in everyday life" (p. 72). Simply, Marcuse offers, that the arts and arts-based learning may offer an *other* way of knowing.

As leaders and management educators seek to find other ways of communicating, creating knowledge, and making sense of the complexities of managing in the New Economy, we are likely to see the continued growth of arts-based learning in organizations. However, while we are likely to see growth, we will also likely continue to experience what Witkin (1990) referred to as the "trivialization of the aesthetic dimension of organizational life" (p. 327). So, while the growth of arts-based learning is asserted, the continued trivialization, or marginalization of aesthetic ways of knowing asserted by Gagliardi (1996, p. 567) and Ottensmeyer (1996, pp. 189-190) is also likely. More optimistically, Strati (1999) views organizational aesthetics to be an emerging discipline—in its infancy. This chapter asserts that, like organizational aesthetics, arts-based learning in management education is also in its infancy.

Regardless, as we continue to rethink management education, this chapter does not suggest that aesthetic epistemology (aesthetic ways of knowing) or arts-based learning can, or should, replace any of the more conventional practices of management education. Mindful of multiple ways of knowing, this chapter seeks to identify arts-based learning as a valuable adjunct to the current dominant pedagogy of management education.

APPENDIX A

Examples of Art as an Organizing Metaphor in Organization and Management Books

Arts Area	Title and Author	Organization/Manage ment Topics
Arts (General)	*Reframing organizations: Artistry, choice, and leadership* (Bolman & Deal, 1991)	using *reframing* to become a more effective leader
	The art of framing: Managing the language of leadership (Fairhurst & Sarr, 1996)	leadership communication
	Smart thinking for crazy times: The art of solving the right problems (Mitroff, 1998)	management problem solving
	Imaginization: The art of creative management (Morgan, 1993)	creative management thinking
	Leadership is an art (De Pree, 1989)	leadership
	Artful work: Awakening joy, meaning, and commitment in the workplace (Richards, 1995)	rethinking work

APPENDIX A (Continued)

Arts Area	Title and Author	Organization/Management Topics
Performing Arts/ Drama	*Unmasking administrative evil* (Adams & Balfour, 1998)	administrative evil
	Voices from the shop floor: Dramas of the employment relationship (Greene, 2001)	labor relations
	The experience economy: Work is theatre and every business a stage (Pine & Gilmore, 1999)	experience marketing
	Managing as a performing art (Vaill, 1989)	management and change
Visual Arts	*The art of the long view* (Schwartz, 1991)	strategic planning/scenarios
	Scenarios: The art of strategic conversation (van der Heijden, 1996)	strategic planning/scenarios
	Sculpting the learning organization: Lessons in the art and science of systemic change (Watkins & Marsick, 1993)	organizational learning and change
Literary Arts	*The poetry of business life: An anthology* (Windle, 1994)	poetic understanding of corporate life
	The heart aroused: Poetry and the preservation of the soul in corporate America (Whyte, 1994)	poetry and workplace spirituality
	Fictions of business: Insights on management from great literature (Brawer, 1998)	fiction as an insight on management
	Good novels, better management: Reading organisational realities in fiction (Czarniawska-Joerges & Guillet de Monthoux, 1994)	novels as organizational reality
Dance/ Movement	*The dance of change: The challenges of sustaining momentum in learning organizations* (Senge, Kleiner, Roberts, Ross, Roth, & Smith, 1999)	change as dance
	Dance lessons: Six steps to great partnerships in business and life (Bell & Shea, 1998)	business partnerships as dance
Music	*Leadership ensemble: Lessons in collaborative management from the world's only conductorless orchestra* (Seifter & Economy, 2001)	leaderless orchestra as model for collaborative management

APPENDIX B

Select Arts-Based Learning and Management Education Web Sites

Music

http://www.facethemusicblues.com/
http://orpheusnyc.com/about/process.htm
http://www.oneworldmusic.com/flashhome.html
http://TheMusicParadigm.com/
http://www.drumcircle.com/vmc/corporations/index.html
http://www.african percussion.com
http://www.jazz-impact.com/about.html
http://www.ubdrumcircles.com
http://www.pianoscapes.com/teachframe.html

Drama

http://www.theatreatwork.com/
http://www.dramaworks.com/
http://www.on-your-feet.com/
http://www.stepsroleplay.demon.co.uk/index.htm*
http://www.actor.demon.co.uk/*
http://www.access-comm.com/what.htm
http://www.cranfield.ac.uk/som/praxis/globe.htm*
http://www.energyspeak.com/main.html
http://www.learnitlive.com/
http://www.energyspeak.com/
http://www.pacificplayback.com
http://www.performanceofalifetime.com
http://www.powerandsystems.com/what_a_way.htm
http://www.moviesforbusiness.com/

Literature

http://www.moversandshakespeares.com/
http://www.hartwick.edu/hhmi/
http://www.poetrysoc.com/places/placeind.htm*
http://www.telescopecomics.com

Visual

http://www.hnl-consulting.com/ifvp.html
http://www.rootlearning.com/home.jsp
http://www.y-core.com/y_fb_fr.html

Cinema

http://www.hartwick.edu/hhmi/
http://www.moviesforbusiness.com/

Dance

http://www.terribledanceofpower.org/dance.htm

Storytelling

http://tech-head.com/dstory.htm
http://www.nextexit.com/
http://cbae.nmsu.edu/~dboje/sto.html
http://cbae.nmsu.edu/~dboje/storytellingorg.html
http://www.stevedenning.com/learn.htm

Miscellaneous

http://www.pair.xerox.com/
http://www.aom.pace.edu/meetings/2000/art/aomart.htm
http://www.artsandbusiness.org/
http://www.aandb.org.uk/*
http://www.jmkac.org/Arts/homepageARTSindustry.html
http://www.aandb.org.uk/html/cf/artswork.html*
http://www.ciis.edu/catalog/exacertificate.html
http://www.saarts.org/
http://www.artandcommunity.com/
http://www.lively-arts.co.uk/business.htm*

* denotes European-centered organizations

ACKNOWLEDGEMENTS

The author would like to acknowledge the following individuals. The article has benefited from the comments and encouragement of: Gene Audette, Elise Ballinger, David Barry, Laura Brearley, John Cimino, Bill Cleveland, Paul Nelson, Chuck Palus, Raymond Saner, Dave Schwandt, Steve Taylor, and the editorial encouragement of Robert DeFillippi and Charles Wankel. A special thank you to Peter Vaill—whose comments and encouragement were invaluable.

NOTE

1. Peter Vaill must be acknowledged as a pioneer of arts-based learning in management education. Vaill (1989) popularized the idea of "managing as a performing art." However, few people may realize that Vaill was thinking of this idea

well before his 1989 publication of *Managing as a Performing Art*. In fact, in 1974, his first year as Dean of the School of Government and Business at George Washington University, Vaill delivered a graduation speech, titled "Management as a Performing Art." In that speech, Vaill said to the graduating class, "I would like to explore a theme that I have been trying on for size in various ways the past few weeks. The more I think about it, the better I like it as a way of talking about education for management ... I would like to suggest that you are graduating from a School of the performing arts. I mean that in just about its literal sense, even though it trespasses, perhaps on the turf of other Schools and departments one finds in a University." Vaill concluded that speech by saying, "Congratulations on your graduation from our School of the performing arts of management." Thus, since 1974 Peter Vaill has been pioneering arts-based learning in management education. Today, he still speaks out – advocating this "other" way of knowing in management education. In one of his most recent writings, *Spirited Leading and Learning*, Vaill (1998) speaks of managerial leadership as a "new kind of liberal art" (p. 4) and asserts the value of "artistic consciousness" (p. 27) in the life of a managerial leader. Vaill has finally (a quarter century later) been joined by other contemporary management educators, such as Schein (2001), who also seeks to explain, "why should managers learn anything about art" (p. 81).

REFERENCES

Adams, G., & Balfour, D. (1998). *Unmasking administrative evil*. Thousand Oaks, CA: Sage.

African Percussion (2001). *African percussion home page*. <http://www.africanpercussion.com> (March 12).

Albion, M. (2001). The ballet of business. *Fast Company*, (February), 1-4.

Alvarez, J., & Merchán, C. (1992). The role of narrative fiction in the development of imagination for action. *International Studies of Management and Organization*, 22(3), 37-45.

Armstrong, D. (1992). *Managing by storying around: A new method of leadership*. New York: Doubleday.

Arts & Business (2001). *Arts & Business Home Page*. <http://www.aandb.org.uk/html/cf/artswork.html> (May 7).

Arts & Business Council. (2001). *Arts & Business Council Home Page*. <http://www.artsandbusiness.org/> (May 7).

Arts/Industry (2001). *Arts/Industry Home Page*. <http://www.jmkac.org/Arts/homepageARTSindustry.html> (May 7).

Atik, Y. (1994). The conductor and the orchestra: Interactive aspects of the leadership process. *Leadership and Organizational Development Journal*, 15(1), 22-28.

Augustine, N., & Adelman, K. (1999). *Shakespeare in charge: The bard's guide to leading and succeeding on the business stage*. New York: Hyperion.

Autry, J. (1994). *Life and work: A manager's search for meaning*. New York: Morow, William and Company.

Autry, J. (1996). *Confessions of an accidental businessman: It takes a lifetime to find wisdom*. San Francisco, CA: Berrett-Koehler.

Barnard, C. (1940). *The functions of the executive* (2nd ed.). Cambridge, MA: Harvard University Press.

Barrett, F. (1998). Creativity and improvisation in jazz and organizations: Implications for organizational learning. *Organization Science, 9*(5), 605-622.

Barrett, F. (2000). Cultivating an aesthetic of unfolding: Jazz improvisation as a self-organising system. In S. Linstead & H. Höpfl (Eds.), *The aesthetics of organization,* 228-245. London: Sage.

Barry, D. (1994). Making the invisible visible: Using analogically-based methods to surface the organizational unconscious. *Organizational Development Journal, 12*(4), 37-48.

Barry, D. (1996). Artful inquiry: A symbolic constructivist approach to social science research. *Qualitative Inquiry, 2*(4), 411-438.

Barry, D., & Elmes, M. (1997). Strategy retold: Toward a narrative view of strategic discourse. *Academy of Management Review, 22*(2), 429-452.

Barton, Z. (2000, June). Stage coaches: Second City Communications teaches better business through the elements of improvisation.*Fast Company,* 1-3.

Bastien, D. and Hostagier, T. (1988). Jazz as a process of organizational innovation. *Journal of Communication Research, 15*(5): 582-602.

Bastien, D. and Hostagier, T. (1992). Cooperation as communicative accomplishment: A symbolic interaction analysis of an improvised jazz concert.*Communication Studies, 43,* 92-104.

Bell, C., & Shea, H. (1998). *Dance lessons: Six steps to great partnerships in business and life.* San Francisco, CA: Berrett-Koehler.

Bilimoria, D. (1999). Management education's neglected charge: Inspiring passion and poetry. *Journal of Management Education, 23*(5), 464-466.

Björkegren, D. (1993). What can organization and management theory learn from art? In J. Hassard & M. Parker (Eds.), *Postmodernism and organizations,* 101-113. Newbury Park, CA: Sage.

Boje, D. (1991a). Consulting and change in the storytelling organisation.*Journal of Organizational Change Management, 4*(3), 7-17.

Boje, D. (1991b). The storytelling organization: A study of story performance in an office-supply firm. *Administrative Science Quarterly, 36*(1), 106-126.

Boje, D., Fedor, D., & Rowland, K. (1982). Myth making: A qualitative step in OD interventions. *Journal of Applied Behavioral Science, 18*(1), 17-28.

Bolman, L., & Deal, T. (1991). *Reframing organizations: Artistry, choice, and leadership.* San Francisco: Jossey-Bass.

Bowden, R., & Craven, A. (2001). The art in the art and science of organizational development. *Organizational Development Journal, 19*(3), 15-25.

Brady, F. (1986). Aesthetic components of management ethics.*Academy of Management Review, 11*(2), 337-344.

Brant, L., & Harvey, T. (2001). *Choosing and using music in training: A guide for trainers and teachers.* Hampshire, England: Gower.

Brawer, R. (1998). *Fictions of business: Insights on management from great literature.* New York: John Wiley & Sons.

Brearley, L. (2000). *Transitional times: A creative exploration of organisational life.* Presented at the meeting of the Academy of Management, Toronto, Canada. (August).

Brookfield, S., & Preskill, S. (1999). *Discussion as a way of teaching: Tools and techniques for democratic classrooms.* San Francisco: Jossey-Bass.

Browning, L. (1991). Organizational narratives and organizational structure. *Journal of Organizational Change Management, 4*(3), 59-67.

Buchanan, L., & Hofman, M. (2000, March). Everything I know about leadership, I learned from the movies. *Inc.,* 58-70.

Butler, T., & Waldroop, J. (1999). Job sculpting: The art of retaining your best people. *Harvard Business Review, 77*(5), 144-152.

Burden, C., & Mock, V. (1988). *Business in literature.* Atlanta: Georgia State University.

Burnham, J., Augustine, N., & Adelman, K. (2001). *Shakespeare in charge: The bard's guide to learning and succeeding on the business stage.* New York: Hyperion.

California Institute of Integral Studies (2001). *California Institute of Integral Studies Home Page.* <http://www.ciis.edu/catalog/exacertificate.html> (2001, May 7).

Carley, M. (1999). Training goes to the movies. *Training & Development, 53*(7), 15-18.

Carvajel, D. (1999). Forsooth, check this consultant: Once more unto Shakespeare for lessons on leadership. *New York Times* (Business Day), December 22.

Center for the Social Application of the Arts (2001). *Center for the Social Application of the Arts Home Page.* <http://www.saarts.org/> (May 7).

Center for the Study of Art & Community (2001). *Center for the Study of Art & Community Home Page.* <http://www.artandcommunity.com/> (May 7).

Champoux, J. (1999a). Film as a teaching resource. *Journal of Management Inquiry, 8*(2), 206-217.

Champoux, J. (1999b). Animated film as a teaching resource. Anderson Schools of Management, University of New Mexico, Working paper. Albuquerque.

Champoux, J. (2000a). *Organizational behavior: Using film to visualize principles and practices.* Cincinnati: South-Western College Publishing.

Champoux, J. (2000b). *Management: Using film to visualize principles and practices.* Cincinnati: South-Western College Publishing.

Channon, J. (1992). Creating esprit de corps. In *New traditions in business: Spirit and leadership in the 21st century,* 53-66. San Francisco: Berrett Koehler.

Chua, W., & Degeling, P. (1993). Interrogating an accounting-based intervention on three axes: Instrumental, moral and aesthetic. *Accounting, Organizations and Societies, 18*(4), 291-318.

Cimino, J. (1995). Re-thinking the arts as a gateway to executive education. *Mind Play, Newsletter of the Innovative Thinking Network, 2*(6).

Cleveland, W. (2000). *Art in other places: Artists at work in America's community and social institutions.* Amherst, MA: Arts Extension Service Press.

Cohen, S., & Jurkovic, J. (1997). Learning from a masterpiece. *Training & Development, 51*(11), 66-70.

COMPAS/St. Paul Companies (1999). *Arts and diversity project report, 1998-1999* [Brochure]. St. Paul, Minnesota.

Conrad, C. (1988). Work songs, hegemony, and illusions of self. *Critical Studies in Mass Communication, 5*(3), 179-201.

Corrigan, P. (1999). *Shakespeare on management: Leadership lessons for today's managers.* London: Kogan Page.

Crossan, M., White, R., Lane, H., & Klus, L. (1996). The improvising organization: Where planning meets opportunity. *Organizational Dynamics,* (Spring), 20-35.

Czarniawska, B. (1998). *A narrative approach to organization studies.* Thousand Oaks, CA: Sage.

Czarniawska, B. (1999). Management she wrote: Organization studies and detective stories. *Studies in Cultures, Organizations and Societies, 5,* 13-41.

Czarniawska-Joerges, B., & Guillet de Monthoux, P. (1994). *Good novels, better management: Reading organisational realities in fiction.* Chur, Switzerland: Harwood Academic Press.

Czarniawska-Joerges, B., & Jacobsson, B. (1995). Political organizations and *commedia dell'arte. Organization Studies, 16*(3), 375-394.

Davies, G., & Hancock, R. (1993). Drama as a learning medium. *Management Development Review, 6*(2), 11-13.

De Ciantis, C. (1995). *Using an art technique to facilitate leadership development.* Greensboro, NC: Center for creative leadership.

DeMott, B. (1989). Reading fiction to the bottom line. *Harvard Business Review,* (May-June), 128-134.

Denning, S. (2001). *The springboard: How storytelling ignites action in knowledge-era organizations.* Boston: Butterworth-Heinemann.

De Pree, M. (1989). *Leadership is an art.* New York: Doubleday.

DeVita, M. (1999). *Engaging the entire community: A new role for permanent collections* [Brochure]. New York: Lila Wallace-Reader's Digest Fund.

Di Ciantis, C. (1995). *Using an art technique to facilitate leadership development.* Greensboro, NC: Center for Creative Leadership.

Dobson, J. (1999). *The art of management and the aesthetic manager: The coming way of business.* Westport, CT: Quorum Books.

Drama Works. (2001). *Drama Works Home Page.* <http://www.dramaworks.com> (February 14).

Ebers, M. (1985). Understanding organizations: The poetic mode. *Journal of Management, 11*(2), 51-62.

Face the Music (2001). *Face the Music Web Page.* <http://www.facethemusicblues.com> (February 14).

Face the Music (n.d.). *Face the music and go beyond the corporate blues.* [Brochure]. Woodstock, NY.

Fairhurst, G. & Sarr, R. (1996). *The art of framing: Managing the language of leadership.* San Francisco: Jossey-Bass.

Ferris, W. (2001). *An innovative technique to enhance teambuilding: The impact of Image Theater.* Paper presented at the annual meeting of the Academy of Management, Washington, DC. (August).

Finn, D., & Jedlicka, J. (1998). *The art of leadership: Building business arts alliances.* New York: Abbeville Press.

Forbesfyi (2000). The bard in the boardroom. *Forbesfyi,* Spring 2000.

Gagliardi, P. (1996). Exploring the aesthetic side of organizational life. In S. Clegg, C. Hardy, & W. Nord (Eds.), *Handbook of organizational studies.* London: Sage.

Garaventa, E. (1998). Drama: A tool for teaching business ethics. *Business Ethics Quarterly, 8*(3), 535-545.

Gargiulo, T. (2001). *Making stories: A practical guide for organizational leaders and human resource leaders.* Westport, CT: Quorum.

Gelernter, D. (1999). *Machine beauty: Elegance and the heart of technology.* New York: Basic Books.

Gerde, V., Shepard, J., & Goldsby, M. (1996). Using Film to examine the place of ethics in business. *Journal of Legal Studies Education, 14*(2), 199-214.

Gershman, E. (2000). Managing to music: Orchestra inspires business leaders. *Stamford Advocate.*

Giacalone, R., & Jurkiewicz, C. (2001). Lights, camera, action: Teaching ethical decision through the cinematic experience. *Teaching Business Ethics, 5*(1), 79-87.

Gilbert, D. (1997). A critique and a retrieval of management and the humanities. *Journal of Business Ethics, 16*(1), 23-35.

Grant, D., Keenoy, T., & Oswick, C. (1998). *Discourse + Organization.* London: Sage.

Greenberg, E., & Miller, P. (1991). The player and the professor: Theatrical techniques in teaching. *Journal of Management Education, 15*(4), 428-446.

Greene, A. (2001). *Voices from the shop floor: Dramas of the employment relationship.* Burlington, VT: Ashgate.

Greene, M. (1995). *Releasing the imagination: Essays on education, the arts, and social change.* San Francisco: Jossey Bass.

Hansen, J., Porter, S., Kemp, M. (2000). *The physician's art: representations of art and medicine.* Raleigh, NC: Duke University Press.

Harris, C. (1999). *Art and innovation: The Xerox PARC artist-in-residence program.* Boston, MA: MIT Press.

Hartwick Humanities in Management Institute (n.d.). *Hartwick Classic Leadership Cases: Case Catalog* [brochure]. Oneonta, NY: Hartwick Humanities in Management Institute.

Harvard Management Update (1999). Dramatic training. *Harvard Management Update, 4,* 11.

Hatch, M. (1997). Jazzing up the theory of organizational improvisation. *Advances in Strategic Management, 14,* 181-191.

Hatch, M. (1998). Jazz as a metaphor for organizing in the 21st century. *Organization Science, 9*(5), 556-557.

Hatch, M. (1999). Exploring the empty spaces of organizing: How improvisational jazz helps redescribe organizational structure. *Organization Studies, 20*(1), 75-90.

Hawkins, L. (1998). Management consultants break out guitar, piano. *Milwaukee Journal Sentinel.* October 8.

Höpfl, H. (1995). Performance in customer service: The cultivation of contempt. *Studies in Cultures, Organizations and Societies, 1,* 47-62.

Houden, L. (1997). *Co-creating sacred space: The use of theatre in the transformation of conflict.* Unpublished dissertation, The Fielding Institute.

Huey, J., & Okrent, D. (1999). *Fortune: The art of covering business.* Salt Lake City, Utah: Gibbs-Smith.

Jackson, B. (2001). Art for management's sake: The new literary genre of business books. *Management Communication Quarterly, 14*(3), 484-490.

Jacobson, M. (1993). *Art for work: The new renaissance in corporate collecting.* Boston: Harvard Business School Press.

Jazz Impact (2001). *Jazz Impact Home Page.* <http://www.jazz-impact.com> (February, 14).

Jones, M. (1991). What if stories don't tally with the culture. *Journal of Organizational Change Management, 4*(3), 27-34.

Jones, M. (1984). Special section: Works of art, art as work, and the arts of working—implications for improving organizational life. *Western Folklore, 43*(3), 172-178.

Jones, M., & Shibley, J. (1999). Practicing relevance. In P. Senge, C. Roberts, R. Ross, B. Smith, G. Roth, & A. Kleiner (Eds.), *The dance of change: The challenges of sustaining momentum in learning organizations,* 190-192. New York: Doubleday.

Journal of Aesthetic Education (1996). Special issue: The Aesthetic face of leadership. *Journal of Aesthetic Education, 30*(4), 1-121.

Journal of Management Education (1997). Special issue: The art of good teaching. *Journal of Management Education, 21*(4), 443-524.

Kemske, F. (1995). *Human resources: A corporate nightmare.* New Haven, CT: Catbird Press.

Kennedy, E., & Lawton, L. (1992). Business ethics in fiction. *Journal of Business Ethics, 11,* 187-195.

Kennedy, C., Sell, J., & Zube, E. (1988). Landscape aesthetics and geography. *Environmental Review, 12*(3), 31-55.

Knights, D., & Willmott, H. (1999). *Management lives: Power and identity in work organizations.* London: Sage.

Koppett, K. (2001). *Training to imagine: Practical improvisational techniques to inspire creativity, enhance communication and develop leadership.* Sterling, Virginia: Stylus.

Leveson, D. (1988). The geologist's vision. *Journal of Geological Education, 36*(5), 306-309.

Levitt, T. (1993). Advertising: The poetry of becoming. *Harvard Business Review, 71*(2), 134-137.

Lieber, R. (2000). Leadership ensemble. *Fast Company, 34*(May), 286-291.

Link, A., & Boger, M. (1999). *The art and science of business valuation.* Westport, CT: Quorum Books.

Linstead, S., & Höpfl, H. (2000). *The aesthetics of organization.* London: Sage.

Lubins, P. (1999). Orchestrating success. In Rehm, R. (Ed.), *People in charge: Creating self managing workplaces.* Gloucestershire, Great Britain: Hawthorne Press.

Mangan, K. (1996). Teaching poetry to business students. *Chronicle of Higher Education,* (November 29), A10.

Manning, J. (1998). Will firms find art fits their palette? *CityBusiness,* (October 30) 5 and 37.

Marcuse, H. (1977). *The aesthetic dimension.* Boston: Beacon Press.

Martorella, R. (1990). *Corporate art.* New Brunswick, NJ: Rutgers University Press.

Mayer, D., & Clemens, J. (1999). *The classic touch: Lessons in leadership from Homer to Hemingway.* New York: Contemporary Books.

McAdams, T., & Koppensteiner, R. (1992). The manager seeking virtue: Lessons from literature. *Journal of Business Ethics, 11,* 627-634.

McKee, J. (1979). Literature and the land. *Journal of Geologic Education, 27*(3), 96-98.

McKenzie, G. (1988) Scope of metageology and geomusic, *Geological Society of America Abstracts with Programs, 19*(4): 233.

McNatt, R. (1998). The bard as business guru. *Business Week,* October 12, 1998.

Melhorn, W., & Kaplan, P. (1982). The geological observations of general George A. Custer. *Journal of Geological Education, 30,* 80-85.

Merritt, S. (1995). *Aesthetic experiential learning.* Unpublished manuscript. Polaroid Creativity Laboratory.

Mintzberg, H. (1987). Crafting strategy. *Harvard Business Review, 65*(4), 66-75.

Mintzberg, H. (1998). Covert leadership: Notes on managing professionals. *Harvard Business Review, 76*(6), 140-147.

Mirvis, P. (1998) Practice improvisation, *Organization Science, 9*(5): 586-592.

Mitroff, I. (1998). *Smart thinking for crazy times: The art of solving the right problems.* San Francisco: Berrett-Koehler.

Mitroff, I., & Kilmann, R. (1975). Stories managers tell: A new tool for organizational problem solving. *Management Review,* (July), 18-28.

Morgan, G. (1993). *Imaginization: The art of creative management.* Newbury Park, CA: Sage.

Movers & Shakespeares. (2000). *The Movers & Shakespeares Web Page.* <http://www.moversandshakespeares.com> (September 6).

Morgan, G. (1993). *Imaginization: The art of creative management.* Newbury Park, CA: Sage.

Moshavi, D. (2001). Yes and introducing improvisational theatre techniques to the management classroom. *Journal of Management Education, 25*(4), 437-449.

Movies for Business (2001). *Movies for Business Home Page.* < http://www.moviesforbusiness.com/> (May 7).

Muoio, A. (2000). The change agent blues. *Fast Company, 34,* 46.

Mullen, C. (1999). Reaching inside out: Arts-based educational programming for incarcerated women. *Studies in Art Educatino, 40*(2), 143-161.

Murnighan, J., & Conlon, D. (1991). The dynamics of intense work groups: A study of British quartets. *Administrative Science Quarterly, 36,* 165-186.

The Music Paradigm. (2000). *The Music Paradigm Web Page.* <http://TheMusicParadigm.com> (April 26).

Nelson, P. (1995). Telling organizational tales: On the role of narrative fiction in the study of organizations. *Organization Studies, 16*(4), 625-649.

Nissley, N. (1999a). Aesthetic epistemology: A proposed framework for research in human resource development. *Proceedings of the 1999 Conference on Human and Organizational Studies,* Ashburn, VA: The George Washington University, 306-356.

Nissley, N. (1999b). *Viewing corporate art through the paradigmatic lens of organizational symbolism: An exploratory study.* Unpublished doctoral dissertation, George Washington University, Washington, DC.

Nissley, N. (2000). *Tuning-in to organizational song as aesthetic discourse.* Paper presented at the European Institute for Advanced Studies in Management, Workshop on Organising Aesthetics, Sienna, Italy.

Nissley, N. (2001). *The trapeze artist, the museum, and arts-based learning in management education: Art & the Workplace.* Paper presented at the Midwest Academy of Management Meeting, Toledo, OH. (March).

Nissley, N., & Jusela, G. (2001). Using arts-based learning to facilitate knowledge creation: The art of intellectual capital at Equiva Services. In J. Phillips (Ed.), *Measuring and monitoring intellectual capital.* Alexandria, VA: American Society for Training and Development.

On Your Feet. (2000). *The On Your Feet Web Page.* <http://www.on-your-feet.com> (2000, January 23).

One World Music. (2000). *The One World Music Web Page.* <http://oneworldmusic.com> (September 13).

Organization Science (1998). Special issue on jazz improvisation and organizing. *Organization Science, 9*(5).

Orpheus. (2001). *The Orpheus Web Page.* <http://orpheusnyc.com> (2001, February 15).

Oshry, B. (Writer). (2001). *What a way to make a living: The search for partnership in organizational life* [Play].

O'Toole, J. (1995). *Leading change: Overcoming the ideology of comfort and the tyranny of custom.* San Francisco: Jossey-Bass.

Ottensmeyer, E. (1996). Too strong to stop, too sweet to lose: Aesthetics as a way to know organizations. *Organization, 3*(2), 189-194.

Pacific Playback. (2001). *The Pacific Playback Web Page.* <http://www.pacificplayback.com> (September 15).

Palus, C., & Horth, D. (1996). Leading creatively: The art of making sense.*The Journal of Aesthetic Education, 30*(4).

Palus, C., & Horth, D. (1998). Leading creatively.*Leadership in Action, 18*(2), 1-8.

Palus, C., & Horth, D. (2002). *The Reader's edge: Six creative competencies for navigating complex challenges.* New York: Wiley.

Parker, M. (1990). *Creating shared vision: the story of a pioneering approach to organizational revitalization.* Oslo, Norway: Norwegian Center for Leadership Development.

Parker, M., Higgins, M., Lightfoot, G., & Smith, W. (2001).*Science fiction and organizations.* New York: Routledge.

Parkin, M. (1998). *Tales for trainers: Using stories and metaphors to facilitate learning.* London: Kogan Page.

Parkin, M. (2001). *Tales for coaching: Using stories and metaphors with individuals and groups.* London: Kogan Page.

Peiken, M. (2000, June 14). Art/work: A Woodbury insurance company's artist-in-residence is giving new meaning to 'corporate culture.'*Saint Paul Pioneer Press,* 1E-2E.

Performance of a Lifetime (2001). *The Performance of a Lifetime Home Page.* <http://www.performanceofalifetime.com> (September 15).

Perry, L. (1996). Strategic improvising: How to formulate and implement competitive strategies in concert. *Organizational Dynamics,* 51-64.

Pestrong, R. (1968). Metageology: Science plus aesthetics.*Journal of Geological Education, 16*(4), 137-138.

Phillips, N. (1995). Telling organizational tales: On the role of narrative fiction in the study of organizations. *Organization Studies, 16*(4), 625-649.

Pimsler, S. (1996). Toward a new folk dance: Caregivers and other partners.*High Performance, 74*(Winter), 19-22.

Pine, J., & Gilmore, J. (1999). *The experience economy: Work is theatre and every business a stage.* Boston: Harvard Business School Press.

Pink, D. (1998). Metaphor marketing.*Fast Company, 14,* 214.

Pitcher, P. (1996). *The drama of leadership: artists, craftsmen, and technocrats and the power struggle that shapes organizations and society.* New York: John Wiley and Sons.

Plummer, C. (1988) Music to soothe the savage physical-geology student,*Journal of Geological Education, 36,* 88-89.

Pogacnik, M. (1999). Music, listening, and freedom: Some principles for coaching the senses. In P. Senge, C. Roberts, R. Ross, B. Smith, G. Roth, & A. Kleiner (Eds.), *The dance of change: The challenges of sustaining momentum in learning organizations,* 152-157. New York: Doubleday.

Porteous, J. (1986). Inscape: Landscapes of the mind in the Canadian and Mexican novels of Malcolm Lowry. *Canadian Geographer, 30*(2), 123-131.

Poetry Places (2001). *Poetry Places Home Page.* <http://www.poetrysoc.com/places/placeind.htm> (May 10).

Power and Systems (2001). *Power and Systems Home Page.* <http://www.powerandsystems.com/what_a_way.htm> (September 15).

Pratt, K. (2000). A pound of cure: Drum circles capture the cadence of the new economy while shaking up traditional notions about team-building. *Fast Company,* (May), 1-3.

Praxis: The Centre for Developing Personal Effectiveness (2001). *Praxis: Centre for Developing Personal Effectiveness Home Page.* <http://www.cranfield.ac.uk/som/praxis/globe.htm> (2001, May 7).

Quigley, M. (1998). Leadership as a performing art. *Executive Excellence, 15*(5), 13-14.

Ramírez, R. (1996). Wrapping form and organizational beauty. *Organization, 3*(2), 233-242.

Ramsey, S. (1996). Aesthetic interventions: The art of composing organizational renewal and well being. *OD Practitioner, 28*(4), 40-49.

Ramsey, S. (1997). Aesthetic interventions: The art of composing organizational well being. *OD Practitioner, 29*(4), 29-34.

Ratzan, R. & Carmichael, A. (1991). *Medicine: A treasury of art and literature.* New York: Beaux Arts Editions.

Reflections (2001). The arts in business and society [special section]. *Reflections (The Society for Organizational Learning Journal), 2*(4).

Reimer, B. & Smith, R. (1992). *The arts, education, and aesthetic knowing: Ninety-first yearbook of the National Society for the Study of Education (Part II).* Chicago, IL: University of Chicago Press.

Richards, D. (1995). *Artful work: Awakening joy, meaning, and commitment in the workplace.* San Francisco: Berrett-Koehler.

Rivette, K., & Kline, D. (1999). *Rembrandts in the attic: Unlocking the hidden value of patents.* Boston: Harvard Business School Press.

Robbins, S. (1990). *Law: A treasury of art and literature.* New York: Beaux Arts Editions.

Root Learning (2001). *Root Learning Home Page.* <http://www.rootlearning.com> (February 14).

Root Learning (n.d.). [Brochure]. Perrysburg, Ohio.

Rothman, J. (1997). *Resolving identity-based conflict in nations, organizations, and communities.* San Francisco: Jossey-Bass.

Rowntree, J. (2001). Learning, not logos—A new dialogue between arts and business. *Reflections* (Journal of the Society for Organizational Learning), 4(2), 76-79.

Sandberg, L., & Marsh, J. (1988). Focus: Literary landscapes—geography and literature. *Canadian Geographer, 32*(3), 266-276.

Saner, R. (2000). *The expert negotiator: Strategy, tactics, motivation, behaviour, leadership.* Amsterdam: Kluwer Law Publisher.

Schein, E. (2001). The role of art and the artist. *Reflections (Journal of the Society for Organizational Learning), 4*(2), 81-83.

Schmitt, B., & Simonson, A. (1997). *Marketing aesthetics: The strategic management of brands, identity, and image.* New York: The Free Press.

Schreyögg, G. (2001, August). *Organizational theatre and organizational change.* Paper presented at the annual meeting of the Academy of Management, Washington, DC.

Schwartz, P. (1991). *The art of the long view: The path to strategic insight for yourself and your company.* New York: Doubleday Currency.

Sciolino, E. (2001, July 26). Allegro, andante, adagio and corporate harmony: A conductor draws management metaphors from musical teamwork. *New York Times,* p. B1.

Seifter, H. (2001). The conductor-less orchestra. *Leader to Leader,* (Summer), 38-44.

Seifter, H., & Economy, P. (2001). *Leadership ensemble: Lessons in collaborative management from the world's only conductorless orchestra.* New York: Henry Holt & Company.

Senge, P., Kleiner, A., Roberts, C., Ross, R., Roth, G., & Smith, B. (1999). *The dance of change: The challenges of sustaining momentum in learning organizations.* New York: Doubleday.

Shafritz, J. (1999). *Shakespeare on management: Wise business counsel from the bard.* New York: Harper Collins.

Shaw, G. (1992). Using literature to teach ethics in the business curriculum. *Journal of Business and Technical Communications, 6*(2), 187-199.

Shaw, G., Brown, R., & Bromiley, P. (1998). Strategic stories: How 3M is rewriting business planning. *Harvard Business Review,* (May-June), 1-8.

Shea, J. (2000). Special edition: Geology and art. *Journal of Geoscience Education, 48*(3), 258-402.

Sicca, L. (2000). Chamber music and organization theory. *Studies in Cultures, Organizations and Societies, 6*(2).

Simmons, A. (1999). Using art in training. *Training & Development, 53*(6), 32-36.

Simmons, A. (2001). *The story factor: Inspiration, influence, and persuasion through the art of storytelling.* Cambridge, MA: Perseus Books.

Sims, D. & Doyle, J. (1995). Cognitive sculpting as a means of working with managers' metaphors. *Omega, International Journal of Management Science, 23*(2), 117-124.

Sittenfeld, C. (1999). How to wow an audience every time. *Fast Company, 27,* 84.

Stafford, B. (1997). Think again: the intellectual side of images. *Chronicle of Higher Education,* (June 20), B6-7.

Standish, D. (2000). *The art of money: The history and design of paper currency from around the world.* New York: Chronicle Books.

Stewart, T. (1997). The dance steps get trickier all the time. *Fortune,* (May 26), 157-160.

Strati, A. (1992). Aesthetic understanding of organizational life. *Academy of Management Review, 17*(3), 568-581.

Strati, A. (1999). *Organization and aesthetics.* London: Sage.

Tamarkin, B., Krantz, L., & Labarre, G. (1999). *The art of the market: Two centuries of American business as seen through its stock certificates.* New York: Stewart, Tabori, & Chang.

Taninecz, G. (1996). Following the muse: Artistic endeavors provide a creative outlet for executives, and could prove to be the key to tomorrow's corporate success. *Industry Week,* (August 19), 111.

Taylor, S. (2000). Aesthetic knowledge in academia: Capitalist pigs at the Academy of Management. *Journal of Management Inquiry, 9*(3), 304-328.

Taylor, S. (Writer & Director). (2001). *Soft targets* [Play].

Telescope Comics (2001). *Telescope Comics Home Page.* <http://www.telescopecomics.com> (September 15).

Tellijohn, A. (2001). Improvising business: Jazz impact brings musical concepts to the business world. *CityBusiness,* (March 30), 13 and 19.

The Terrible Dance of Power (2001). *The Terrible Dance of Power Home Page.* <http://www.terribledanceofpower.org/dance.htm> (September 15).

Theatre at Work (2001). *Theatre at Work Home Page.* <http://www.theatreatwork.com> (February 14).

Theatre at Work (n.d.). [Brochure]. St. Paul, Minnesota.

Theatre Techniques for Business People (2001). *Theatre Techniques for Business People Home Page.* <http://www.energyspeak.com/> (May 7).

Thomas, R. (1994). *What machines can't do: Politics and technology in the industrial enterprise.* Berkeley, California: University of California Press.

Traub, J. (1996). Passing the baton: What CEOs could learn from the Orpheus Chamber Orchestra. *New Yorker,* (September 2), 100-105.

UpBeat Drum Circles (2001). *UpBeat Drum Circles Home Page.* <http://www.ubdrumcircles.com> (March 12).

Vaill, P. (1974). *Management as a performing art.* Presented at the Commencement Address, School of Government and Business Administration, George Washington University, Washington, DC. (May).

Vaill, P. (1989). *Managing as a performing art: New ideas for a world of chaotic change.* San Francisco: Jossey-Bass.

Vaill, P. (1996). *Learning as a way of being: Strategies for survival in a world of permanent whitewater.* San Francisco: Jossey-Bass.

Vaill, P. (1998). *Spirited leading and learning: Process wisdom for a new age.* San Francisco: Jossey-Bass.

Valiga, T. & Bruderle, E. (1997). *Using the arts and humanities to teach nursing: A creative approach.* New York: Springer.

van der Heijden, K. (1996). *Scenarios: The art of strategic conversation.* New York: John Wiley.

Village Music Circles. (2000). *Village Music Circles Web Page.* <http://drumcircle.com> (2000, December 6).

von Krogh, G., Ichijo, G., & Nonaka, I. (2000). *Enabling knowledge creation: How to unlock the mystery of tacit knowledge and release the power of innovation.* New York: Oxford University Press.

Watkins, K., & Marsick, V. (1993). *Sculpting the learning organization: Lessons in the art and science of systemic change.* San Francisco: Jossey-Bass.

Weick, K., (1990). Organised improvisation: 20 years of organizing. *Communication Studies, 40,* 241-248.

Weick, K. (1998). Improvisation as a mindset for organizational analysis. *Organization Science, 9*(5), 543-555.

Weick, K., Gilfillan, D., & Keith, T. (1978). The effect of composer credibility on orchestra performance. *Sociometry, 36,* 435-462.

Weisbord, M. (1992). *Discovering common ground: How future search conferences bring people together to achieve breakthrough innovation, empowerment, shared vision, and collaborative action.* San Francisco: Berrett-Koehler.

Weisbord, M., & Janoff, S. (1995). *Future search: Finding common ground for action in organizations and communities.* San Francisco: Berrett Koehler.

Westlake, D. (1998). *The Ax.* New York: Mass Market.

White, D. (1996). "It's working beautifully!" Philosophical reflections on aesthetics and organization theory. *Organization, 3*(2), 195-208.

Whitney, J., & Packer, T. (2000). *Power plays: Shakespeare's lessons in leadership and management.* New York: Simon & Schuster.

Whyte, D. (1994). *The heart aroused: Poetry and the preservation of the soul in corporate America.* New York: Doubleday.

Whyte, D. (2001). *Crossing the unknown sea: Work as a pilgrimage of identity.* New York: Riverhead Books.

Whyte, D. (2001). *Crossing the unknown sea: Work as a pilgrimage of identity.* New York: Riverhead Books.

Wilkins, A. (1984). The creation of company cultures: The role of stories and human resource systems. *Human Resource Management, 23*(1), 41-60.

Williams, A. (1976). The art of geomorphology. *Journal of Geological Education, 24,* 18-20.

Williams, O. (1997). *The moral imagination: How literature and films can stimulate ethical reflection in the business world.* South Bend, IN: University of Notre Dame Press.

Windle, R. (1994). *The poetry of business life: An anthology.* San Francisco: Berrett-Koehler.

Witkin, R. (1990). The aesthetic imperative of a rational-technical machinery: A study in organizational control through the design of artifacts. In P. Gagliardi (Ed.), *Symbols and artifacts: Views of the corporate landscape,* 325-338. Berlin: Walter de Gruyter.

Wolff, M. & Clemens, J. (1999). *Movies to manage by: Lessons in leadership from great films.* New York: Contemporary Books.

Yanow, D. (2001). Learning in and from improvising: Lessons from theater for organizational learning. *Reflections (Journal of the Society for Organizational Learning), 4*(2), 58-62.

Yasso, W. (1972). Learning geological concepts through classroom and museum study of landscape art. *Geological Society of America Abstracts with Program, 4,* 711.

Young, D., & Dixon, N. (1995). Extending leadership development beyond the classroom: Looking at processes and outcomes. In E. Holton (Ed.), *Academy of Human Resource Development 1995 Conference Proceedings.* Austin, TX: Academy of Human Resource Development.

CHAPTER 3

SERVICE-LEARNING
Creating Community

Anne M. McCarthy, Mary L. Tucker, and Kathy Lund Dean

Institutions of higher education face many challenges as they prepare students for multiple roles: employees in an ever-changing economy, citizens in a democracy, and participants in their communities. Yet, some charge that universities are places that credential students and tenure faculty, but do not engage in activities that are "particularly relevant to the nation's most pressing civic, social, economic, and moral problems" (Boyer, 1996, p. 14).

Pedagogically, service-learning is a response to both Boyer's critique as well as to students' increasing demands for learning based in the real world. Service-learning reconnects universities to their communities by engaging students in projects that assist non-profit, community agencies. Service-learning can serve as a mission congruent, student centered classroom technique, whether in a public, private, secular, or religiously affiliated institution. Thus, service-learning integrates the university with its community and, in the process, prepares students for productive careers (Zlotkowski, 1996), citizenship (Cohen, 1994; Newman, 1985; Smith, 1994), and community involvement (McCarthy & Tucker, 2002; Myers-Lipton, 1998). For business schools, service-learning fulfills the challenge by

Rethinking Management Education for the 21st Century
A Volume in: Research in Management Education and Development, pages 63–86.
Copyright © 2002 by Information Age Publishing, Inc.
All rights of reproduction in any form reserved.
ISBN: 1-930608-21-7 (cloth), 1-930608-20-9 (paper)

Porter and McKibbin (1988) to link classroom theory and real world practice.

First, this chapter defines service-learning and discusses its theoretical basis, followed by a review of anecdotal and empirical research regarding its efficacy. The chapter ends with an overview of how to integrate community service learning into management courses.

WHAT IS SERVICE-LEARNING AND WHAT DOES IT HAVE TO OFFER?

The National Society for Experiential Education defines service-learning as "any carefully monitored service experience in which a student has intentional learning goals and reflects actively on what he or she is learning throughout the experience" (Kendall & Associates, 1990, p. 3). Service-learning, also known as community service learning or more recently as community based learning, is a type of experiential learning in which students directly apply what they are learning in the classroom as they perform service work at a community agency (Jacoby, 1996; Kolb, 1984; Luce, 1988).

It is important to distinguish service-learning from volunteer work. Volunteers, motivated by altruism, donate time and energy to a worthy cause, while students in service-learning experiences gain practical knowledge through the application of classroom theories to real world problems. The service is a graded experience, for which academic credit is awarded for the learning gained from the experience and not only for the service (Howard, 1993). Community based learning projects are also distinct from internships. An internship usually involves pay for performance and is the content of the entire course, whereas a service-learning project is embedded in a course as an assignment and is not paid for by the service organization.

Service-learning differs from other forms of experiential learning as a result of its basis in reciprocity and reflection (Giles & Freed, 1985). Ideally, there is reciprocity between what the student learns and how community needs are addressed, in which both student and agency teach and learn. Thus, service-learning involves students in community programs that lead to personal and academic development as well as community benefit (Tucker, Powell, & Cleary, 1999; Zlotkowski, 1996).

Like other forms of experiential learning, service-learning projects require students to reflect on their experience in terms of what they have learned about theories and concepts presented in class, and how it has impacted their lives. In some instances, an additional goal of reflection is to foster a critical understanding of the social conditions that make the work of non-profits necessary as well as the development of the learners' understanding of their roles and responsibilities as citizens of the community. In other words, reflection assists in synthesizing the connection between the service experience and course theories as well as the connection between student efforts and community well being (Kobrin & Mareth, 1996).

Professors, students, university entities, or community organizations can generate projects. See Appendix 1 for resources. Community based learning projects take many forms and can involve diverse community partners. Activities range from straightforward, individual projects to complex, team projects. Time requirements can vary from a few to over 50 hours and from two to sixteen weeks. The entire class may work with one non-profit community organization or students may choose from several organizations. In the case of Bentley College, service-learning is integrated across a majority of the curriculum (Kenworthy, 1996). Evaluation of student performance usually involves input from the outside agency and student deliverables.

Theoretical Basis of Service-learning

Most service-learning advocates trace the theoretical underpinnings of service-learning to the writings of John Dewey (Giles & Eyler, 1994a; Saltmarsh, 1996). Even those who primarily reference other education theorists or philosophers, e.g., Kolb (Cone & Harris, 1996), Rorty (Liu, 1995) or Mills (Hironimus-Wendt & Lovell-Troy, 1999), acknowledge that these theorists are rooted in Dewey.

Dewey's emphasis on experience, inquiry, and reflection as the conditions leading to knowledge forms the foundation of a "theory of knowing in service-learning" (Giles & Eyler, 1994a, p. 79). For Dewey (1933), acting and reflective thinking are essential components of learning. He proposes that, to be considered "educational," an experience should: generate interest, be intrinsically worthwhile, awaken creativity and a search for information, and take place over time. In addition, five dimensions from Dewey's writings contribute a theoretical basis that can be applied to service-learning. These dimensions are

1. linking education to experience,
2. enacting a democratic community,
3. participating in social service,
4. engaging in reflective inquiry, and
5. educating for social transformation (Saltmarsh, 1996).

Hironimus-Wendt and Lovell-Troy (1999) offer a theoretical base specifically for justifying the incorporation of community service learning into the field of sociology. Similar to other disciplines, there is little in sociology that provides a theoretical justification for service-learning as an alternative pedagogy with the exception of Myers-Lipton (1998), who advocates it as a pedagogy of social change. Agreeing with him that transformation is important, Hironimus-Wendt and Lovell-Troy use Myers-Lipton as a starting point in developing a broader theoretical foundation "in order to encourage other educators to consider its adoption and implementation" (p. 363) by drawing on the writings of Dewey and C. Wright Mills. Mills (1959) proposes that the ultimate goal of social science is to make the world more humane, reasoned, and free through activist social scientists rather than lecturers of textbook knowledge. Neither Dewey nor Mills, however, explicitly consider the possibility of students working in the community as part of their learning experience. Hironimus-Wendt and Lovell-Troy help to make the transition from theory to practice. They posit that, "by conceptualizing education as an active process requiring reflective thinking about experience, by linking school and community, by embedding educational ideas in a larger hope for social melioration, the service-learning movement owes much to" the work of Dewey and Mills (Hironimus-Wendt & Lovell-Troy, 1999, p. 366).

Since service-learning involves students in the community, it delivers on the promise of education that Dewey and Mills envision, according to Hironimus-Wendt and Lovell-Troy (1999). They propose that the "primary goal of service-learning is to rebuild moral community through a form of education grounded in experiential knowledge" (p. 366). Indeed, research suggests that participation in service-learning can lead to greater social responsibility and community service (Kendrick, 1996; McCarthy & Tucker, 2002).

Liu (1995) explicitly expands the discussion to the epistemological level. Drawing upon the works of Rorty (1979) and West (1989), Liu (1995) presents pragmatism as an alternate epistemology that leads to the pedagogical values of community, diversity, and engagement. Pragmatism, as opposed to dualism, maintains that knowledge is derived within the context of human discourse (Rorty, 1979). Liu (1995) proposes that pragmatism's principles of community, diversity, and engagement provide the context for discourse to occur. Hence, knowledge results within a context of community based discourse that integrates diverse views and engages people in exploring relations between concepts, activities, and people. If this context is the condition for knowledge, then it is also the context in which people learn. As Liu notes, "the connection between an alternative epistemology and service-learning is now clear: The pedagogical virtues implicated by pragmatism are among the defining features of service-learning" (Liu, 1995, p.16).

In a refinement of Liu's arguments, Richman (1996) asserts that if community based pragmatism is to serve as the epistemological justification for service-learning, then two conditions must hold. First, "the learning component must involve dialogue with the community served" (p. 10). Second, the community members must be experts on or have personal experience in the topics addressed in the dialogue. Thus, Richman argues, not all courses are appropriate for service-learning projects, since many courses involve theories and concepts of which community members have no relevant knowledge or experience (e.g., quantum physics).

Drawing from Kolb (1984), Moore (1990), and Freire (1994), Cone and Harris (1996) present a six-stage model to capture the individual, psychological and the interpersonal, socio-cultural nature of service-learning. Their model begins with the learning needs of the student, and then moves to the issues faced by the instructor in shaping the service experience. The third part of the model deals with the service experience as different from standard classroom pedagogy, which therefore should challenge students to broaden their perspectives. The fourth and fifth stages involve reflection. The fourth stage asks students to reflect in oral and written form using both their intellectual and emotional abilities. The fifth stage involves the instructor as guide and mentor in facilitating the student's learning. In the final stage, the emphasis returns to the students, where success is measured by the ability of students to undertake dialogue at an abstract level and to develop an overarching perspective of both their experience and the community. Cone and Harris believe that "service-learning needs to consider the personal and intellectual growth of both the student and community" (p. 32).

Like others (Dewey, 1938; Giles & Eyler, 1994a; Hironimus-Wendt & Lovell-Troy, 1999), Cone and Harris draw the distinction that the service experience does not necessarily bring about learning. They argue that the service project may even serve to confirm stereotypes and existing false perspectives. Instead of developing empathy, students "may fall into the trap of blaming the victim" (Hironimus-Wendt & Lovell-Troy, 1999, p. 367). In fact, Smith (1994) cautions that students can best make the connection between service and citizenship when the service is linked strategically to course objectives. It is, therefore, critical that the faculty member provides structure and guidance so that the students do not simply interpret the experience within their existing conceptualizations. If this occurs, then learning does not take place in terms of personal transformation.

All service-learning theorists view community based learning as a different way of understanding theory and, therefore, of learning class material. In addition, some see community service learning as a different way of knowing about the world in which we live. Thus, theorists range from viewing service-learning as an alternative pedagogy for integrating theory and practice, which brings both together in service to the community, to a pedagogy for integrating theory and practice with transformation of both the student and society. As seen in Figure 1, three themes emerge from theory: learning, skill development, and civic responsibility.

Service-learning leads to student learning even if personal or social transformation does not take place. Learning theory and skills can still occur if

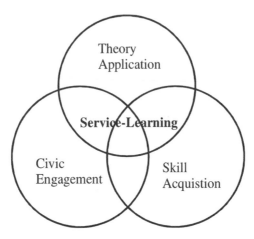

FIGURE 1
Learning Components in Service-learning

the conditions that Dewey sets forth are present in the project. That is, in acting and reflecting about theory and their skills, students learn even if they do not experience a dialogue with community members that results in personal transformation and increased civic responsibility. In fact, it is too narrow to limit the definition of service-learning to transformation through dialogue. Figure 2 shows how instructors can combine theory application, skill development, and civic engagement in differing degrees. The four quadrants represent the array of service-learning implementation currently found in higher education. However, there is some disagreement as to whether each quadrant truly represents service-learning.

In quadrant I, *forced volunteerism*, neither learning nor transformation regarding social ills is present. In this instance, the instructor, though well

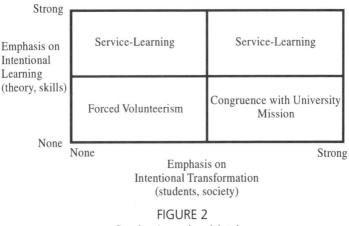

FIGURE 2
Service-Learning Matrix

intentioned, forces students to undertake community service in a misguided attempt to serve the community. For example, students may be required to clean up trash along a local river or work at the local humane society; yet, the activity is not tied into the course learning objectives. Even though the community benefits from the service, no link is created to course theories in the mind of the student.

In quadrant II, *congruence with university mission,* students participate in service projects that may or may not be directly related to the course, but are related to the institution's mission of encouraging civic participation. Although students may not be applying theories or refining skills relevant to a particular course, they are likely learning the values of serving others and realizing the need for social change. For advocates of values-based education (Bennett, 1993), this would be an appropriate use of service-learning. Advocates of service-learning at religiously affiliated or community based institutions argue that service-learning is a perfect vehicle for students to experience the values and culture of the university. Moreover, integration of service-learning in this manner fits such institutions' external stakeholder values. Yet, this type of service would not be viewed as service-learning within the theoretical context presented in this chapter, because it does not link course content to the service experience.

Quadrants III and IV, *service-learning,* represent the continuum of true community based learning applications in terms of intentionally creating opportunities for theory/skills learning and personal/social transformation. Which quadrant a particular project falls into depends in large part upon the learning goals of the course. Not all courses are appropriate for service-learning (Richman, 1996). Further, we argue that within the realm of appropriate courses, not all projects are equally suited for theory application and skill building as well as social and personal transformation. In quadrant III, projects concentrate on theory and skills. Such a concentration does not necessarily negate personal or social transformation only that it is secondary to learning theory and skills. In quadrant IV, equal emphasis is placed on theory, skills, and transformation. Yet, in some courses, like business ethics or the social environment of business, the emphasis is likely to be on the transformation end of the continuum.

What are some implications of service-learning theory for management faculty? As teachers in professional schools within universities, few business instructors see their role as encouraging social transformation as part of class content (Hogner, 1996). Rather, the goal of most faculty members is to teach theory (management, finance, marketing, etc.) and foster the skills to apply that theory. In this scenario, community based learning offers one way to build students' skills by connecting theory with practice in a real world setting. Is there a place, then, for the transformative goals of the service-learning theory continuum in the business curriculum? Some believe that, in classes focused on corporate social responsibility and ethics, service-learning offers a way for students to experience how organizations can improve the fabric of community life and transform society as well as to question an organization's "institutional separateness from society" (Hogner, 1996, p. 35). The growing stream of research reflects these themes; some researchers focus on theory application and skill building, other researchers focus on moral development and civic engagement leading to social change.

Service-Learning Research

The popularity of community service learning may be doomed to fade if evidence of its efficacy relies mainly on disjointed or personal reporting (Cohen & Kinsey, 1994). The risk that service-learning becomes yet another management education fad is real. While theoretical support is critical to its success, community service learning is more likely to become a permanent part of curricula if its effectiveness can be reliably demonstrated. Yet, even though service-learning has existed as a field of education since 1967, until the 1990s little effort was devoted to documenting the success of community based learning (Cohen, 1994; Giles & Eyler, 1994b).

In response to calls for research support, efforts are underway in a range of categories to substantiate community based learning as a legitimate pedagogy. Although the majority of service-learning articles focus on anecdotal observations of small groups by instructors, empirical studies are growing in interest and number. While relatively new research fields need empirical support, it is important not to discount anecdotal studies about the benefits of service-learning, which serve as launching sites for empirical work. Further, because community service learning bases its value in application, the growing literature of anecdotal evidence provides useful schema for instructors who want to integrate service-learning into their courses.

Some advocates focus on promoting the benefits of service-learning (Dillon & Van Riper, 1993; Jacobs, 1994), while others work toward establishing service-learning as a legitimate educational tool (Bringle & Hatcher, 1996; Sims & Sims, 1991; Zlotkowski, 1996). Others claim that community service learning can make classroom pedagogy more relevant. Nathan and Kielsmeier (1991) argue that service-learning creates new roles for students and teachers, makes use of action-based instructional methods, and leads to the learning of meaningful, real world content. Lund Dean (2001b) reports using service-learning as the organizing teaching model in a management capstone course in response to several consistent course frustrations, including textbook case obsolescence, an over-reliance on the rational/analytic decision-making model, and the lack of immediacy for student knowledge application. In her class, students analyzed and made real-time strategic decisions for their service organizations, bringing a fresh approach to the traditional case analysis in a capstone course.

Research focusing on student outcomes from participation in community based learning can be divided into the three themes derived from theory centering on theory application, skill acquisition, and civic engagement.

Theory Application

Anecdotal evidence on theory application is provided by Godfrey (1999), Lund Dean (2001b), and Kinsley (1993). In creating service projects, Godfrey's students practice marketing, finance, analytic skills, oral presentations, interviewing and data collection, project development, and accounting. The generative nature of the project allows students unique depth in skill applicability. Godfrey reports that students gain insight into the impact of organizational structure and differences in outside stakeholders' influence.

Lund Dean (2001b) found that combining theory with service tasks provides structure for students in confronting the often ambiguous environment of a service organization. In her strategic management course, students interview executive directors from service organizations about aspects of their mission and strategic plans. As a result, students integrate course concepts and develop an awareness of the bigger picture, both organizationally and socially. Similarly, based on an analysis of interviews and surveys, Kinsley (1993) reports that students learn basic skills and apply theory as a result of their service project.

Empirical studies have also shown that service-learning significantly enhances learning and improves grades. When compared to students taught by traditional methods, students in service-learning sections received significantly higher course grades (Kendrick, 1996; Markus, Howard, & King, 1993). In addition, students in the service sections were more likely than the students in traditional sections to agree that they performed at their potential and applied principles learned in the course. Cohen and Kinsey (1994) also reported significantly increased motivation and contextual understanding of specific, substantive course material.

Skill Application

Kenworthy-U Ren (1999) encourages instructors to focus less on the moral or citizenship arguments and more on the opportunity to acquire skills that service-learning provides. In an anecdotal report, she advances the position that instructors should not proffer a moral or ethical stance in their teaching role. Her students are, "...not expected to serve as volunteers, rather, they are professional consultants" (p. 381). The imperative here is a skills-based service to the community, in which students gain critical application experience.

Other anecdotal studies indicate that leadership skills can be developed and refined through community based learning projects (Dillon & Van

Riper, 1993). Students are exposed to management and leadership theories in organizational behavior, strategy, and general management courses; service-learning takes such abstract concepts and allows students to experience these theories. Dillon and Van Riper (1993) note:

> As future leaders, today's students require the understanding, skills, confidence, and motivation necessary to take actions that will ensure a sustainable and secure world. The service experience is taken back to the classroom where it is researched, analyzed, evaluated, and reflected on. Then, students apply their findings not only to the immediate problems of the community, but to the wider context of problems in the global community. (p. 48)

Service-learning, then, makes leadership come to life and requires action, analysis, reflection, retrenchment, and projection.

Working in community service learning projects also improves communication skills (Dillon & Van Riper, 1993; Lund Dean, 2001b; Tucker, et al., 1998; Tucker & McCarthy, 2001). Students have the opportunity to interact with each other in an environment that often requires adapting different ways of relating because the environment is new and ambiguous. Students reflecting on their service often report an increased mastery of communication skills, because working in unfamiliar environments forces them to draw upon different and/or auxiliary communication styles, when their comfortable and reflexive communication styles are no longer effective (Lund Dean, 2001a,b; Tucker, McCarthy, Hoxmeier, & Lenk, 1998). In such settings, students enrich communication competencies when working with agency management, clients, or their peers, mimicking role-based communication in the work world.

This is substantiated in an empirical study by Tucker and McCarthy (2001), which demonstrates that community service learning projects significantly increase students' presentation self confidence. Their experimental study of 127 undergraduate business students confirmed that students completing the service-learning project significantly increased their presentation self efficacy across multiple types of audiences compared to students in the sections without the service-learning project. Further, students with the most negative sense of self efficacy experienced the greatest improvement. Thus, participation in a community based learning assignment can increase students' confidence in their leadership and communication skills by achieving success in settings that cannot be reproduced in a university classroom.

Civic Responsibility

A number of researchers have found that service-learning develops caring skills that lead to higher levels of moral reasoning. Based on anecdotal observation, Godfrey (1999) reports that some of the most effective and lasting learning occurs when a service-learning experience humanizes problems and allows students access to such amorphous issues as homelessness or abandonment. He writes from the perspective that the capitalist market mechanism, and correspondingly the private enterprise, "hold the moral authority to set the social agenda for the United States" (p. 363-364). The imperative is to show students how to perform in organizations in ways that combine social justice with profitability.

Kinsley (1993) observes that, through service-learning, students develop a sense of community. Kinsley's case study, based on interview analyses and student surveys, concludes that community based learning projects provides students with the opportunity to experience a sense of community by creating community within the classroom, school, neighborhood, and city. Gorman and others, as reported in Newman (1985), compared students in a service-learning course, who worked with disadvantaged people, with students in an ethics course. They found that the service-learning participants scored significantly higher on a test measuring principled moral reasoning and conclude that these students exhibit an increase in "personal responsibility, public interest, self confidence, and the capacity to achieve needed for civic learning" (p. 63).

Kolenko, Porter, Wheatley and Colby (1996) reviewed nine community service learning programs in schools of business and found that service-learning expands the repertoire of concrete experiences necessary to develop fully as a manager. These authors argue that business school educators have a complex teaching agenda that includes technical learning as well as student self-diagnosis and understanding. They note that, "only recently has the responsibility for personal growth and community service entered this crowded agenda. Quests for self-knowledge and redefinition of the self through learning are relatively new demands on most business educators" (Kolenko, et al., 1996, p. 134). While service-learning fosters ethical behavior and social responsibility, Kolenko et al. focus primarily on the affective learning outcomes that community based learning pedagogy can offer, and echo Schein (1990) when they assert student needs for self discovery as a means to acquiring effective leadership skills.

In other studies (Kendrick, 1996; Markus et al., 1993), students in service-learning sections demonstrate significant increases in their assessment of the importance of several factors, including: helping people in need, working toward equal opportunity, improving the community, giving to charity, making a difference in the world, and tolerating and appreciating others. In a study of 226 liberal arts undergraduates, Batchelder and Root (1994) scored student journal entries along three dimensions: cognitive approaches to social problems, prosocial moral development, and identity development. When compared to students in traditional courses, service-learning students demonstrated a significantly greater resolve to engage in prosocial behavior and a greater awareness of social problems. Similarly, using pre-post data on 56 students, Giles and Eyler (1994b) found that, as a result of a community service learning experience, college students showed a significant increase in their beliefs that they

1. can make a difference,
2. should be involved in community service, and
3. would perform volunteer service in the near future.

Boss' (1994) research supports the assertion that community service incorporated into course requirements provides students with greater gains in moral reasoning. Using Rest's Defining Issues Test, she found that service work in combination with a discussion of relevant moral issues moved students into the post-conventional stage of principled moral reasoning. "Community service not only improves sensitivity to moral issues, but helps students overcome negative stereotypes that often act as a barrier to interacting with other people" (Boss, 1994, p. 194).

Another empirical study, conducted nationally by Eyler, Giles, and Braxton (1997), reports a significant impact from service-learning programs on students' attitudes, values and skills as well as how they perceive social issues over the span of one semester. In this study,

> feeling connected to community, seeing the systemic or political nature of social problems, feeling a need to give priority to greater social justice as well as increased perspective-taking capacity were uniquely affected by service-learning. Providing opportunities for students to link community service with their classroom experience adds value to their college experience and enhances qualities of understanding and commitment that lead to effective citizenship participation. (p. 13)

These research efforts serve to strengthen the legitimacy of service-learning and are critical steps to gaining greater pedagogical acceptance for community based learning in higher education. Clearly, service-learning has an impact on students in terms of improving their ability to apply theory, strengthening their skills, and developing their sense of social responsibility. Given all the benefits, it becomes appealing to incorporate service-learning into management courses, since at its root it is an experiential learning tool. The next section discusses how this can be accomplished.

INCORPORATING SERVICE-LEARNING
INTO MANAGEMENT COURSES

Where skill acquisition is a major goal of the course, service-learning provides an outlet for students to practice what they learn (Kenworthy-U Ren, 1999). For example, management students put into practice organizational development concepts by conducting analyses and survey feedback programs as well as facilitating planning sessions for organizations. Where learning theory is important, community based learning, again, provides a powerful vehicle that brings to life complex, ambiguous, and sometimes nebulous concepts. For example, students in a leadership class confront the concept of powerlessness while working with disadvantaged groups as they learn about the effective use of power by leaders (Bies, 1996). Finally, where civic involvement is a goal along with theory application and skill building, service-learning provides a sound pedagogical method. Thus, strategic management or entrepreneurship students practice planning skills by writing business plans for ventures that promote business development and social goals in low-income neighborhoods (Collins, 1996). The results are a win-win for all involved. This section presents the key steps for implementing service-learning into management courses.

Successful adoption of community service learning into any course depends upon thorough planning and administration. It is critical to remember that the service activity is not an add-on component, but rather an integrated, experiential way to teach skills and concepts (Bringle & Hatcher, 1996; Kendall, 1990). Thus, as indicated by theory, faculty should

1. plan the service-learning activity with course objectives at the forefront and assess what essential learning points can be introduced or reinforced through the activity (Cone & Harris, 1996);
2. determine community needs;
3. structure the service activity, with due dates and evaluation methods;
4. prepare the students for the activity, including training; and
5. reflect and assess.

Start with Learning Objectives

Starting with course objectives enables the instructor to identify which theories and/or skills might best be learned in an applied setting. Theory emphasizes the need for careful planning so that the student is intellectually challenged and the activity is truly educational (Dewey, 1933; Giles & Eyler, 1994a; Hironimus-Wendt & Lovell-Troy, 1999). As identified by a number of writers in the field, if service-learning initiatives are to become a permanent part of classroom pedagogy, then each community based learning project needs to be closely tied to the content of the course (Cone & Harris, 1996; Kendall, 1990; Strage, 2000). Even general types of learning objectives such as better critical thinking and writing skills may be explicitly linked to service-learning activities (Vogelgesang & Astin, 2000).

It is possible that one type of service-learning project may be used in different management classes, with relative emphasis placed on the aspect of the project that is more salient in a particular class. For example, students in both leadership and communication courses can mentor elementary students in reading. Mentoring projects are an excellent way for students to be introduced to community service. Each student works one on one with an elementary student and can schedule mentoring meetings around class and work constraints. Leadership students practice such activities as modeling, inspiring, encouraging, and serving others while mentoring elementary students (Kouzes & Posner, 1987). Conversely, in a communication class, students can write a press release about their community service learning project or design a marketing brochure to promote the program, thereby practicing different skills.

Determine Community Needs

Clearly articulated learning goals are only half of the equation. The other half is how the service activity aids the community. Faculty implementing service-learning must investigate and prepare appropriate service sites that fit with the course goals. Instructors should not define needs *for* the community partner, but rather *with* the partner (Ferrari & Worrall, 2000). For example, a strategic management professor may want the students to practice strategy formulation skills for local agencies. Yet, the more pressing need of the majority of agencies might be in designing and implementing human resource recruiting procedures, budget programs, or computer information systems.

For a first time implementation, it is helpful for the instructor to visit the service site(s). These visits become less necessary for repeated activities with the same community partner. Through discussion with agency directors, the instructor can tailor the activity to fit both classroom goals and agency requirements.

During the initial planning visit with community partners, faculty can describe what students have to offer by outlining learning objectives, possible time commitment, and potential logistic limitations. It is useful for instructors to gather pertinent information, including contact person, location relative to the university, availability of public transportation, number of students that can be accommodated, orientation and training requirements, and hours of service.

Structure the Activity

Once the service-learning activity is aligned with course objectives and designed to meet community needs, the project can be formally structured. Time spent before the course begins will contribute to increased satisfaction for students and community partners.

One formal way to structure the activity is to incorporate the community based learning project into the course syllabus. That involves building course objectives for the community project and providing a detailed explanation of the project, along with expected deliverables. Deliverables for the service agency are defined by the activity to be engaged in and/or the content to be delivered in the form of written reports or oral presentations. Deliverables to be graded as part of the class assignment might include writing assignments (papers, journals), discussion topics, presentations, reports to the agency, and other activities that provide a means for linking the service activity to the course content (Jacoby, 1996).

Another way of establishing student expectations is to ask students to sign a formal agreement or write their own contract, which is discussed later. In the formal agreement, students affirm, for example, that they understand the rationale for the service-learning component of the course. See Table 1 for an example of a formal agreement. It is also helpful to provide students with a list of criteria for measuring a successful out-

TABLE 1
Example of Student Agreement

Student Agreement
• I understand the rationale for the service-learning component of this course.
• I agree to arrange my schedule during this term to participate in the service-learning experience for a minimum of 10 hours.
• I agree to participate actively and professionally in the service-learning experience by making every appointment and arriving on time.
• I agree to reflect on my service-learning experiences at least weekly and use the highlights in the service-learning reflection paper.
• I agree to participate in any opportunities for photographic, audio, and video recording of parts of my service-learning experience.
• I agree to allow my reflections to be used to promote service-learning.
• I agree to coordinate with the instructor in obtaining legal release forms prior to any photographic, audio, or video recording.
• I agree to display the utmost in professionalism as a representative of this course, the College of Business, and the university during my service-learning experiences.
↔↔↔↔↔↔↔↔↔↔
• I agree to communicate with the instructor as soon as possible if there are any problems that arise with any aspect of this course.
Sign Name   Date
Print Name

come. Formalization of the service-learning activity provides the foundation for faculty to prepare the students.

Prepare the Students

It is critical for the instructor to communicate the intended outcomes to the students in order to provide a framework for what is likely to be a new educational experience for the students. Careful planning "involves providing students with pre-service training and theoretical concepts that the student will be expected to apply and understand" (Cone & Harris, 1996, p. 33). To best prepare students, instructors need to discuss the service on the first day as part of the overview of the course—providing a clear link between course theories, the service activity, and assessment of student learning (Lund Dean, 2001a,b; Markus et al., 1993; Tucker & McCarthy, 1999). The instructor may want to stress that the community service learning activity is another way of learning course materials, as are exams and papers (McCarthy & Tucker, 1999).

Faculty should describe the benefits of service-learning, the relevance to the course objectives, and the means for assessing learning. Previous students' testimonials can also inspire students to embrace something that often pushes them outside their comfort zone or challenges their expectations regarding formal education. Inviting agency representatives to visit the class or hosting a panel presentation, if multiple community partners are involved, is also effective.

Be prepared for overt resistance from a few students. The majority will not say anything, but still may be skeptical. A small percent will embrace the idea and instructors can build on their positive attitudes. The more the instructor openly addresses student concerns, fears, and expectations regarding the service experience, the more easily students will overcome these barriers (Hogner, 1996). The instructor must prepare students with adequate skills, while also allowing students their own discovery process.

Some service-learning supporters advocate that faculty consider having an alternative for those students who are legitimately unable to participate in the service experience (Tucker et al., 1999). Since the service is a learning activity, the instructor may want to use the example of a paper, project or exam in negotiating with the student what content the student needs to learn, how he or she will learn it, and when the alternate assignment will be due. Faculty can help students avoid the inevitable temptation to procrastinate by providing a timeline or benchmarks for contacting the agency, meeting with supervisors and signing contracts as well as beginning and completing the service.

Instead of a formal agreement, instructors may have students write a contract for the activity as an effective way to help them organize what needs to be done; it also reinforces course content and expected outcomes (Zlotkowski, 2000). Contracts delineate several operational issues in the form of an individual project plan, including the:

- name of the service organization,
- type of clients served,
- work to be done (deliverables),
- course-related competencies students expect to develop, and
- professional standards for performance (timeliness, reliability, dress, etc).

Some contracts also include a commitment by the students to seek advice from the instructor or agency personnel if difficulties arise. By completing a contract that includes an individual project plan, students reinforce their commitment to the activity.

Reflect and Assess

Student reflection is most effective when it takes place during and at the completion of the activity. Assessment involves evaluating student performance as well as obtaining feedback from the agency partner(s) and the students.

Student Reflection

Periodically, during the project, classroom discussions can tie theory to the activity and maintain a culture for continued commitment. Thus, it is important that faculty devote class time to dialogue with the students as the project is progressing. Short, frequent discussions are crucial in helping students link theory with experience (AAHE, 1998; Kohls, 1996), celebrate personal triumphs or growth events, and share personal issues—such as handling discomfort or overcoming fear and ambiguity. In addition, reflection upon project completion provides an opportunity for students to revisit the entire project and connect how the activity led to learning and growth.

It is important that faculty avoid the assumption that students are familiar with or competent at reflection work; students may need to be taught how to reflect. Conducting reflection throughout the semester familiarizes students with the different skill sets and ways of thinking about an activity that make reflection a unique and fruitful endeavor. Consequently, students are more comfortable with completing a formal reflection at the end of the activity. Structured reflection questions provide a foundation for students with little or no reflection experience yet allow a tremendous degree of latitude for students to personalize their work. See Table 2 for an example of a reflection assignment.

Evaluating Student Performance

Grading is usually based on several components: successful completion of the service contract hours, community partner evaluation, and instructor assessment. Instructors can assess the first and second components by asking the service agency to complete an evaluation of each student's performance. Table 3 contains an example of a community partner evaluation form. For the third component, instructors can assess learning on a number of dimensions, including theory integration, analytical skills, communication skills, critical thinking and synthesis. This is usually accomplished through journals, reflection papers and/or final reports for the community partner. While some portion of credit can be awarded for completing the assignment, the bulk credit is awarded for the learning gained from the experience as measured by class assignments.

TABLE 2
Example of Agency Rating Form

Agency Rating Form	
Student Instructions: Give this form to your supervisor at _____ to fill out.	
Supervisor Instructions: Please fill out this form and return to the principal 1-10 with 10 being 'Stellar''	
Student's Name:_____	*Rating*
1. This student kept each appointment	_____
2. This student was always prompt.	_____
3. This student was able to _____ (insert skill to be practiced)	_____
4. This student represented the university in a professional manner.	_____
5. This student set a good example, _____ (insert additional skill)	_____
TOTAL	/50
Comments:	
Rater's Signature:_____	

TABLE 3
Example of Instructions for a Reflection Paper

Community Service Learning (CSL) Reflection Paper

Introduction—Your CSL Project

Where your CSL Project was completed

- Teacher
- Class
- Students(s)

Reflection on your CSL Experience

Describe your CSL Experience

- Look back at your first day. How did you feel that day, and how is that different from the way you feel there now? What has changed? Why has it changed?
- What was fun or satisfying about this project?
- What was the best thing that happened to you there? Why was it the best?
- What was the most difficult part of being there? Why?

Evaluate your CSL Experience

- How does your service experience link to the content covered in your class? What theories from class did you utilize and reinforce in this project? What makes the connection meaningful to you?
- What business skills did you learn in this project that will be helpful to you in your career?
- What are some of the benefits of integrating service and academic learning?
- What did you learn about the community through your service-learning experience? Did your service-learning experience alter your perception of the community? How?
- Did your service-learning experience alter your perception of yourself? In what way?
- How has the community benefited from your service experiences?

Synthesis

- How has this activity affected the way you view your leadership and emotional intelligence?
- What aspects of leadership and emotional intelligence will you plan to develop further because of this service-learning experience?
- In what ways are you a better leader because of this experience?

Obtaining Project Assessment from the Community Partner and Students

It is important to assess the project by asking for input from the community partner as well as from students. In order to achieve continuous improvement, faculty will want to contact the community partner at least once mid-project and at the end of the project to seek feedback. Similarly, student input may shed light on the content of the project and the degree of cooperation from the agency. Instructors may consider ending a relationship with an agency that is not responsive. Group feedback, when appropriate, provides a way for instructors to assess the effects of group dynamics and intra-group mechanics on the service experience. Finally, instructors may encourage students to comment on the service-learning experience on the end-of-semester course evaluation form.

By paying close attention to all these implementation details, the instructor is more likely to create a community based learning project that is effective and enjoyable for the students and the service agency.

SUMMARY

Increasingly, university instructors are charged with creating real world learning opportunities in order to prepare students for employment and develop within students a sense of citizenry and moral responsibility (Kolenko et al., 1996). Community service learning can serve to integrate the university with its community and, in the process, prepare students for productive careers, citizenship, and community involvement. In addition, service-learning fulfills the need to link classroom theory to real world practice. Service-learning is a type of experiential learning in which students directly apply what they are learning in the classroom while performing service work at a community agency.

John Dewey's (1933) advocation of doing and reflecting as well as his five dimensions of learning form the theoretical underpinning for service-learning, including

1. linking education to experience,
2. enacting a democratic community,
3. participating in social service,
4. engaging reflective inquiry, and
5. educating for social transformation.

Cone and Harris (1996) propose a six-stage framework for service-learning that captures the individual, psychological and the interpersonal, socio-cultural nature of community based learning. Lui (1995) and Richman (1996) ground service-learning in pragmatic epistemology that emphasizes learning through dialogue with community members.

While theoretical support is crucial to its success, community service learning must also validate its effectiveness in order to become a permanent part of the curriculum. Research begun in the 1990s focuses on student outcomes from participation in service-learning and confirms that service-learning has a significant impact on students in terms of improving their learning, strengthening their skills, and developing their sense of social responsibility through real world experience. Given these benefits, service-learning is a highly effective pedagogy for enhancing student learning. When deciding how to make our management courses more effective, we need to remember an old adage from Confucius:

I hear, I forget
I see, I remember
I do, I understand
    —Confucius

APPENDIX 1. SERVICE-LEARNING DEVELOPMENT RESOURCES

Community service learning projects are versatile tools that can be adjusted to fit the needs of each classroom. The Corporation for National Service provides guidance on developing campus community service-learning offices. Similarly, Campus Compact at Brown University has a list of business programs with service-learning courses.

www.compact.org Campus Compact

http://umn.edu/~serve is the National Service Learning Clearinghouse

www.aahe.org/service/srv-lrn.htm American Association for Higher Education S-L site

http://Csf.colorado.edu/sl/ The Colorado Service-Learning home page

www.umich.edu/~ocsl/MJCSL/ Michigan Journal of Community Service Learning

REFERENCES

American Association for Higher Education, (2002). *Assessment Forum.* http://www.aahe.org/assessment/web.htm

Batchelder, T. H., & Root, S. (1994). Effects of an undergraduate program to integrate academic learning and service: Cognitive, prosocial cognitive, and identity outcomes. *Journal of Adolescence, 17,* 341-355.

Bennett, W.J. (Ed.). (1993). *The book of virtues: A treasury of great moral stories.* New York: Simon & Schuster

Bies, R. J. (1996). "Down and out" in D.C.: How Georgetown M.B.A. students learn about leadership through service to others. *Journal of Business Ethics, 15*(1), 103-110.

Boss, J. (1994). The effect of community service work on the moral development of college ethics students. *Journal of Moral Education, 23*(2), 183-198.

Boyer, E. L. (1996). The scholarship of engagement. *Journal of Public Service & Outreach, 1*, 11-20.

Bringle, R. G., & Hatcher, J. A. (1996). Implementing service-learning in higher education. *Journal of Higher Education, 67*(2), 221-223.

Cohen, J. (1994). Matching university mission with service motivation: Do the accomplishments of community service match the claims? *Michigan Journal of Community Service Learning, 1*, 98-104.

Cohen, J., & Kinsey, D. (1994). "Doing good" and scholarship: A service-learning study. *Journalism Educator,* (Winter), 4-14.

Collins, D. (1996). Serving the homeless and low-income communities through business and society/business ethics class projects: The University of Wisconsin-Madison plan. *Journal of Business Ethics, 15*(1), 67-85.

Cone, D. & Harris, S. (1996). Service-learning practice: Developing a theoretical framework. *Michigan Journal of Community Service Learning, 3*(1), 31-48.

Dewey, J. (1933). *How we think.* Boston: Heath.

Dewey, J. (1938). *Experience and education.* New York: Macmillan.

Dillon, P., & Van Riper, R. (1993). Students teaching students: A model for service and study. *Equity & Excellence in Education, 26*(2), 48-52.

Eyler, J., Giles, D. E., Jr., & Braxton, J. (1997). The impact of service-learning on college students. *Michigan Journal of Community Service Learning, 4*, 5-15.

Ferrari, J.R. & Worrall, L. (2000). Assessments by community agencies: How 'the other side' sees service-learning. *Michigan Journal of Community Service Learning, 7*, 35-40.

Freire, P. (1994). *Pedagogy of the oppressed.* New York: Continuum.

Friedman, S. D. (1996). Community involvement projects I Wharton's MBA curriculum. *Journal of Business Ethics, 15*(1), 95-101.

Giles, D. E., Jr. (1991) Dewey's theory of experience: Implications for service-learning. *Journal of Cooperative Education, 27*(2), 87-90.

Giles, D. E., Jr., & Eyler, J. (1994a). The theoretical roots of service-learning in John Dewey: Toward a theory of service-learning. *Michigan Journal of Community Service Learning, 1*, 77-85.

Giles, D. E., Jr., & Eyler, J. (1994b). The impact of a college community service laboratory on students' personal, social, and cognitive outcomes. *Journal of Adolescence, 17*, 327-339.

Giles, D. E., Jr., & Freed, J. (1985). *The service learning dimensions of field study: the Cornell human ecology field student program.* Paper presented at the National Conference on Service-Learning, Washington, D.C. (March).

Godfrey, P.C. (1999). Service-learning and management education: A call to action. *Journal of Management Inquiry, 8*(4), 363-378.

Hironimus-Wendt, R. J., & Lovell-Troy, L. (1999). Grounding service-learning in social theory. *Teaching Sociology, 27*, 360-372.

Hogner, R. H. (1996). Speaking in poetry: Community service-based business education. *Journal of Business Ethics, 15*(1), 33-43.

Howard, J. (1993). Principles of good practice in community service learning pedagogy. *Praxis I: A faculty casebook for community service learning.* Ann Arbor, MI: OCSL Press.

Jacoby, B. (1996). Service-Learning in today's higher education. In B. Jacoby (Ed.), *Service learning in higher education: Concepts and practices,* 3-25. San Francisco, CA: Jossey-Bass Inc.

Jacobs, J. (1994). Service-learning: A new approach in higher education.*Education*, 97-98.

Kendall, J. C. & Associates (Eds.) (1990). *Combining service and learning: A resource book for community and public service*, 1-33. Raleigh, NC: National Society for Internships and Experiential Education.

Kendrick, J. R., Jr. (1996). Outcomes of service-learning in an Introduction to Sociology course. *Michigan Journal of Community Service Learning*, 3, 72-81.

Kenworthy, A. L. (1996). Linking business education, campus culture and community: The Bentley service-learning project. *Journal of Business Ethics*, 15(1), 121-131.

Kenworthy-U Ren, A.L. (1999). Management students as consultants: An alternative perspective on the service-learning 'call to action.' *Journal of Management Inquiry*, 8(4), 379-387

Kinsley, C. W. (1993). Community Service learning as a pedagogy.*Equity & Excellence in Education*, 26(2), 53-59.

Kobrin, M. & Mareth, J. (1996). *Service matters: A source book for community service in higher education.* Denver, CO: Campus Compact/ The Education Commission of the States.

Kohls, J. (1996). Student experiences with service learning in a business ethics course. *Journal of Business Ethics*, 15(1), 45.

Kolb, D.A. (1984). *Experiential learning.* Englewood Cliffs, NJ: Prentice Hall.

Kolenko, T. A., Porter, G., Wheatley, W. & Colby, M. (1996). A critique of service-learning projects in management education: Pedagogical foundations, barriers, and guidelines. *Journal of Business Ethics*, 15, 133-142.

Kouzes, J. M. & Posner, B. Z. (1987). *The leadership challenge.* San Francisco: Jossey-Bass Publishers.

Liu, G. (1995). Knowledge, foundation, and discourse: Philosophical support for service-learning. *Michigan Journal of Community Service Learning*, 2(1): 5-18.

Luce, J. (Ed.). (1988). *Service-learning: An annotated bibliography linking public service with the curriculum.* Raleigh, NC: National Society for Internships and Experiential Education.

Lund Dean, K. (2001a). From "Yes, service-learning has great potential, but what about my course goals?" to "Yes, service-learning is a part of my course, and it really fits!" Paper presented at the Organizational Behavior Teaching Conference, Harrisonburg, VA. (June).

Lund Dean, K. (2001b). "But how will this get me a job?" Instrumentalism and service-learning in the management classroom. Paper presented at the meeting of the Academy of Management, Washington, D.C. (August).

Markus, G. B., Howard, J. P. F., & King, D. D. (1993). Integrating community service and classroom instruction enhances learning: Results from an experiment. *Educational Evaluation and Policy Analysis*, 15(4), 410-419.

McCarthy, A. M., & Tucker, M. L. (1999). Student attitudes toward service-learning: Implications for implementation. *Journal of Management Education*, 23(5): 554-573.

McCarthy, A. M., & Tucker, M. L. (2002). Encouraging community service through service-learning. *Journal of Management Education*, 26, in press.

Mills, C. W. (1959). *The sociological imagination.* New York: Oxford University Press.

Moore, D. T. (1990). Experiential education as critical discourse. In J. Kendall (Ed.), *Combining Service and Learning*, 273-283. Raleigh: National Society for Internships and Experiential Education.

Myers-Lipton, S. (1998). Effect of a comprehensive service-learning program on college students' civic responsibility. *Teaching Sociology, 26*, 243-258.

Nathan, J., & Kielsmeier, J. (1991). The sleeping giant of school reform.*Phi Delta Kapan, 72*(10), 738-742.

Newman, F. (1985). *Higher education and the American resurgence.* Princeton, NJ: Carnegie Foundation for the Advancement of Teaching.

Porter, L. W., & McKibbin, L. E. (1988). *Management education and development: Drift or thrust into the 21st century?* New York: McGraw Hill.

Richman, K. A. (1996). Epistemology, communities and experts: A response to Goodwin Liu. *Michigan Journal of Community Service Learning, 3*, 5-12.

Rorty, R. M. (1979). Philosophy *and the mirror of nature.* Princeton: Princeton University Press.

Saltmarsh, J. (1996). Education for critical citizenship: John Dewey's contribution to the pedagogy of community service learning.*Michigan Journal of Community Service Learning, 3*, 13-21.

Schein, E.H. (1990). *Discovering your real values.* San Diego: Pfeiffer.

Sims, R. R. & Sims, S. J. (1991). Increasing applied business ethics courses in business school curricula. *Journal of Business Ethics, 10*, 211-219.

Smith, M. W. (1994). Community service learning: Striking the chord of citizenship. *Michigan Journal of Community Service Learning, 1*, 37-43.

Strage, A. A. (2000). Service-learning: Enhancing student learning outcomes in a college-level lecture course. *Michigan Journal of Community Service Learning, 7*, 5-13.

Tucker, M. L. & McCarthy, A. M. (2001). Presentation self-efficacy: Increasing communication skills through service-learning.*Journal of Managerial Issues, 13*(2), 227-244.

Tucker, M. L., McCarthy, A. M., Hoxmeier, J. A., & Lenk, M. M. (1998). Community service learning increases communication skills across the business curriculum. *Business Communication Quarterly, 61*, 88-99.

Tucker, M. L., Powell, K. S., & Cleary, C. A. (1999). Incorporating Community Service Learning into the Business Communication Class,*Delta Pi Epsilon, 41*(2), 42-52.

Vogelgesand, L.J. & Astin, A.W. (2000). Comparing the effects of community service and service-learning. *Michigan Journal of Community Service Learning. 7*, 25-34.

West, C. (1989). *The American evasion of philosophy: A genealogy of pragmatism.* Madison: University of Wisconsin Press.

Wutzdorff, A. (1993). Service-learning belongs. *Journal of Career Planning and Employment, 33.*

Zlotkowski, E. (1996). Opportunity for all: Linking service-learning and business education. *Journal of Business Ethics, 15*(1), 5-19.

Zlotkowski, E. (2000). Early example of student and agency contract. In*Linking Citizenship and Scholarship through Service-Learning: A National Imperative.* Teleconference resource packet. (Available from the National Resource Center for the First-Year Experience & Students in Transition, University of South Carolina, 803-777-6029, http://www.sc.edu/fye)

SECTION II

RETHINKING MANAGEMENT EDUCATION IN CYBERSPACE

CHAPTER 4

CREATING AN ONLINE M.B.A. PROGRAM

Veronica M. Godshalk and Ellen Foster-Curtis

Distance education, online learning, e-learning, clicks-and-mortar—all of these terms are becoming synonymous with the latest approach to providing high quality educational offerings. What differentiates these approaches from the traditional bricks-and-mortar, ivy-clad educational environment of the college campus is that typically no physical campus exists. The Internet has allowed colleges, corporate universities and for-profit businesses to begin offering degrees and executive education via the Web. In fact, this segment of the education market appears to be the fastest growing when compared to the traditional market. International Data Corporation estimates that the online corporate education market may total $11.4 billion by 2003, up from $234 million in 2000. By 2002, online Master of Business Administration degree offerings are expected to grow substantially from today's 5,000 enrolled students to 50,000, and students taking all types of distance learning programs should total 2.2 million (Schneider, 2000a, 2000b). The "e-learning revolution" has just begun (Werry, 2001).

Distance education may be defined as a learning environment where the student and instructor overcome the restrictions of both same-time

Rethinking Management Education for the 21st Century
A Volume in: Research in Management Education and Development, pages 89–108.
Copyright © 2002 by Information Age Publishing, Inc.
All rights of reproduction in any form reserved.
ISBN: 1-930608-21-7 (cloth), 1-930608-20-9 (paper)

and same-place learning by the use of technology (Swift, Wilson & Way-land, 1997). Interaction with the instructor and with other students may occur via videoconferencing or teleconferencing. When using computers, interaction may take place in asynchronous (email or bulletin board) sessions or synchronous (chat room) sessions. Still other technologies for distance education include the more traditional methods of closed circuit television or mailed videotapes. The intent of the instructor in these long distance environments should be to create a community of learners (Moller, Harvey, Downs, & Godshalk, 2000), where students interact with each other and the instructor just as if they were physically together. The focus of this distance learning environment is on student outcomes and attitudes (Phipps & Merisotis, 1999; Webster & Hackley, 1997; Yellen, 1998).

Knowledge building is encouraged through information exchange and social reinforcement. The learning community contributes to effective learning by fostering cognitive development through communication, argumentation and critical analysis. The learning community also allows for greater potential collaborative learning than a traditional classroom (Alavi, 1994; Fussell & Benimoff, 1995; Leidner & Jarvenpaa, 1995). The community concept suggests emotional support is also needed for growth or intellectual risk-taking behaviors to occur. It is doubtful that online learners would engage in substantive and rich conversation without the feelings of acceptance that a learning community provides (Moller et al., 2000). These feelings of acceptance replicate but cannot replace the experience of the face-to-face classroom.

This suggests that the successful distance-learning environment is significantly based on the atmosphere created by the instructor. In fact, Webster and Hackley (1997) found that instructor attitude was positively related to student learning outcomes in technology-mediated distance education environments. Also, this dependence on the instructor's attitude is magnified when the instructor is starting to transfer knowledge into a web-enabled environment for the first time. Alavi, Yoo, and Vogel (1997) found that the instructor's first experience with web-based instruction resulted in cognitive overload, which could be very demoralizing for the instructor.

Cognitive overload is a result of the instructor learning to interact within a virtual classroom, which is very different from a traditional classroom. The distance education instructor needs to redesign the course, reconsider student assignments, provide for student-to-student and student-to-instructor interactions, and establish systems for document management (Arbaugh, 2000; Berger, 1999; Bilimoria, 1997/1999). Additionally, the instructor needs to learn to deal with the avalanche of student electronic communications that does not necessarily exist within a face-to-face class, since many questions are fielded by the instructor in class (Berger, 1999). Once the virtual learning environment is mastered, the instructor is then free to enjoy the many benefits distance education allows for the student.

The learning environment distance education provides appears to be best suited for the graduate and corporate learner. Online learners experience high levels of freedom and control over their time, learning space, method and frequency of interaction with other students and faculty. This student-managed learning environment can be a double-edged sword. Those students who do not have the necessary time management skills or motivation, most often traditional full-time undergraduates, may sink in the virtual learning space of distance education (Thomas, 2000). Thus, it has been surmised that the successful online learner is the part-time student, full-time employee (Lankford, 2001) or one who may have historically felt removed from access to a university education (Fornaciari, Forte, & Mathews, 1999). The Internet allows the enterprising employee to pick the degree, certificate or training program most necessary for enhancing one's career (Kaeter, 2000). Therefore, the focus of this chapter will be on the types of M.B.A. distance education programs universities may offer for part-time students who are also full-time employees.

This chapter investigates the many processes through which educational institutions may offer online, distance education graduate programs. M.B.A. program offerings will be explored through a framework that analyzes each graduate degree offering along with faculty and curricular issues, organizational funding and commitment, technology options, and impact on extant programs. Several university offerings at various stages of their development will be discussed. Implications for the direction of online graduate education will be suggested.

Common Models for Distance Education

The once almost visible line between corporate training and higher education is blurring. Distance education is causing this convergence. Kaeter (2000) suggests that this convergence is creating a common field of battle for colleges, corporate universities, and for-profit training and development businesses. The development of corporate-university partnerships around online learning offerings is opening up new roles for academic institutions to play. Students benefit from being able to choose from among the best programs in the country (or world), instead of being limited by geography and time. Education becomes a convenience, and a route for career advancement, instead of a chore.

Four models are suggested as a framework for universities to use to develop online courses: the classic approach, educational portals, tailored training, and university spin-off (Kaeter, 2000). We briefly describe and evaluate each model below and provide examples of current MBA programs based on each model.

The classic approach follows the traditional tuition reimbursement model in that students apply for a particular degree or set of course offerings, are admitted, and register for their courses. Students take courses from the college's standard curriculum, but take their courses at a distance. In this model, at a distance sometimes means that students are sent videotapes of faculty members' lectures in "live" classes or in an empty TV sound stage (Kaeter, 2000). On the other hand, students may log onto a website where they follow a syllabus and complete the instructor's assignments. Courses usually have a synchronous component, where students discuss topics in chat rooms, or critique papers and projects in a team setting. Regis University in Denver has offered an online M.B.A. since 1996 using this method.

The benefit for the university in this model is that they develop a library of courses they can literally "pull off the shelf" for course delivery. Also, universities can bring in guest lecturers from academia or industry via videotape or live video feeds. The Pennsylvania State University is in the process of developing an online M.B.A. degree following the classic approach.

Educational portals, or use of a third party website to offer curriculum, gives students access to a variety of courseware offerings, regardless of the originating source (Kaeter, 2000). Oftentimes, a commercial supplier (the third party) hosts the website and works with a number of universities to offer course work. The third party supplier benefits by being able to leverage their off-the-shelf courseware and technology for a number of university clients, and the university benefits by not taking on the risk of the hardware and software investment, as well as the investment in support personnel.

Until recently, the courseware in this environment was minimally customized, and corporate clients and executive education were the main focus of this delivery system. However, more than 200 universities, including Johns Hopkins and the University of Pennsylvania, have contracted with portal providers, such as eCollege (Kaeter, 2000). eCollege offers a platform for courseware delivery and supports Internet based education. Now educational institutions are crafting their own curricula and using companies like eCollege as the portal provider. Drexel University, in Philadelphia, Pennsylvania, offers a technology based M.B.A. using eCollege as its portal provider. Drexel and eCollege are partners in the delivery of this degree program.

While the first two models proposed tend to involve large-scale libraries of online courseware, the tailored training approach allows the university to offer a curriculum that is focused to the needs of the corporate client or targeted market. Certificate programs, structured to provide students with content mastery in a few courses, allow students to master a specific piece of information, and use that information at work the next day. Duke University uses this approach, and rounds out their executive education program offerings by putting basic information (like reading a balance sheet) on the web. Then students who need that resource can access it; others who do not can ignore it (Kaeter, 2000; Schneider, 2000a).

Accountability and demonstrable achievement are important tenets of this model. Pat Postma, assistant dean of degree and nondegree executive education at the University of Tennessee's College of Business, stated that certificate degrees benefit both the student and the corporation. "Companies want more certificate programs because it shows that people have mastered something...Employees want it too because they can show competence on a resume" (Kaeter, 2000, p. 120). The University of Tennessee has also pursued the tailored training approach in its offering of a Physician Executive M.B.A. program. This program, while initially developed for a specific health care provider organization, has been opened to physicians worldwide wanting to pursue an Executive M.B.A. since 1998.

The final model involves the university spinning off business ventures to pursue the market. In Bloomington, Indiana, a company named Wisdomtools.com was founded when the Indiana University's Center for Excellence in Education decided that its research had produced a viable commercial product for student interaction in a distance classroom (Kaeter, 2000). The Kelley School of Business at Indiana University has also spun off Kelley Direct that creates all of its online M.B.A. courseware. Duke has spun off Duke Corporate Education, Inc. in order to run its custom executive education program (Schneider, 2000a). Duke's plan is to repackage the materials it creates for executives into online courses and market courses to the general workforce. Babson University, in Wellesley, Massachusetts, has created Babson Interactive LLC, to put content on the web that will support part-time M.B.A. students and corporate clients. Consortiums are also forming to offer for-profit courseware. The most notable is the Cardean University, an online business school, with courses developed by an amalgamation of professors from Carnegie Mellon, the London School of Economics, Stanford University, and the University of Chicago (Lankford, 2001). As the market for online education grows, and it will by all accounts, more universities will consider for-profit options as a serious alternative.

The Classic Approach

The classic approach to offering an online M.B.A. provides the face-to-face offering via a new delivery method. Typically, the courseware developed for the traditional classroom is replicated into a distance education format. At Regis University, students can mix online and face-to-face courses held at the Denver, Colorado campus. According to Dr. Michael Goess, Chairman of the Regis M.B.A. online program, approximately 15% of the in-house students also take online course (M. Goess, personal communication, April 30, 2001). This is partially due to the eight-week format of both the online and in-house course offerings running concurrently. Students self-select and pursue the online course offerings due to personal or professional reasons. Regis' average online M.B.A. student is a 32-year-old professional who must have at least two years of full-time significant work experience prior to entering the program. Regis' class size is usually 12-15 students per faculty member.

At the Pennsylvania State University, the University's Board of Trustees has recently approved an online M.B.A. offering. While the courseware is similar in content to that offered by the four M.B.A. granting locations within the state system, an entirely new curriculum has been developed for the program. Faculty from the four state-wide campuses, the Smeal College of Business in State College, the Behrend College in Erie, the School of Business in Harrisburg, and the Great Valley School of Professional Studies in Malvern, came together to create a curriculum that follows the guidelines for the Association to Advance Collegiate Schools of Business (AACSB International) accreditation as well as following the strategic mission of the program. That mission includes offering a high quality professional M.B.A. with timely and purposeful content focused on today's digital economy. Penn State intends to have 25-30 students per cohort entering each semester. The program is targeted at an adult population with at least three years of management experience. It is expected that students will range in age from 30 to 44 years old. The University plans on offering online M.B.A. courses in early 2002.

Faculty and Curricular Issues

Regis' online M.B.A. program is a 30 credit hour, ten course degree that can be completed in two years. It is a part-time "track" program, in which students follow a prescribed course of study. Courses are offered in the same sequence as the in-house program. This allows students to take face-to-face courses if they are so inclined. Regis' online program does not require a residency, so students reside throughout the country (and the world).

Regis offers a variety of content over a variety of media. Students learn via streaming audio and video lectures (if the student has the appropriate hardware and software technology), usually in ten-hour segments. Each course includes weekly assignments to help the students stay focused, motivated and on track. Faculty members host panel discussions with students and industry experts. CD ROMs are provided to students with course content. Comprehensive course guides are also offered to students with transcriptions of lectures, notes, Microsoft PowerPoint slides, and cases covered. Threaded discussions and chat rooms facilitate conversation among students. Regis uses WebCT software for this purpose.

Students are assigned two faculty members as advisors throughout their program. One Regis faculty member is assigned as the student's academic advisor. This academic advisor serves as the student's primary contact with the University. In addition, for each course taken, an evaluating faculty advisor is assigned. This faculty advisor is the student's main contact for the course. Regis' faculty members are located throughout the country, so often student/faculty matches are made based on time zones when possible.

Faculty involvement in course creation was originally performed on a volunteer, contracted basis. Teaching in the program is also based on a contract with the faculty member. Tenured faculty members may or may not participate in the online program. Regis is working with Bisk Publishing in Tampa, Florida to provide instructional design, marketing and technology assistance.

Penn State's online M.B.A. program is a 48 credit hour program, with courses varying in credits from one to four credits. The program is a two and a half year track program where students take online courses along with an introductory and closing week long residency experience. Courses in the program were developed with the four main tenets of the AACSB accreditation guidelines in mind: domestic and global economic environments, human behavior in organizations, creation and distribution of goods and services, and financial reporting, analysis and markets. Unlike Regis, few courses in the online program are the same as those offered in the face-to-face programs, which does not allow for crossover class credits between programs.

The structure of each course is focused on high interactivity between the faculty member, the students, and planned guest presenters. Courses are integrated across the curriculum so that knowledge gained in one course will be used in other courses. In fact, the residency weeks are planned not only to bring everyone together, but also to cumulate the students' knowledge into group projects and presentations. Curriculum development, instructional design and technology implementation for each course will be done by Penn State's in-house, web-oriented technology organization, the World Campus. The World Campus is specifically chartered by the University to provide online courseware for a variety of program offerings. The World Campus has already been responsible for offering undergraduate and graduate degrees, as well as continuing education certificates, online. The World Campus is staffed by instructional designers, technical writers, and hardware and software specialists. The main task of the World Campus staff is to facilitate the move of the faculty members' course content into the web-enabled environment. Recent surveys of students taking World Campus courses found that 94% were highly satisfied with their use of the technology and 75% were very satisfied with student interaction using the courseware (J. May, personal communication, March 28, 2001).

Faculty involvement in the Penn State program is voluntary. Faculty from each of the four M.B.A. granting locations were involved in program and curricular development, and course delivery. Faculty members will teach in the online program as part of their normal teaching load. The program has been structured so that students will have faculty advisors, in addition to access to the faculty teaching each course they take.

Funding and Commitment to Success

Regis University's online M.B.A. program is a subset of the in-house M.B.A. program, and hence is funded internally by the University. With Regis' tuition costing less than $10,000, it is an efficient organization and self-sustaining entity within the School of Graduate Professional Studies. The University is committed to the success of the program, since the online M.B.A. program is consistent with the focus of the University's mission of developing exceptional adult leaders.

At Penn State, there is a strong commitment at all levels of the university, including the president, Dr. Graham Spanier, to providing the "Penn State experience" to a broader student population. It is expected that the program, targeted to professionals in mid-career, will provide a high quality, significantly differentiated course offering at the right price point. Given that Penn State is perceived as one of the top degree granting institutions in the country, tuition for the degree is expected to be greater than $40,000.

Faculty and administrators at the four M.B.A. degree-granting locations within the State system are committed to the success of the Penn State online program. Significant tangible (financial, faculty time) and intangible (faculty notes and courseware) investments were made prior to approval by the Board of Trustees. The University funds activities by World Campus staff. Also, Penn State has received several Sloan Foundation grants to develop the online M.B.A. program.

Technology

All courses in the Regis online M.B.A. were originally hosted on a dedicated University server. Many course materials are accessible through the Internet. Others are shipped to students via the mail. However, Regis has recently partnered with Bisk Publishing to provide dedicated servers and instructional design assistance.

Penn State's courses will all be hosted on World Campus servers located in State College, PA. World Campus is the in-house entity responsible for providing technical, hardware and software support, as well as instructional design and course development assistance for faculty. Faculty at different locations will have access to both local and World Campus instructional designers for help when designing and developing courses. The World Campus is also responsible for distribution of all class materials, either electronically or via the mail.

Impact on extant programs

Dr. Goess of Regis remarked that the online M.B.A. program minimally impacted their existing in-house program (M. Goess, personal communication, April 30, 2001). The online program provides access to audiences that the traditional program does not reach, thus increasing the school's total enrollments. In fact, the online program provides a great benefit to the face-to-face learners by allowing these students to take online equivalents of the face-to-face classes when work or family do not allow the student to continue with the traditional classroom experience.

Penn State's faculty was very cognizant of the effect of potential impact on current M.B.A. course offerings. The online curriculum was designed to try to minimize direct competition from current offerings. This allows each of the Penn State M.B.A programs to maintain its own identity. Specific characteristics that differentiate each of the offerings include full-time versus part-time, online versus face-to-face, curricular content and focus, price, proximity to work and home. It is expected that students will select from these four Penn State M.B.A. offerings one that is best suited for the individuals' needs.

The Educational Portal Approach

This approach is similar to the "outsourcing" many corporations are doing today. Using this model, a university identifies its "non-core business," such as non-knowledge generating activities like technology maintenance or accounts payable, and contracts with outside companies to take over responsibility for those activities. In distance education, universities are contracting with companies such as eCollege to provide them with the technical and instructional design assistance necessary to outsource an entire online program. Drexel University is an example of an online M.B.A. program that is managed by both internal Drexel personnel in concert with eCollege personnel. Courses for its first cohort entering in the Fall of 1998 ran on internal college servers. The first year's volume of activity was so intense that Drexel decided to outsource the management of the servers and help desk to eCollege. eCollege assists Drexel faculty with the creation of courses in a web-enabled environment, and sends personnel to the Drexel campus when necessary. eCollege supports students by providing around the clock technical help, while directing curricular content or assignment issues to Drexel faculty. There is no additional charge to Drexel students for this 24-hour assistance from eCollege.

Faculty and Curricular Issues

Drexel's online M.B.A. program is "technology management" oriented, both in its medium of delivery and its curricular content. Five new courses were added to the standard M.B.A. curriculum to strengthen the program's focus on technology. The student profile is a technically savvy individual who has several years of experience in business. Entering students must meet prerequisite requirements through ten required foundation level courses or may be given credit for previous coursework if certain conditions are met. After meeting the prerequisites, students take sixteen advanced M.B.A. courses or a total of 48 advanced credits. In some instances, students can complete the entire online program in less than two years. Most students take three years to complete the program.

Advanced level courses are offered in a lock-step cohort model. Cohorts begin as a group of 20-25 students and proceed through the program together. Students interact throughout the program in faculty-guided threaded discussions, which act as structured conversations where the faculty member works with the students to discuss and analyze the topic at hand. As part of their advanced work, students are required to attend three four-day weekend residencies at the beginning, middle and end of the program. The final residency experience is abroad at the London, England or Warsaw, Poland campuses. These residencies are structured as concentrated workshops. When students return, they complete online those projects and group activities begun at the residencies.

Faculty members in the online program are members of the College of Business and Administration at Drexel. They typically have taught the courses face-to-face as well as in the online mode, and are experienced teachers in their field. Selection of the faculty was based both on content area expertise, and the faculty member's interest and ability to teach in an online environment. Drexel recognized early on that not all faculty members would have the desire and "personality" to keep pace with the online students. According to Dr. Thomas Wieckowski, Director of the Master's Programs in Business, approximately 25% of faculty members teaching in the program are tenured (T.J. Wieckowski, personal communication, April 3, 2001). Most are teaching courses as an overload to their normal teaching schedule. Students have access to both the faculty teaching the course, and to their program advisors.

Funding and Commitment to Success

Drexel took a top down approach when committing to the development of an online M.B.A. offering. The Dean of the College of Business and Administration, as well as the University President, Dr. Constantine Papadakis, were very supportive of this initiative. Dr. Wieckowski and several other faculty members put together a plan to establish and market the online M.B.A. The commitment from the faculty was a result of the strong similarity between the structure of both the traditional and online programs. The faculty saw a synergy as well as a commitment to quality by going in this direction. Five technology management-related courses were newly developed for the online program, and are only offered in this mode. Drexel's faculty members are also committed to the program because students are admitted through the same admissions criteria as traditional students, again maintaining the quality of the Drexel M.B.A. degree.

Drexel has received some developmental grants from eCollege and from within the University to fund the early development of new courses for the online program. If a student is required to take the ten foundation courses, the cost for those courses is approximately $12,000. If the foundation courses are fulfilled, then charges for the advanced level courses are greater than $32,000. Costs for travel to the residency locations are excluded.

Technology

Today, Drexel's program is entirely run off of multiple servers at eCollege. Drexel participates in eCollege's premier program that gives Drexel's internal technical support team and students access to eCollege's technical and instructional design support personnel. Drexel's team has a significant role in the development of the "look and feel" of the software that the students use on eCollege's hardware infrastructure. Most students are unaware of the fact that there is a third party involved between Drexel and the student. While Dr. Wieckowski suggests that though there are some managerial issues that Drexel and eCollege need to address regarding this outsourced arrangement, Drexel is very pleased with the performance of the eCollege system and so are its students.

Impact on Extant Programs

Drexel pursued the online market in order to strengthen existing ties the University has outside of the greater Philadelphia area. Drexel had potential students in the Pacific Rim and Europe through connections with faculty members in those countries, and an online program would allow potential students to experience Drexel in their home country. Developing an online M.B.A. program proved to be much less costly than establishing campuses in those countries. Drexel actively marketed the online M.B.A. program nationally and internationally, through airline magazines such as *Attaché*. Because Drexel did little marketing of the online M.B.A. program in the Philadelphia area, it experienced little impact on enrollments in its onsite M.B.A. program. Some local students, who because of professional obligations cannot attend a traditional program, opted for Drexel's online M.B.A. Drexel actually increased its enrollments in the Greater Philadelphia area, because that type of student would have chosen an online program regardless of local university options. Now Drexel can offer students either the traditional or online options.

The Tailored Training Approach

The Center for Executive Education at the University of Tennessee in Knoxville offers a variety of executive programs, all tailored at specific segments of the executive education market. The most mature of these programs is the Physician Executive M.B.A. program. This program, started in 1998, was originally designed as a tailored training program for a healthcare provider. The Hospital Corporation of America (HCA) asked Tennessee to develop an Executive M.B.A. that physicians throughout the country working for HCA could participate in with little disruption to their medical practices. The driving principle of the program's development was "time is money." Physicians participating in the program would need to utilize time effectively. The University began working on an online program that allowed physicians to study at night and on weekends to pursue a M.B.A. while maintaining their normal workload. The typical physician-student is 43—45 years old and has fifteen years work experience (M. Stahl, personal communication, April 23, 2001).

Due to corporate restructuring, HCA had to back out of active involvement in the development of the program after the first year. The University completed development of the Physician E.M.B.A. program on its own and opened the program to physicians around the world. Thirteen percent of the student population is located outside the United States. The program is seeking to build greater brand recognition through its tailored approach to the target market.

Faculty and Curricular Issues

The Physician E.M.B.A. program is a 45 credit hour program that physicians can complete within one calendar year. The program begins in January with a residency week, and cohort groups meet again in July before completing the program in December. The cohort groups enter each year with approximately 30 physician-students, and are broken into five person teams.

Between eight and twelve tenured faculty members were instrumental in constructing the curriculum from scratch. These faculty members were advised by outside physicians, and some were physicians themselves. Dr. Michael Stahl, Distinguished Professor of Management and Director of the Physician E.M.B.A. program, stated that the program was truly a collaborative effort on part of the Tennessee faculty, working in conjunction with the ultimate consumer, the physician (M. Stahl, personal communication, May 23, 2001). The program is tailored to the management needs of these individuals, while still retaining the necessary content areas typical of most M.B.A. programs. For its novel approach, the program was recognized with the Princeton Award for Innovation in Education.

Funding and Commitment to Success

The program received some initial funding from the HCA for development of the tailored training program. Once HCA withdrew from active participation, the University took on the remainder of the funding for the program. According to Dr. Stahl, the program is widely supported throughout the University, and faculty members who were initially involved in the development of the program are still guiding forces in program changes. The Physician E.M.B.A. program has gained a great reputation amongst those in the medical industry, and there is more demand yearly for the program than capacity. Costs for the program, including books, other course materials, residency meals and special events are $48,000. Travel to the Tennessee campus is excluded.

Technology

The program is run on innovative Centra software that enables the Saturday morning cyber-classes to run using both synchronous and asynchronous communication techniques over the web.

Centra allows two-way text and audio transmissions among the instructor and physician-students. Video transmission is also possible with the appropriate hardware and line bandwidth. These interactive components allow for a virtual classroom experience much like a face-to-face classroom where the instructor can lecture and show Microsoft PowerPoint slides and the students can respond and ask questions—both in real time. The faculty member can ask students to go into virtual breakout rooms to discuss topics on their own, and then the groups can come back together into the "lecture hall" to discuss each group's findings. Alternatively, the group can send a Microsoft PowerPoint slide or Microsoft Word document to the other groups and the instructor to report on their findings. The Centra technology is very sophisticated in allowing true interactivity among the physician-students and the instructor. These Saturday sessions occur 40 times throughout the year, with discussions continuing between cyber-classes. Centra and Tennessee have partnered to provide the necessary software and hardware technology assistance to the physician-students. Dr. Stahl claims that the physician-students have a short learning curve to get up and running with the technology.

Impact on Extant Programs

Due to the tailored nature of the Physician E.M.B.A. program, and the student market niche it addresses, there has been no impact on other M.B.A. programs offered by the University of Tennessee. The Executive M.B.A. program may learn from the Physician E.M.B.A. experience and offer some modules of the program in a distance format using Centra software. This E.M.B.A. program had been run more asynchronously and now will become even more asynchronous using the software. Dr. Stahl's team is working with other departments within the University to provide such assistance.

The University Spin-off Approach

The Kelley School of Business at Indiana University and Babson University are two examples of major business schools that have spun-off business ventures to create and deliver online M.B.A. programs. Kelley Direct produces all distance education programs, degreed or non-degreed, offered by the Kelley School. Babson Interactive LLC is a for-profit venture that develops distance learning programs and business simulations in conjunction with the Olin Graduate School of Business and the Babson School of Executive Education. The structure of the M.B.A. degrees and the role played by the delivery units differ for the two institutions.

The Kelley Direct M.B.A. evolved from the Indianapolis-based evening M.B.A. program. In 1997, in response to requests from students for more flexible access to courses, the program created and launched alternative delivery channels for web-based electives. Based on the enthusiastic response to these offerings, and supported by Indiana University's *Oncourse* class management system, Dr. Richard Magjuka, then chair of the part-time M.B.A., and currently the chair of distance education at Kelley, proposed the development of an online degree program (R. Magjuka, personal communication, April 4, 2001). By the summer of 1999, the first cohort began coursework.

Babson has developed a hybrid model, 50% on-line, 50% face-to-face instruction, and launched the model as a custom M.B.A. program for employees of Intel Corporation in May 2001. Babson's faculty hold classes once a month at Intel locations. The remaining instruction uses e-learning techniques. The program's first year parallels the curriculum of Babson's full-time integrated M.B.A. The second year will consist of discrete elective courses.

Faculty and Curricular Issues

Kelley Direct used course titles and course content that already existed in the part-time evening M.B.A. program. The 48-credit program centers around 15 web-based courses and a one-week residential experience at the beginning of each academic year. Faculty involvement in course creation was originally performed on a volunteer, extra compensation basis. Teaching in the program now comprises part of the faculty's regular workload. Tenured faculty members from the Kelley School of Business do almost all of the teaching in this program.

Babson Interactive LLC subcontracts with Babson University faculty to develop and teach courses. Cenquest, Babson Interactive's technology partner, provides the instructional design platform and technical support to students and faculty. Defining the intellectual property rights on the courseware is one of the most pressing issues among the faculty.

Funding and Commitment to Success

Kelley Direct grew internally from funds provided by Indiana University, the Kelley School of Business, and Kelley Executive Partners (KEP), a stand-alone corporation for executive education. The first cohort of students in 1999 was limited to managers from KEP's corporate clients. Based on that class's success, Kelley Direct opened the program to the public for the 2000-2001 academic year. The tuition for the online M.B.A. is $31,200, comparable to the residential M.B.A. in Bloomington, Indiana. Average cohort size is 42 students. Based on the number of applications to date, Dr. Magjuka anticipates running two to three entering cohort classes in 2002 and subsequent years.

The Olin Graduate School of Business, the School of Executive Education, and Cenquest provided startup funds for Babson Interactive LLC. Tuition for the Intel Corporation custom M.B.A. program is $52,000, approximately 10% higher than the Babson residential M.B.A. program. The first cohort contains 28 students. Babson plans future expansion of the program, first to other corporate clients, and eventually to the public. According to Thomas Moore, CEO of Babson Interactive and Dean of the School of Executive Education, other future plans include increasing the online portion of the program from 50% to 70%, and leveraging the online courseware to enrich the full-time and evening M.B.A. programs with an increased use of technology (T. Moore, personal communication, April 11, 2001).

Technology

All courses in the Kelley Direct M.B.A. are hosted on a dedicated Indiana University server. Course materials are accessible through the Internet. *Oncourse* is the proprietary online teaching and learning environment students use. The *Oncourse* software system manages and maintains the courseware and provides multimedia content and real-time chat rooms. Kelley Direct Help Desk provides technical support to program participants. One component of the M.B.A. course materials is Time Revealed Scenarios (TRS), a customized, integrative web-based learning tool. TRS uses authentic business situations in a narrative revealed over time. TRS presents students with the opportunity to solve problems and discuss issues with peer groups in online facilitated forums.

The Babson Intel program uses e-learning techniques for 50% of the coursework. Cenquest personnel work with the faculty to develop the online portions of the program, including Web hosting for student interaction, guest lecturers, chats, and message boards. Cenquest provides technical support to students and faculty. Babson Interactive is currently exploring hiring its own technical design staff and outsourcing technical support to additional contractors. This is due in part to the volatile business environment in which e-learning firms are operating. Several such firms have recently gone out of business.

Impact on extant programs

Both Dr. Magjuka of Kelley Direct and Dr. Moore of Babson Interactive perceive that the new online M.B.A. programs will impact their existing programs in a positive way. Both programs will provide access to audiences that the traditional programs did not reach, thus increasing their schools' total enrollments. Additional benefits include enhancing the curricula of their other programs through the use of online courses, increased flexibility in delivering executive and continuing education programs, and continuing faculty development in the uses of technology.

Implications for Online Graduate Education

Online M.B.A. programs will be one of the fastest growing markets throughout the first decade of the 21st century. This is due not only to the continued value of the degree, but also to the new media through which a degree may be received. The examples shown in this chapter demonstrate that there is a variety of content, residency requirements, and price points from which to choose.

Universities face the decision of if and how they add an online M.B.A. degree to the graduate degrees they offer. The university must also decide which strategy best suits the distance education vision and direction of the university. Fornaciari et al. (1999) suggest that academic institutions consider Porter's (1980) model of generic strategies to achieve competitive market advantage. A cost leadership strategy is based on the goal of achieving a lower cost position than the university's competition. The university may charge a lower tuition, at the same time achieving a low cost position by controlling operating costs. Also, Fornaciari et al. (1999) suggest that large, low-tuition-cost universities may want to adopt a cost leadership strategy due to their ability to be efficient in offering coursework in high volume to an expansive market. Institutions like Indiana and Penn State may be poised to consider a cost leadership strategy as they pursue distance education M.B.A. offerings.

Another strategy that may be pursued is one of differentiating the university's product so that significant value is perceived by the student. The goal of a differentiation strategy is to avoid price-based competition by earning student loyalty through a unique and highly valued product offering (Fornaciari et al., 1999). This unique product offering implies expensive cost structures along with special features for which the student may be willing to pay. With their specific market niches, Babson University and the University of Tennessee seemed to be pursuing a differentiation strategy.

A focus strategy is the final alternative strategy a university may follow. Universities that employ a focus strategy compete either on the basis of cost leadership or differentiation. "The primary difference from the aforementioned strategies is that the focus organization attempts to establish and sustain an advantage from a specific market segment or a small number of segments" (Fornaciari et al., 1999: 713). These researchers suggest that small schools with regional reputations may be most effective when they implement a focus-cost leadership-based strategy. Regis University is an example of this type of focus-cost leadership strategy in action. Fornaciari et al. (1999) also state that small schools with regional reputations which offer high cost M.B.A. programs may differentiate themselves by focusing on a specific niche. Drexel University seems to have done this with their technology-based M.B.A. program.

If a university decides, based on its desired strategy, to offer such a M.B.A. program, it will have to decide which approach—the classic, educational portal, tailored training, or spin-off—to take. Each approach has its advantages and disadvantages. Several factors need to be considered prior to entry into such an offering.

The classic approach may be the easiest for the initial development of online degrees. A university simply takes classes it already offers and moves them to a web-enabled environment. Once in the web-enabled environment, the university faces the challenges of maintaining the hardware, software and network communication lines. The continued upkeep of such a system is a significant undertaking and should not be entered into lightly. If the university does not have the personnel or internal funding to support this distance-learning environment (and the support needed to make the faculty and students successful), then pursuit of an online degree is destined to failure.

The outsourced education portal represents a significant investment decision for a university. When managed well, partnerships with third party educational portal companies provide some distinct advantages. The companies provide expertise in the field not necessarily available at all learning institutions. There are economies of scale associated with educational portal companies, since they provide the same type of service for many similar customers. While initially this may seem like another easy approach to offering an online degree, partnerships with third party companies can create challenges for all involved. Universities must make sure that their website is differentiated from the other university offerings, and is protected from potential system hackers. If the third party should go out of business, or merge with another company, the university could be left without a technology partner. Drafting contract language to protect the university and its students presents significant challenges. If the issues are addressed successfully, educational portals may be the best alternative for a university to pursue an online degree.

The tailored training approach is probably most appropriate for universities that already have an infrastructure that supports a Center for Continuing Education (CE). Such centers work with organizations to develop tailored training for their employees. University employees working in CE are "selling" the assets of the university to develop specialized training for local companies. University of Tennessee's Physician Executive M.B.A. program originated from a contact made by their Center for Executive Education. Universities with such centers are well-prepared to develop tailored training for specific market niches. An online M.B.A. degree then becomes one of several alternatives in the university's product line of customized offerings.

The spin-off approach is appropriate for the organization that can fund the establishment of a separate organization to offer the online degree. Kelley and Babson are two examples where the culture of both universities was entrepreneurial enough to consider spinning-off companies to develop online programs. Not all universities are capable of such entrepreneurial insights. Depending on the agreement made with the spun-off company, the university may have a majority or minority investment in the firm (and therefore significant or menial initial cost outlays). The benefit to the university of a spin-off organization is that the newly created firm becomes a for-profit entity, and hence supports itself over time. This hands-off approach by the university also benefits the spun-off firm by enabling it to make more entrepreneurial decisions than it may have as part of the larger institution. These decisions can aid in the innovative development of both content and delivery processes for the online program and its potential customer base.

At first glance it appears that everyone may benefit in this scenario. Closer examination reveals some disturbing possibilities. Potential pitfalls may include questions of maintaining academic quality and rigor. Intellectual property issues for faculty still have not been solved. As more and more programs are created as quasi-independent profit-seeking enterprises, how will the face of graduate education change? Only time will tell.

REFERENCES

Alavi, M. (1994). Computer-mediated collaborative learning: An empirical evaluation. *MIS Quarterly, 18,* 159-174.

Alavi, M., Yoo, Y., & Vogel, D.R. (1997). Using information technology to add value to management education. *Academy of Management Journal, 40*(6), 1310-1333.

Arbaugh, J.B. (2000). Virtual classroom versus physical classroom: An exploratory study of class discussion patterns and student learning in an asynchronous Internet-based MBA course. *Journal of Management Education, 24*(2), 213-233.

Berger, N.S. (1999). Pioneering experiences in distance learning: Lessons learned. *Journal of Management Education, 23*(6), 684-690.

Bilimoria, D. (1997). Management educators: In danger of becoming pedestrians on the information superhighway. *Journal of Management Education, 21,* 232-243.

Bilimoria, D. (1999). Emerging information technologies and management education. *Journal of Management Education, 23,* 229-232.

Brindle, M. & Levesque, L. (2000). Bridging the gap: Challenges and prescriptions for interactive distance education. *Journal of Management Education, 24*(4), 445-457.

Drexel University (2002). *Bennett S. LeBow College of Business website.* http://mbaonline.lebow.drexel.edu.

Fornaciari, C.J., Forte, M., & Mathews, C.S. (1999). Distance education as strategy: How can your school compete? *Journal of Management Education, 23*(6), 703-718.

Frost, P.J. & Fukami, C.V. (1997). Teaching effectiveness in the organizational sciences: Recognizing and enhancing the scholarship of teaching. *Academy of Management Journal, 40*(6), 1271-1281.

Fussell, S.R. & Benimoff, N.I. (1995). Social and cognitive processes in interpersonal communications: Implications for advanced telecommunications technologies. *Human Factors, 37*(2), 228-250.

Indiana University (2002). *Kelley Executive Partners website.* http://kep.indiana.edu/

Kaeter, M. (2000). Virtual cap and gown. *Training, 37*(9), 114-122.

Lankford, K. (2001). Do online MBAs measure up? *Kiplinger's Personal Finance,* May, www.kiplinger.com/magazine/archives/2001/May/managing/webMBAs.html.

Leidner, D.E. & Jarvenpaa, S.L. (1995). The use of information technology to enhance management school education: A theoretical view. *MIS Quarterly, 19,* 265-291.

Moller, L. A., Harvey, D.M., Downs, M., & Godshalk, V.M. (2000). Identifying factors that effect learning community development and performance in asynchronous distance learning. *Quarterly Review of Distance Education, 1*(4), 293-305.

Phipps, R. & Merisotis, J. (1999). *What's the difference? A review of contemporary research on the effectiveness of distance learning in higher education.* Washington, D.C: The Institute for Higher Education Policy.

Porter, M.E. (1980). *Competitive strategy: Techniques for analyzing industries and competitors.* New York: Free Press.

Regis University (2002). *Regis University—MBA program website.* http://www.mbaregis.com.

Schneider, M. (2000a). Duke's B-School goes into business. *Business Week,* June 30.

Schneider, M. (2000b). Look who's building online classrooms. *Business Week,* July 25.

Swift, C.O., Wilson, J.W., & Wayland, J.P. (1997). Interactive distance education in business: Is the new technology right for you? *Journal of Education for Business, 73*(2), 85-89.

Thomas, R. (2000). Evaluating the effectiveness of the Internet for the delivery of an MBA programme. *Innovations in Education and Training International, 37*(2), 97-104.

University of Tennessee (2002). *The University of Tennessee Center for Executive Education website. http://thecenter.utk.edu.*

Webster, J. & Hackley, P. (1997). Teaching effectiveness in technology-mediated distance learning. *Academy of Management Journal, 40*(6), 1282-1309.

Werry, C. (2001). The work of education in the age of e-college. *First Monday,* 6 (5). *http://firstmonday.org/issues/issue6_5/werry/index.html.*

Yellen, R.E. (1998). Distant learning students: A comparison with traditional studies. *Journal of Educational Technology Systems, 26*(3), 215-224.

CHAPTER 5

eLEARNING BUSINESS MODELS
Strategies, Success Factors, and Best Practice Examples

Sabine Seufert

As the Internet changes almost every sector, it influences management education worldwide as well. Due to the interactivity and ubiquity of the Internet, learning is possible without spatial and temporal barriers. The globalization of education is increasing rapidly. Students and corporate employees now can access courses and other eLearning resources from such diverse sources as the Open University in Great Britain to MIT's teaching. Students and instructors connect through digital media transcending physical, geographically delimited meeting spaces. Education around the world is becoming strongly networked and we are beginning to see fundamental changes in the organization of education. We no longer have geographical isolation at the college and university level. The long-term implications are a worldwide network and a real marketplace for university and college level education. This will expand naturally into vocational and adult training as well. Online education will become a major

Rethinking Management Education for the 21st Century
A Volume in: Research in Management Education and Development, pages 109–132.
Copyright © 2002 by Information Age Publishing, Inc.
All rights of reproduction in any form reserved.
ISBN: 1-930608-21-7 (cloth), 1-930608-20-9 (paper)

export for some countries. Competition among universities is ever increasing and universities are under pressure to find new strategies and business models to produce and deliver educational products.

Similarly, company training is dramatically changing as well. Multinational companies already train their employees via online learning global networks. eLearning as a new buzzword for web-based education and web education support services (e.g., business strategies, technologies, applications, etc.) is an expanding market. Companies are spending more than ever on training to respond to a growing need for new information and knowledge required to cope with, manage, and drive new challenges. The business environment is transforming due to increased interdependencies, complexity, and uncertainty associated with radical changes in information technology and other emerging technologies, globalization, shifting industry boundaries, changing customer demands, increased expectations for social responsibility, rapid shifts in business practices, and other changes that are placing new stresses on the organization and its people and changing their requirements for success (Glotz, 1999, 10). These ever-changing new technologies require more and quicker means of teaching and training employees.

Beyond doubt: eLearning has been a promotional boon for companies, universities and other educational institutions. It has led to the phenomenal growth in the use of web-based learning and experimentation with multimedia, video-conferencing, and Internet-based technologies. According to several forecasts, by the Gartner Group and the International Data Corporation for example (International Data Corporation, 2000), eLearning is a promising and tremendously growing market. Conversely, announcements of failures and closings of eLearning providers, such as Governors University or Pensare, show how instable and dynamic this new market is. The true actualization of promising forecasts is questionable. However, due to the limited capacity of physical locations and the time and place constraints of students' eLearning offers, innumerable advantages accrue, ranging from technology issues and didactics to the convenience of students and faculty (Porter, 1997, 12). A new learning paradigm based on students' self-organization and collaborative approaches appears essential to cope with the challenges of a learning organization.

New eLearning strategies are needed to implement the new learning paradigm and to react to the changes in the competitive and global education market. They will reshape the role of training and education in the organization and create enduring advantages for firms, universities and educational institutions. The purpose of this chapter is

a. to introduce the changes in the education market and to explain eLearning as the convergence of several forces,
b. to outline a framework for eLearning business models for the implementation of the changes,

c. to demonstrate best practice examples for the different eLearning business models, and

d. to analyze some trends and critical success factors for achieving a leading position in the eLearning market. The last section

e. briefly summarizes this article and concludes with the main implications for management institutions as well as for management educators.

eLEARNING AND THE CHANGING EDUCATION MARKET

eLearning is a very broad term for Internet-based learning in general. Distance education, online learning, eLearning—all of these terms are becoming synonymous with the latest approach to providing high quality educational offerings. eLearning can be defined as technology-supported learning and the delivery of content via all electronic media. Compared to computer-based training (CBT) eLearning places greater emphasis on interaction and communication. Interaction with the instructor and with other students may occur via Internet-channels, videoconferencing or teleconferencing, in asynchronous (email or bulletin board) sessions or synchronous (e. g., chat room, Whiteboard, application sharing) sessions (Seufert et al., 2001, 35).

Furthermore, the term eLearning has developed promotional caché over the last couple of years that supports marketing considerations. Indeed, eLearning as a fashionable eWord has become a buzzword, used by marketing strategists and by educational institutions to boost the eLearning trend. The Internet has enabled colleges, corporate universities and for-profit businesses to offer degrees and executive education via the web. Definitions or articles about eLearning go back only to 1999, revealing the newness of the term. That was the time when companies offering computer-based training established so-called eLearning solutions. One of the largest companies in this business field "CBT systems" renamed itself Smartforce in 1999, introducing the trademark The eLearning Company. Today, this company holds the market leader position in delivering integrated eLearning solutions (Urdan & Weggen, 2001).

According to several forecasts, this segment of the education market is growing faster than the traditional market. International Data Corporation estimates that the online corporate education market may total $11.4 billion by 2003, up from $234 million in 2000 (International Data Corporation, 2000). John Chambers, president and CEO of Cisco Systems promotes eLearning on its corporate website: "There are two fundamental equalizers in life: the Internet and education. eLearning eliminates the barriers of time and distance creating universal, learning-on-demand opportunities for people, companies and countries" (quoted from the website: www.cisco.com). He emphasized at a keynote speech to the Fall 1999 Comdex Trade Show in Las Vegas that "the biggest growth in the Internet, and the area that will prove to be one of the biggest agents of change, will be in eLearning" (Rosenberg, 2000, xv). Is it just a pushy marketing strategy or is there truly a global market that is potentially worth hundreds of billions of dollars? Why do all forecasts agree on the dramatic growth of eLearning?

A reasonable answer has to consider diversified and multiple factors. Technological developments, pedagogical advances and changing learning patterns, the demands of corporate training and the business aspects of eLearning as a "window of opportunity" are determining factors. Therefore, eLearning represents the convergence of many factors from different fields; for example technological drivers, changes in society, edutainment drivers, changing corporate training and the new learning paradigm, which describes the shift from training to learning (Meister, 1997, 22). The new learning paradigm emphasizes the following critical issues:

Self-organized learning, focus on metacognitive learning strategies and preparing life-long learning skills,

- Emphasis on process-oriented learning (to focus on "learning to learn") instead of product oriented learning,
- Shift from training to self-responsible learning,
- Student- and team-oriented methods and collaborative learning based on constructive learning theories, building a community of learners, experts, facilitators, and coaches,
- High flexibility, personalized and individualized learning (according to different learning types, personal preferences).

eLearning represents the convergence of several factors. Conversely, the growth of eLearning and distance education has converging effects on the educational market (see Figure 1). The once almost visible line between the academic and corporate sector is disappearing. Companies and universities become both customers and suppliers of the new eLearning business models.

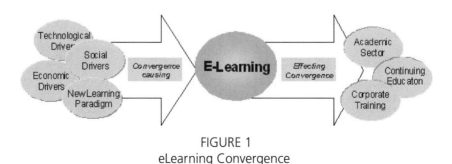

FIGURE 1
eLearning Convergence

BUSINESS MODELS FOR eLEARNING STRATEGIES

Introduction

What are the challenges and strategies for universities and for companies? Who are the competitors in a converging education market? Who are the key players of eLearning? What are the new business models in this converging market?

First of all, what challenges do emerging business models face in delivering eLearning strategies? The literature about electronic commerce is inconsistent in the usage of the term business model. Timmers (2000, 3) gives the following definition of business model:

- An architecture for the product, service and information flows, including a description of the various business actors and their roles, and
- A description of the potential benefits for the various business actors, and
- A description of the sources of revenues.

Based on these definitions the different business models of the eLearning market will be introduced in the following section.

Framework of eLearning Business Models and Best Practice Examples

The education market landscape has developed several models to produce and deliver educational products (Brockhaus et al., 2000, 140). Some have their roots in the academic sector, some in the business sector. But as noted in the previous section, the line between both academic education and corporate training sectors is blurring (demonstrated in Figure 2). Among innovative eLearning business models, one may distinguish between the alma mater multimedialis, which describes a traditional university in the transformation process focusing on implementing the new learning paradigm, and several models offering new ways of delivering education, which include Virtual Universities, University Networks, Corporate Universities, Education Providers and Education Consortia.

New entrant eLearning players have developed mostly by deconstructing the traditional educational value-chain. With reference to the e-commerce terminology one may distinguish between three different business fields:

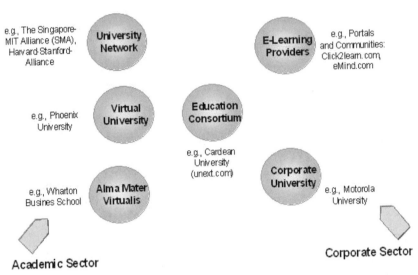

FIGURE 2
Landscape of eLearning

- E2B = Education to Business (corporate eLearning),
- E2E = Education to Education, University, Professors, other educational institutions (university eLearning),
- E2C = Education to Consumers (eLearning focusing on the private sector).

Alma Mater Virtualis/Multimedialis

Traditional universities, the classic alma mater, will probably exist in two different forms in the future. First, only a few elite institutions, recognized as centers of excellence, will offer their specialized expertise to a global market. The best masters in a field will provide education as customized learning. Second, the alma mater will survive by offering a lower education quality but will be confronted with global competition from the academic and corporate sectors. The traditional university can evolve to a kind of alma mater virtualis/multimedialis by creating a learning and community platform for their students and developing a library of online courses. Hybrid-concepts will be used for teaching in the form of method mix and a combination of face-to-face seminars and self-conducted online-course components (dual mode institutions). The benefit for the university will be

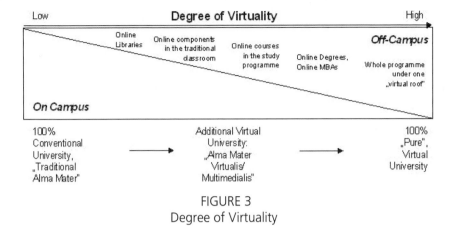

FIGURE 3
Degree of Virtuality

in a better study (information, communication and cooperation) infrastructure and the improved personal contact between the students and their professors and tutors.

The business actors will be mainly universities and private students, which means the alma mater virtualis/multimedialis represents a typical form of E2C Business. E2B Business plays mostly a role in the field of executive education. The elite institutions in particular will offer and deliver executive education modules to companies and to other universities (E2E-Business). The sources of revenue are mainly university fees and fees for courses and eLearning products.

The main motivation of media-enabled teaching is different for virtual universities. As the next figure demonstrates, the degree of virtuality differentiates between traditional universities using media and Internet technologies to improve the quality of teaching, to organize self-study components, and to integrate innovative teaching concepts and those virtual universities using off-campus teaching as the dominant course delivery mode. Furthermore, the options for universities to act on the eLearning market depend on their cooperation strategies, shown as degree of cooperation in the next figure. Implementing key partnerships and building networks with corporate partners should be seen as key success factors to secure a strong position in the eLearning market. According to Figure 4, three models are suggested as a framework for traditional universities to use to develop online courses and to act on the eLearning education market:

- *University-wide Approach.* This cooperation model focuses internally on the organization itself: whether a university follows a broad eLearning trategy for undergraduate and graduate degrees. It includes the classic tuition reimbursement model where students have to pay for

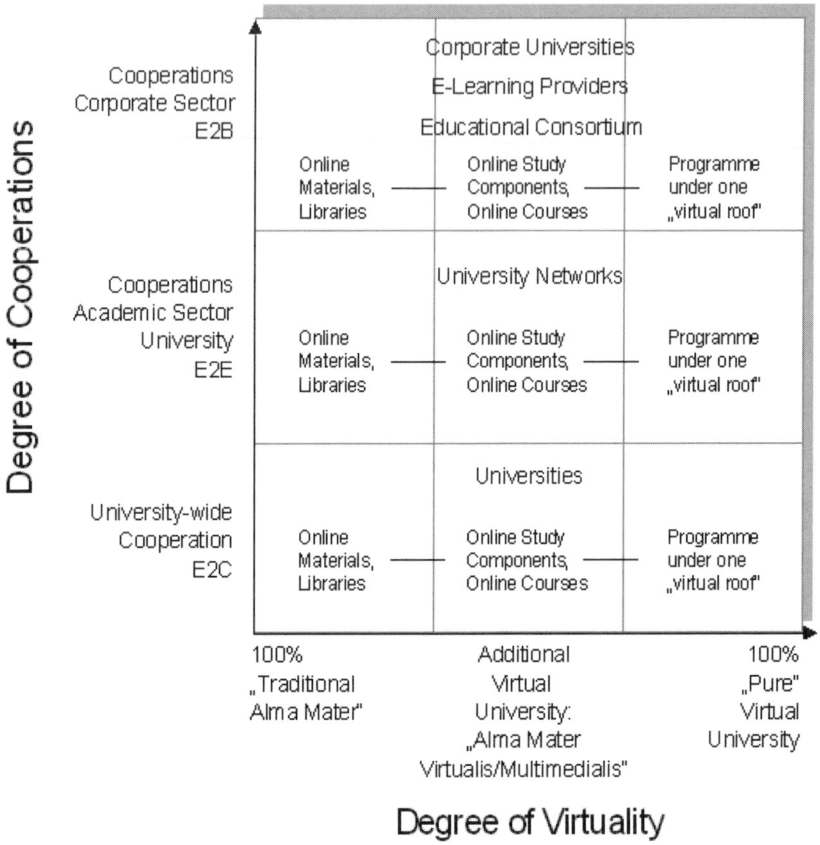

Degree of Cooperations (vertical axis label)

	Corporate Universities E-Learning Providers Educational Consortium		
Cooperations Corporate Sector E2B	Online Materials, Libraries	—— Online Study Components, Online Courses ——	Programme under one „virtual roof"
Cooperations Academic Sector University E2E	University Networks		
	Online Materials, Libraries	—— Online Study Components, Online Courses ——	Programme under one „virtual roof"
University-wide Cooperation E2C	Universities		
	Online Materials, Libraries	—— Online Study Components, Online Courses ——	Programme under one „virtual roof"
	100% „Traditional Alma Mater"	Additional Virtual University: „Alma Mater Virtualis/Multimedialis"	100% „Pure" Virtual University

Degree of Virtuality

FIGURE 4
Degree of Virtuality and of Cooperation of Universities

attending (virtual or traditional classroom) courses. The benefit for the university in this model is that universities can enter new markets and enhance potential customer segments because non-regional students are provided access from a distance via the Internet. Also, universities where the production of online material and courses are organized efficiently in centralized departments and learning centers can benefit from economies of scale.

- *Cooperations Academic Sector.* Traditional universities have the option to cooperate with other universities in developing course material and eLearning products. The benefits from this approach are sharing costs and reaching critical masses of students for specialized study programmes. This approach leads to the business model University Networks which will be explained in 3.2.3.

- *Cooperation with the Corporate Sector.* Universities have the option to cooperate with corporate universities, educational providers, as well as with educational consortia. Universities may offer their content and courses to corporate universities (see 3.2.4). Oftentimes a commercial education provider or broker (third party) hosts a website and works with a number of universities to offer course work. A third party supplier benefits by being able to leverage their off the shelf courseware and technology by providing it to a number of corporate clients. Educational institutions are crafting their own curricula and using companies like eCollege.com as portal providers. The business model of educational providers will be explained in section 3.2.5. A university also has the option to spin-off business ventures to pursue the market, as the Duke Corporate Education spin-off from Duke University illustrates. In section 3.2.6 the eLearning business model of educational consortia is assessed for integrating partners from the academic and corporate sector.

One best practice example of the type alma mater multimedialis is Wharton Business School of the University of Pennsylvania (www.wharton.upenn.edu). Wharton, one of the world's preeminent business schools, initiated several Internet-projects to become a leader in technology for academic research. Wharton's Director of Advanced Technology Development, Kendall Whitehouse, built the desktop environment and intranet-based information service Spike http://www.wharton.upenn.edu/spike/ for students (Aragon, 1997, 29). Spike is not an acronym, and the name does not have any kind of hidden meaning. Students can download course materials and class notes, gain access to the university library and its electronic resources, bid for a seat in a Wharton course, send email, chat in Spike's webcafe and explore the Internet and other areas on Wharton's intranet. Furthermore, Wharton developed an enormous research database "knowledge@wharton" and a Internet-based business data service "Wharton Research Data Services (WRDS)".

Virtual Universities

The term virtual university is often not clearly defined and is used to refer to both conventional campus-based universities offering online courses (hybrid institutions, brick-and-mortar) and virtual universities in a pure form in the sense that *all* their activities are delivered online via the Internet. A virtual university may be defined as an institution that is involved as a direct provider of learning opportunities and uses the Internet to deliver its programs and courses while receiving tuition support (Ryan et. al. 2000, 2). Virtual universities belong to the academic sector, are often accredited, and have core activities that are the same as those of conventional universities. The business actors are the universities and their students, privately employed people, who are mainly studying part-time (E2C business). The benefit for a university is that it can unite the whole program of a conventional university under one virtual roof. Students benefit from virtual universities because they can learn anytime and anywhere in a very flexible way to guarantee their continuing professional education. eLearning environments guarantee access to digital libraries and to student teams and tutors to support their learning processes. Sources of revenues are similar to traditional universities and are mainly universities fees and tuition fees for online courses

Four models are suggested as a framework for virtual universities to use to act on the eLearning education market:

- *Model 1: Pure Virtual University.* A virtual university exists instead of a traditional campus-based university. This is the model of a pure virtual university. All core activities are delivered online.
- *Model 2: Additional Virtual University.* A traditional university includes a virtual university as well. This model is very similar to the alma mater multimedialis model. Here, an eLearning strategy is organized university-wide with a programme complementary to the conventional university.
- *Model 3: Academic Sector Cooperation.* Several traditional campus-based universities are the founding partners of an additional virtual university. This model is a special type of a university network explained in 3.2.5.
- *Model 4:Corporate Sector Cooperation.* In this scenario a university cooperates with corporate sector partners, e.g., with education vendors or as a member of a consortium, which will be analyzed in the following sections.

A best practice example of model 1 is the University of Phoenix (UoP) online.uophx.edu. On May 31, 2001, UoP Online had degree enrollments of 25,700 students of the UoP consolidated degree enrollment of 116,800 students (*Baltimore Business Journal,* 2001). UoP Online components are the most prominent part of each study programme (click-and-mortar-strategy). The University of Phoenix Online was formed in 1989 as a for-profit organization and belongs to the Apollo Group. The target group of the University of Phoenix Online is working adults pursuing continuing education, mainly in the subject fields of business administration and information technology. It currently enrolls more than over 15,000 online students. They work in small groups of three to four students who correct each other's weekly homework before they are submitted to the instructors. Each class shares its own group mailbox using Microsoft Outlook Express, which serves as an electronic classroom. While communication between individuals is common, each class uses a group forum where students put their work and ideas before classmates for comment. This upgrades the quality of most work before its more formal, academic review by the instructor. Students can also access research material from the university's Electronic Library. The online program is designed to fit the requirements of working adults: courses are offered one at a time, in sequence. There are no semesters, so students can begin a course of study any month of the year. A student can concentrate on one subject at a time and can learn at his or her own speed. The key advantage for the students and working professionals is the flexible concept of anytime and anywhere learning in combination with an accredited programme.

University Networks

eLearning affects networking among universities in the global market. For long-lasting competitive advantage, universities form university networks. The members of such a network have access to a pool of eLearning products. The general practice of such networks is a hybrid of online learning environments and face-to-face teaching. Courses and degrees are largely compatible. The business actors are universities who offer their courses to other university members of the network (E2E business). The multimedia product format is usually not of the same high quality standard as that of institutions from the corporate sector (e.g., corporate universities). Therefore online course fees are much more affordable for partners. University networks also serve the continuing professional education market but they mainly offer their courses to small and medium enterprises (E2B business), which cannot afford to develop online courses by themselves. At present, the main focus of existing university networks is the development of specialized study programmes such as an MBA programme in eCommerce or New Media. The benefits for universities are sharing online course development costs (economies of scale) and gaining a competitive advantage in a highly competitive market.

Harvard Business School and Stanford University have founded a strategic alliance to strengthen their market positions in the field of executive education. Another best practice example is the SMA University network (the Singapore MIT Alliance) (web.mit.edu/SMA). The Singapore-MIT Alliance (SMA) was founded in 1998 and is an engineering education and research collaboration among the National University of Singapore (NUS), Nanyang Technological University (NTU), and the Massachusetts Institute of Technology (MIT). A primary goal of SMA is the creation of a center of excellence for graduate education and research in engineering, which features the most technologically advanced distance learning facilities available. The center will provide opportunities for private-sector organizations to share in SMA's research, collaborate with its students, and recruit potential employees.

Corporate Universities

Corporate universities have been around for the last forty years. General Electric's Corporate University was launched in 1955. However, the real surge of interest in launching the corporate university structure as a strategic umbrella for managing an organization's employee learning and development began in the late 1980s (Meister, 1998, 2). The last ten years have seen the number of corporate universities grow from 400 to 1000.

Business training departments may have, depending on their type of corporate universities, internal (all employees, work groups, top management) and external target groups (suppliers, customers). The sources of revenue are dependent on the type of corporate university as well. The flexible and fast eLearning can be an immense benefit to such companies. Conventional training is usually too procedural and fragmented to deal with the demands of fast knowledge turnover. Just-in-time learning and learning-on-demand are requirements of corporate training. In the words of Douglas McKenna, General Manager, Executive and Management Development at Microsoft:

> Learning is the most valuable benefit we can offer employees and our ability as a company to learn faster and better than competitors is our most valuable competitive resource. The implications if this combination are quite staggering. When it comes to learning, what's good for employees is the same as what's good for the company (Aubrey, 1999, 33).

In the eLearning literature, many typologies of corporate universities already exist. Based on the common frameworks developed by Aubrey (1999), Deiser (1998) and Fresina (2000) five models are summarized below:

- Model 1: Training Department, Qualification Center:
  - Target group: all employees, internal focused,
  - Strategic goal: reinforce and perpetuate (evolution),
  - Business Logic: incentives for professional education, certificates for the employees,
  - Curriculum focus: technology development, service development,
  - Knowledge aspect: general, fundamental knowledge and enterprise specific knowledge,
  - eLearning aspect: learning anytime and anywhere, just-in-time, innovative learning methods.
- Model 2: Top Management Lessons
  - Target group: top management,
  - Strategic Goal: manage change (Revolution),
  - Business Logic: incentives for the top management, cooperation with top business schools,

- Curriculum focus: people development, customized executive seminars at top business schools,
- Knowledge aspect: general and brand-new management know-how,
- eLearning aspect: interactive discussion forums, F2F seminars, virtual cooperation partners and networks.
- Model 3: Standardization Engine
  - Target group: all employees, customers, suppliers,
  - Strategic goal: reinforce and perpetuate (evolution).
  - Business Logic: Economies of scale, costs are reducing the more people are involved in the corporate university,
  - Curriculum focus: technology development, service development,
  - Knowledge aspect: transfer of work practices,
  - eLearning aspect: development of mass products, interactive learning systems for a broad target group, standardized programs.
- Profit Center, Education Vendor
  - Target group: all employees, customers, suppliers, other companies, consumers,
  - Strategic goal: reinforce and perpetuate (evolution).
  - Business Logic: profit, revenues (e. g., corporate fees, fees for online courses, etc.),
  - Curriculum focus: technology development, service development, enterprise-specific knowledge
  - Knowledge aspect: transfer of knowledge, content delivery
  - eLearning aspect: killer application on the Internet, mix of educational products, interactive and innovative learning forms, learning anytime and anywhere, just-in-time, marketing of eLearning products (e.g., education portals).
- Learning Lab, Strategic Change Engine
  - Target group: all employees, customers, suppliers,
  - Strategic goal: drive and shape (vision),
  - Business Logic: sustained competitive advantage on the basis of a learning culture, strong relationship to knowledge management,
  - Curriculum focus: not extremely focused, technology, service, people development, certificates are irrelevant,
  - Knowledge aspect: creation of new knowledge, initiate innovations,
  - eLearning aspect: work-out programs as knowledge exchange and creation places, direct communication, interactive learning processes.

As a best practice example, Motorola University represents a combination of a qualification center and a learning lab (http://mu.motorola.com). Motorola University was established 1981 and designed as a "center for strategic thinking and a major catalyst for change" (Aubrey 1999, 37).

Therefore, the effort required a strong commitment from the top. At present, 130,000 employees and a huge number of customers and suppliers in five continents are users of Motorola University. Motorola manages what it considers a strategic competency of the company: a learning strategy that includes customer satisfaction, manufacturing supervision, negotiation, and communication. Teaching methods range from face-to-face classroom training led by professional instructors to original coursework developed by line managers to learning on the job concepts of shop-floor workers teaching their peers essential job skills. The media based environment builds the Internet, CD-ROMs (as just-in-time lectures technology), and the web-based training administration system (TAS). Despite the term university, theory-based education is not the focus of Motorola University. One best practice example of the curriculum is Motorola's innovative leadership development program, the China Accelerated Management Program (CAMP), where learning is always tied to a real business issue and includes case discussions and action-based exercises. Underlining the strategic importance of learning, Motorola University has its own board of trustees, which includes Christopher Galvin and the heads of the company's major business (Aubrey, 1999, 37).

Commercial Suppliers, Educational Providers

Commercial suppliers or educational providers represent eLearning ventures mostly as new entrant eLearning players by deconstructing the classic educational value-chain as Figure 5 shows. Financial capital to launch new ventures comes from the corporate sector. Companies are investing in the eLearning market as it is a business field of dramatic growth. The business actors are the education providers, both companies

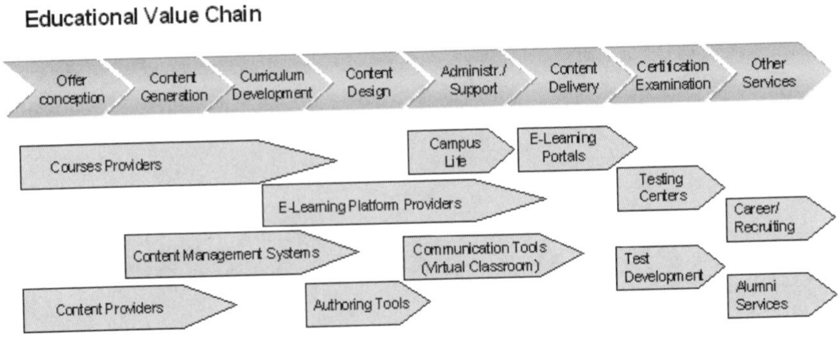

Educational Value Chain

FIGURE 5
New eLearning Providers by Deconstructing the
Educational Value-chain

and universities as suppliers or customers and private consumers. The whole portfolio of eLearning is represented:

- *E2C Business:* The target groups are students and adults interested in supplemental learning. For example, GEN.com (Global education network) is a content factory and service provider seeking to provide a strong core curriculum in liberal arts. Acclaimed professors supply the content but GEN provides the technology to video-tape and disseminate courses.
- *E2E Business:* Customers are universities and university professors as the example of WebCT.com (www.webct.com) demonstrates. WebCT's main area of business is providing web packages that allow faculty to develop, deliver and administer web-based courses.
- *E2B Business:* eLearning ventures provide corporations with interactive web-based training courses affiliated with universities (e.g., Quisic.com) or unaffiliated with any universities (Emind.com).

Sources of revenue range from advertising, course fees, books, subscriptions, to university fees and corporate fees. New entrant eLearning players have developed by deconstructing the traditional educational value-chain. Three basic Internet-based education business models have emerged seeking to offer the benefits of the Internet:

- *Model 1: Integrator.* Similar to a virtual university or an online business school, the educational provider in this model develops and delivers every single process of the educational value-chain, including offer conception, content development and delivery, and other customer services.
- *Model 2: Broker.* An education broker collaborates with other partners along the educational value-chain. In this model the value-chain is deconstructed and the broker has the function of coordinating the different processes. A strong network of academic and corporate partners is a hallmark of this model. Partners include corporate universities, traditional universities, and other education providers who can be both customers and suppliers. This model is almost identical with the eLearning model of an education consortium explained in the next section.
- *Model 3: Specializer.* Some eLearning companies concentrate on a specific service within the educational value-chain, e.g., authoring tool development, eLearning platform provision or testing center.

As a best practice example, the eLearning site Quisic (www.quisic.com) demonstrates a corporate content provider. Quisic is a content factory that provides education products mainly to corporations. These products are typically unavailable to individual students through university programs.

University professors help to develop content and Quisic offers corporations tailored programs or pre-MBA programs. Quisic's strategy is to provide the best quality of online education. Quisic has won more than 50 awards for educational excellence. The site provides a full range of products from a library of books and articles to undergraduate, graduate and corporate courses. The sources of revenue are mainly universities, corporate fees and institutional funding. In the education market since 1996, Quisic continues to grow as it recently purchased IEC, a 17 year old custom corporate training development company. Quisic is also planning to deliver courses with E-ducavia through a $96 million joint venture with Cisco, IBM, and Telefonica. The partners plan to create an online business school for Spanish, Portuguese and Latin American markets.

International Education Consortium

An international education consortium is a group of companies who come together to pool their training resources, offering their education products and services to working adults. Such a consortium acts as a training broker, acquiring content from traditional institutions of higher education or even corporate universities and then offering this back to the open market in the form of an electronic education mall. In this scenario, corporate universities as well as traditional universities become both customers and suppliers to the consortium.

A variety of incentives can motivate companies to form a consortium. The following best practice example, The Global Wireless Education Consortium (GWEC), brings together companies with common interests to create an educational solution for an entire industry. GWEC was formed in late 1996 by the founding partners Ericsson, AT&T Wireless Services, Lucent Technologies, AirTouch Communication, and Motorola, along with Mankato State University, South Central Technical College, and the University of Texas at Dallas. Each organization in this network has been confronted with the same problems in recruiting and retention because of a huge and growing need for wireless technicians and engineers in an industry that is growing exponentially. Misty Baker, executive director of GWEC, stated: "This is a people problem and we can either sue each other, like the software industry is doing, or we can collaborate to solve the problem" (Meister, 1997, 219). The industry decided on a collaborative solution. GWEC represents an education model where corporations and academia come together as partners to solve a common problem. The consortium has been established as a means of effectively creating a pool of skilled wireless technicians. Additionally, the advantage of this collaboration is that the participating companies can share their costs for training development and high quality multimedia courseware.

Another best practice example represents the international education consortium UNext.com (www.unext.com). Unext stands for the Next Generation University and was created to deliver world-class education. Whereas GWEC was initiated by companies to collaborate to solve a common problem (internally focused), Unext offers eLearning products to the open market (externally focused). The entrepreneur behind this start-up company is Andrew M. Rosenfield, a business consultant and University of Chicago alumnus. The first investor for the company, which was founded in December 1997, was Knowledge University (20% ownership stake without voting rights, Guernsey, 1999, 24). It is a company that establishes and invests in companies delivering education services in all different areas (higher education, corporate training, consumer training, etc.). Under the brand names "Cardean" and "Cardean University" unext.com offers next-generation business courses online, mainly to companies in association with academic consortium members, leading top business schools such as London School of Economics, Stanford University, Columbia University, University of Chicago and Carnegie Mellon. Members of the academic advisory board are Nobel Prize winners Kenneth Arrow, Gary S. Becker and Merton H. Miller. The Internet is the basis for the learning processes and the knowledge transfer. The learning environment allows a combination of self-study and interactive teamwork. Integrated feedback and performance control systems as well as the support of group work should help to provide a user- and student-centered learning environment.

eLEARNING TRENDS AND SUCCESS FACTORS

Corporate eLearning is one of the fastest growing markets. While the market is currently relatively small and early-stage, it is poised to explode if one believes the forecasts. The online training market is expected to nearly double in size annually, reaching approximately $11.5 billion by 2003 (International Data Corporation, 2000). However, the corporate eLearning market is characterized by low market transparency and limited knowledge of eLearning products and services. With new content providers, technology suppliers, and service vendors emerging on a weekly basis, it is becoming more difficult for companies to decide which eLearning provider to choose. Quality, price, and sophistication of courses and technology vary widely. Transparency and information flow in the market are still low. Efficient means to compare dozens or even hundreds of similar courses from different vendors are unavailable. The eLearning industry is an immature and dynamic market, still in the defining process.

What are the key trends of this dynamic and nontransparent eLearning market? Whereas new eLearning entrants are mainly developed by deconstructing the education value-chain, the trend is now towards convergence and "one-stop shopping" concepts. The major trends are summarized in the following.

Trend 1: Continuing Convergence

The further trend towards convergence in corporate training can be observed in different areas:

- Since corporate customers, due to the increasing complexity of technology-based learning arrangements, no longer want to employ several different content, services, and technology providers to meet their educational needs, training companies have started to integrate all three segments in their product portfolio in order to offer one-stop-shopping concepts (see trend 4),
- In the content segment the converging trend can be observed as well. Many IT training vendors are expanding their product lines with management and soft skills training. Soft skills training providers have begun to spread out in the technical arena.
- A number of major corporations have begun to centralize their training departments, closing down their stand-alone IT training divisions and integrating them into their core corporate training groups (e.g., by building Corporate Universities).
- eLearning and traditional classroom learning are blending. This means finding an optimal combination of both concepts rather than one ruling out the other. The strongest use of online learning with added-value education services seems to be an extension rather than a replacement for classroom training.

Trend 2: Market Consolidation

The global eLearning sector comprises approximately 5,000 participants offering every imaginable method of eLearning. No single competitor in the e-training market accounts for 5% or more of market share. Recognizing their inefficiencies, market participants have started to consolidate. The currently valid business strategy in the eLearning market seems to be deeply connected with answering the question "eat or be eaten." A highly fragmented market, long development cycles, and other inefficiencies make the eLearning industry attractive for more intense Mergers & Acquisitions (M&A) activities. Small size not only might result in inefficient production but also preclude from creating and capturing brand recognition and market share quickly enough. Another reason for consolidation is the increasing tendency of corporate customers (see continuing convergence) to satisfy all their training needs through one single supplier. Due to the market pressure to offer a complete eLearning solution, eLearning vendors have to buy their way into skills and capacities they do not yet possess.

Trend 3: Branding as Key Strategy

One of the most important reasons why eLearning has not tremendously taken off yet is that the eLearning platforms are still very complex, requiring specific know-how and immense investments (in terms of knowledge and needed time) for decision-makers. Due to the low market transparency and limited knowledge of eLearning products customers will likely be seriously challenged in the next several years. The implication might be that companies prefer the safe choice and retain eLearning providers with established brand names. Brand is and will continue to be the most important factor influencing the competitive landscape. Corporate customers will be willing to pay a higher price for a quality product to avoid even costlier mistakes. eLearning providers are currently addressing the main factors constituting a brand, such as quality, consistency, competency, reputation, and a loyal and recognized customer base (Ziegler, 2001). Customers are increasingly demanding customized training. eLearning success factors include a well-known brand name that stands for quality, differentiated service offering, large direct sales force, and strong partnerships across the value-chain.

Trend 4: One-stop Shopping and Added-Value Services

Corporations increasingly demand a more comprehensive one-stop-shopping approach to meet their training needs, which leads to convergence effects within the e-Training industry (see trend 1). As Internet-based learning becomes an increasingly popular method of delivering training courses, customer priorities are shifting away from stand-alone training courses to more comprehensive and convenient eLearning solutions more often embedded in knowledge management concepts. Currently the mostly demanded services include curriculum design and development, pre- and post-training mentoring, coaching and support, training effectiveness analysis, reporting and tracking tools, and advisory services on how to integrate new e-training solutions into an organization's education strategy.

Trend 5: E-Learning Partnerships and Strategic Alliances

Content providers are entering into strategic alliances and partnerships with education technology vendors, training services suppliers, or other content providers to enhance their product offerings, expand their distribution channels, explore new market segments, and capture a larger share of fast growing IT and soft skills training markets. Others are going together with learning portals or even diversified eCommerce websites, leveraging their distribution channels in order to reach a broader audience. However, part of the value of a partnership is its exclusivity. Currently one might be under the impression that more or less all the players are partnering with each other. Thus, it is doubtful whether partnerships that are easily replicable truly lead to a significant value proposition.

Trend 6: Modularization and Standardization

Modularization of courses and content (knowledge and learning objects) has been a trend for several years. Content and courseware must be reusable, interoperable, and easily manageable at many different levels of complexity throughout the online instructional environment. Corporate customers need to be able to easily track content created by multiple content providers through one training management system. They must be able to search vast local or distributed catalogs of content to identify learning objects or modules on a particular topic. Modularization of content is the key prerequisite to be addressed. Technology infrastructure varies widely and incompatibility between existing learning technologies and current infrastructure is one of the main barriers to adopting web-based training. Open standards are crucial to the continuing successful adoption of eLearning, especially as it begins to transition beyond early adopters into the rapid growth phase of the market. Authoring tools will need to operate across different platforms and communicate with other tools used to build learning systems. The technological barriers are lessening through standardization including modularization of content.

Trend 7: New Learning Models, Communities

One of the highest growth areas in online learning is the creation of Internet-based meeting places for instructor-led classes to provide community, communication, and supplemental materials online (Palloff et. al., 1999, 11). Analysis of how the Internet has power to build communities are only at the beginning. However, one of the biggest challenges for university and corporate learning is labeled under the new buzzword blended learning: how to combine ingeniously the traditional teaching methods with the new Internet-based world. An increasing number of educational institutions and corporations are utilizing online authoring and delivery systems to build surroundings, learning environments that support efficiently the learning and communication process among students, peers, tutors, web-coaches, instructors, etc. New learning models facilitate studying, note-taking, class discussions, and catching up, all of which enhance classroom instruction.

Trend 8: Scalable Business Models

To capture significant market share, it will be imperative for training vendors to leverage their branded content by making it scalable in terms of development, delivery technology, and/or distribution. Scalable business models should be more profitable in the long-run. Successful companies emphasize the production of quality off-the-shelf content using template-based, reusable learning objects to speed up the development. In addition, market participants who license their teaching products to organizations in volume, deploy a course delivery platform able to support millions of users, and utilize multiple and effective distribution channels may be able to enjoy an exponentially growing revenue stream and significant economies of scale. Thereby, these players not only benefit from reduced development cost per unit but also minimize time-to-market, which is a critical competitive factor in the fast-paced world of the Internet.

CONCLUSION

This chapter has shown that trends in the educational market, notably those caused by eLearning developments, run towards greater competition for universities and educational organizations. Traditional university eLearning participants have been confronted with international competitors not only from their field but also from the hardware and software industries, the media industry, and training departments and institutions, which have established corporate and virtual universities. The line between academic and corporate training is blurring. Universities will increasingly invest and focus on continuing education and further cooperate with eLearning vendors.

The most promising market within the education industry seems to be the E2B market, corporate eLearning. Companies face more economic and social pressures to find new ways of training delivery coupled with fewer regulatory, bureaucratic, financial, and technical barriers to implement eLearning solutions than other segments of the education industry. In corporate settings, increasing global competition, rapid technological advances, demographic changes, and the emergence of a service- and knowledge-based economy force organizations to train and re-train their workforce in new ways. The Internet provides companies and universities numerous possibilities for leveraging knowledge and education resources in the context of lifelong learning (Maehl, 2000, 21). It redefines eLearning not only in terms of an easier delivery worldwide but also more current, dynamic educational content, more personalized, based on relevant learning experiences, and more collaboration forms with experts and peers. But currently it is still a relatively small and immature industry. The consolidation process is still going on at a dramatic speed and it is hardly feasible to exactly predict the market. Whereas I doubt the exponential growth many forecasts prognosticate, I am convinced that eLearning will become a stable, consolidated and more transparent market with several market leaders and with some strong market niches.

The main purpose of this chapter was to analyze the changing educational market from an eLearning perspective (section 2), to give an overview of stunning new models for eLearning strategies (section 3), and to investigate eLearning trends and critical success factors influencing the trajectory of development of eLearning (section 4). Finally, this last section concludes with some further considerations and fundamental implications for institutions of management education as well as for management educators. eLearning can be seen as a new challenge for universities and companies in the training industry.

This challenge will impact *Institutions of management* as summarized below:

Given the recent changes in the education market, universities and educational organizations should ascertain their eLearning strategy and positioning in the eLearning market. Usually, the above-described business models for eLearning are not found as pure forms of eLearning activity. For example, many universities support several forms (e.g., cooperation strategies in building strategic alliances, founding spin-offs, offering customized management courses, etc.). It is important for educational institutions to keep in mind their reputation when choosing an eLearning strategy. The strategic decision has to be accompanied by a marketing strategy that emphasizes the image of the university or training company and its services.

The eLearning challenge impacts management educators in university and corporate settings. Educators are confronted with a changing role in eLearning environments. While technology-based learning is unlikely to completely replace the school and university experience, it offers more opportunities for corporate training and continuing education. However, the role will change: management educators will become facilitators, offering guidance and motivation strategies for students who should get used to self-organized study techniques. Educators will be more engaged in providing additional educational services (e. g., dynamic update of knowledge databases, transparent and clear syllabi, reading recommendations, microarticles, etc.) in order to support information and communication processes in learning settings. Human interaction is a critical component for learning. Face-to-face contact is still not comparable with meeting each other on the web. There are situations in which classroom training cannot be replaced. Certain content because of its nature, relative value, or importance, is not suitable for technology-based delivery. Certain groups of employees do not want to miss the "edutainment value" of live experience and desire the total interactivity with a human trainer. Others are simply uncomfortable with computers. For a number of individuals, technology-based training is not the most efficient learning method due to their learning style. The classroom also provides guidance and structure. These elements are important for individuals who lack the motivation and confidence to succeed in a self-study-only program. eLearning may require more dedication and discipline. Often either the organizational environment and climate block efficient learning processes or individuals are likely not trained enough in self-organizing their studies. Frequently, it also does not yet reach the degree of interactivity and collaboration offered by classroom training. Despite these shortcomings eLearning is a practical and convenient way without time and place barriers for the delivery of content and value added education services. Therefore eLearning will find its place in the education and training industry. The existing shortcomings of eLearning will force educators to develop improved pedagogic models and techniques for online learning environments in order to bring measurable participation and results. Media and communication competencies appear to become a key qualification for management educators in online settings (Seufert et. al., 1999, 23).

REFERENCES

Aragon, L. (1997). Wharton's Information Spike. Case Study: Collaboration between students, IT spawns intranet app that simplifies mundane tasks. *PCweek, 14*(September 29), 41,

Aubrey, B. (1999). Best practices in corporate universities. In: Neumann, R. & Vollath, J. (Eds.), *Corporate University. Strategische Unternehmensentwicklung durch massgeschneidertes Lernen*, 33-55. Ahrendt et al.: A&O des Wissens.

Baltimore Business Journal. (2001). University of Phoenix parent's profits up 49 percent, (June 25). http://baltimore.bcentral.com/baltimore/stories/2001/06/25/daily4.html

Brockhaus, M., & Emrich, M.; Mei-Pochtler, A. (2000). Hochschulentwicklung durch neue Medien—Best-Practice-Projekte im internationalen Vergleich. *Online Studium*, 137-158.

Deiser, R. (1998). Corporate Universities—Modeerscheinung oder Strategischer Erfolgsfaktor? *Organisationsentwicklung, 1*, 36-49.

Fresina, A. (2000). The Three Prototypes of Corporate Universities, www.ekw-hrd.com/3_Prototypes.pdf .

Glotz, P. (1999). *Die beschleunigte Gesellschaft. Kulturkämpfe im digitalen Kapitalismus.* Munich: Kindler.

Guernsey, L. (1999). Circuits: Click Here for the Ivory Tower. A Start-up Enlists Elite Schools for Online Learning and Raises Eyebrows, *New York Times,* September 2.

International Data Corporation. (2000). Corporate *ELearning Markets, Forecast and Analysis 2000,* http://www.idccentraleurope.com .

Maehl, W. H. (2000). *Lifelong Learning at its Best: Innovative Practices in Adult Credit Programs.* San Francisco: Jossey-Bass.

Meister, J. C. (1998). *Corporate Universities. Lessons in Building a World-Class Work Force.* New York: McGraw-Hill.

Palloff, R. M., & Pratt, K. (1999). *Building Learning Communities in Cyberspace: Effective Strategies for the Online Classroom.* Cambridge: Jossey-Bass.

Porter, L. R. (1997). *Creating the Virtual Classroom: Distance Learning with the Internet.* New York: Wiley.

Rosenberg, M. J. (2001). *eLearning. Strategies for Delivering Knowledge in the Digital Age.* New York: McGraw-Hill.

Ryan, S., Scott, B., Freeman, H., & Patel, D. (2000). *The Virtual University.* London: Kogan Page.

Timmers, P. (1998). Business Models for Electronic Markets. *EM—Electronic Markets, 8*(2), 3-8.

Seufert, S., Back, A., & Häusler, M. (2001). *eLearning, Cookbook for Internet-based Learning.* Zürich: Smartbook.

Seufert, S., & Seufert, A. (1999). The Genius Approach: Building Learning Networks for Advanced Management Education. *Proceedings of the 32nd Hawaiian International Conference on System Sciences,* Hawaii.

Urdan, T. A., & Weggen, C. C.. (2001). SMTF: In Earnings We Trust: Reiterate Strong Buy Rating. *WR Hambrecht eLearning Research Report,* (September 20). http://www.wrhambrecht.com/research/eLearning/notes/smtf20010920.pdf

Ziegler, R. (2001). eLearning - the same old wine in a brand new bottle? Key note speech at the Learntec 2001, Karlsruhe, Germany, 7 February.

SECTION III

RETHINKING MANAGEMENT EDUCATION FOR EXECUTIVES

CHAPTER 6

DEVELOPING SCHOLARLY PRACTITIONERS
Doctoral Management Education in the 21st Century

Eric B. Dent

Doctoral education in the United States is nearing its 150th anniversary and doctoral education in management is nearing its 75th anniversary. Such milestones occasion an examination of the current state of doctoral education, particularly in management, and a determination as to whether any aspects of doctoral education need rethinking. Certainly, the organizational environment of today is dramatically different from that of the 1850s and 1930s. This changed environment has implications both for the nature of doctoral education and for the study of management at the doctoral level. This chapter will also explore current trends in doctoral education as well as briefly allude to the specific examples of a few university programs. The primary emphasis of the chapter will be to present the Doctor of Management degree at the University of Maryland University College (UMUC)

Rethinking Management Education for the 21st Century
A Volume in: Research in Management Education and Development, pages 135–155.
Copyright © 2002 by Information Age Publishing, Inc.
All rights of reproduction in any form reserved.
ISBN: 1-930608-21-7 (cloth), 1-930608-20-9 (paper)

as a case study. The designers of this program endeavored to rethink all aspects of the traditional Ph.D. and, where necessary, make improvements. Atwell (1996) has called for multiple models of excellence, reflecting different but equally worthy educational missions. UMUC's intention is to develop a model that will become the benchmark doctoral degree for students who want to be scholarly practitioners rather than tenure-track faculty. If history is any predictor, models get locked in and are not easily changed in higher education. Once such a model is formed it may influence doctoral education for over 100 years. The chapter will conclude with a series of ideas for exploration as educators continue to modify and improve doctoral education.

THE CURRENT STATE OF DOCTORAL EDUCATION

The output of universities has long been a tremendous source of progress for the country, government, and economy and has had far-reaching impact worldwide (Walshok, 1995). United States universities are seen as the benchmark throughout the world. Yet the process of doctoral-level education is widely viewed as more problematic than effective. The criticisms of doctoral education span decades but there are few signs of any improvement attempts in the arts and sciences programs at traditional universities. The work of Goodchild and Miller (1997), for example, led them to conclude that the elements of the doctorate are substantially unchanged since 1856. Notable exceptions include the Preparing Future Faculty Program cosponsored by the Council of Graduate Schools and the Association of American Colleges and Universities which provides doctoral students with opportunities to observe and experience faculty responsibilities at a variety of academic institutions and EDAMBA (European Doctoral Programmes Association in Management and Business Administration), which provides doctoral students with exposure to other universities, among other goals.

Three primary criticisms of doctoral education are:

1. The mismatch between doctoral education and the preparation needed for both faculty and non-faculty jobs.
2. The onerous process of doctoral education and the high incompletion rates.
3. The dissertation process and lack of dissemination of doctoral work.

The Doctoral Education Mismatch

Jules LaPidus (1997), former President of the Council of Graduate Schools, has described the present state of doctoral education as a classic mismatch, with universities producing a highly specialized product that the employers do not want. Over 40,000 doctorates are awarded each year (Syverson, 2001). Most of these heavily emphasize education in quantitative research, yet only a small percentage of these degree holders go into academia or similar research positions. In a large, comprehensive study, Golde and Dore (2001) found that

> in today's doctoral programs, there is a three-way mismatch between student goals, training and actual careers. Despite a decade of attention, the mismatch between the purpose of doctoral education, aspirations of the students, and the realities of their careers—within and outside academia—continues. Doctoral students persist in pursuing careers as faculty members, and graduate programs persist in preparing them for careers at research universities, despite the well-publicized paucity of academic jobs and efforts to diversify the options available for doctorate-holders. The result: students are not well prepared to assume the faculty positions that are available, nor do they have a clear concept of their suitability for work outside of research. (p. 5)

The Ph.D. is a research degree. Ironically, although the degree is designed for those who will become faculty members, almost no doctoral programs (excluding Education degrees) have teaching requirements. Many students do get experience teaching, however, by way of teaching assistantships that finance their educations. Yet, teaching assistantships and post-doctorates provide primarily on-the-job experience with little or no intentional mentoring and skill development.

Golde and Dore (2001) also found that even the stated objectives of developing research expertise in Ph.D. programs were not being achieved. Part of this difficulty may be the discord in higher education (David, 1997) that characterizes any discussion of alternative objectives for a doctoral program. Winter, Griffiths, and Green (2000) contend that both the content and research methods of doctoral programs, traditional and practice-based, are entangled in controversy about the value and foundations of knowledge. The lack of consensus about the needed fundamental changes may be solidifying the *status quo*.

The Onerous Process and High Incompletion Rates

One could argue that the mismatch described above results in an enormous waste of human capital. What might represent an even larger waste, though, is the number of years spent by students pursuing doctorates that are never completed. Bowen and Rudenstine (1992) report that fewer than half of all students entering doctoral programs finish. Most of those who do not finish complete all requirements but the dissertation. Several factors contribute to the high incompletion rate. Students enter a doctoral program without a reasonable awareness of the time, money, clarity of purpose, and perseverance that doctoral education entails (Golde and Dore, 2001). Once enrolled, students still do not encounter mechanisms that easily increase their awareness about these matters. Many appear to receive little guidance about how to navigate the doctoral process. Critical success factors for doctoral education remain murky to them throughout their time in graduate school.

These factors take many forms. Surprisingly, most programs do not have clear guidelines about how much time it will take to complete a degree and when exactly a student is eligible for graduation (Golde and Dore, 2001). The process of advisor selection is not explicit and the advising a student receives throughout a doctoral program is subject to the vagaries of the advisor. Ongoing financial support is an issue in many doctoral programs. Fellowships and assistantships may not be renewed in years when a university department is strapped for financial resources.

The Dissertation Process and Lack of Dissemination of Doctoral Work

The critique of the traditional dissertation requirement is so scathing in the literature that one wonders why immediate changes have not been made throughout the country. Typical comments include "the tenacious, unreflective commitment to the traditional rationale of the dissertation makes it one of academe's greatest monuments to non-thought" (Spriestersbach and Henry, 1978, p. 54) and "the typical, traditional dissertation is ill-suited to the task of training doctoral students in the communicative aspects of educational research, and is largely ineffectual as a means of contributing knowledge to the field" (Duke and Beck, 1999, p. 31).

Perhaps some of the ineffectiveness of the process stems from the fact that the conduct of any given dissertation committee appears to be idiosyncratic. One of the positive developments arising from the expanding number of practitioner-oriented doctorates is that dissertation examination procedures are now coming under study. Johnston (1997) discovered that "the examination process for doctoral theses seems to be based on assumptions which [sic] are largely untested and on understandings which [sic] are not necessarily open for discussion" (p. 334).

The traditional dissertation is a unique document. In the field of business and management it is almost never published in that form. As many as half of all dissertations are never disseminated through a presentation, article, or other means (Duke and Beck, 1999). If a doctoral student does not become a faculty member who needs to publish, only the committee members and perhaps a family member of the student may know of a high quality dissertation. Graduates speak of "mining" their dissertation or "extracting" an article from the document. Extracting an article from a dissertation is a non-trivial matter. It is not usually the case that large contiguous chunks of the dissertation can be put into an article. The process is closer in scope to taking ten percent from each page of a 200-page dissertation to create a 20-page article meeting the format and requirements of most journals.

Doctorates in Management Education

Doctoral programs in management are not as plagued by such issues, possibly because these degrees have less history. Doctorates in the field of management have existed only since the 1940s, although these have mostly been in business administration rather than management *per se*. Many of the early doctorates were DBAs (Doctors of Business Administration) rather than Ph.D.s, which also helped skirt some of the problems (graduation criteria, for example, tend to be much clearer). Management doctoral education has also avoided some problems because it has frequently been pursued on a part-time, rather than full-time basis (Miles, 1985). Business schools have typically preferred graduate students who have some career-oriented work experience. Consequently, many doctoral students start their degree programs later in life and continue to be employed full-time while they pursue the degree. It is common for many employers to subsidize the tuition expenses of masters' students, and often even doctoral students, in management.

THE CURRENT ENVIRONMENT OF MANAGEMENT AND ORGANIZATIONS

The current organizational milieu has been described as "permanent white water" (Vaill, 1991). Doctoral students in business and management are faced with a subject matter that is turbulent, fuzzy, chaotic, ambiguous, and emergent. Not only do the students study an environment like this, but they also want to become better practitioners in such an environment. Successful practitioners and executives must be lifelong learners. They must excel at the skill of engaging a set of circumstances for which they have no prior education and experience, and quickly becoming effective in that set of circumstances.

Such a scenario changes the nature of the type of learning that is most helpful. Relational learning, which occurs when individuals acquire skills, competencies, and/or perspectives in dialogue and connection with others (Boyatzis and Kram, 1999), has been shown to be effective in increasing managerial performance (McCall, Lombardo, and Morrison, 1988). Traditional learning is seen as a process of increasing individuation. Relational learning, on the other hand, deepens one's sense of interdependence.

Traditional learning is also seen primarily as an individual activity. However, today's practitioners and executives are increasingly operating in an environment in which they are functioning as part of a team whose basic activity is learning. Consequently, team-oriented learning activities should be part of any doctoral education in management. This form of learning is also important because research shows that much of what leaders do is sense-making, which occurs in a social context. It is in relationship that people test concepts, mutually adjust positions, learn as they communicate, experiment, and develop consensus (Weick, 1995).

Consider four actual situations in which a doctoral education can increase the effectiveness of the manager's response. Each of the four scenarios is followed by a discussion of the relevant aspects of a doctoral education.

a. The owner of a modest-sized business with little technical experience decides the business needs a corporate web presence. How does she choose from among a number of proposals that range in cost from $250,000 - $500,000 and promote different features? What criteria does she use to evaluate the proposals? How will the success of the web presence be measured? Since the web-page developers will almost certainly overemphasize the technical aspects of the proposal, how does the business owner know to include the social, psychological, and cultural dimensions of a web presence (Dent, 1999)? These kinds of questions arise in a number of business settings aside from assessing web pages.

b. A CEO picks up a book in an airport bookstore. The [fictitious] subject is reengineering transformational scorecards. The book is filled with testimonials of success in comparable firms. Should the CEO institute reengineering transformational scorecards in his company? How does a CEO determine what will endure and what will fade away? What philosophical foundation is the CEO working from and what are the advantages and disadvantages of that perspective? Many organizations embraced Deming's TQM philosophy, for example, without realizing that, while it is a great model for a high-quality organization, the philosophy has no change process implicit within it. Is transformational leadership a fad? Is knowledge management? How does a senior executive know?

c. The CFO of a large company is evaluating a funding proposal for a deferred compensation plan for the CEO. The total sum involved exceeds $100 million over a period of many years. Although the CFO evaluates financial proposals every day, this transaction has some features that the CFO is not trained to evaluate. How should the CFO decide whether to accept the funding proposal? The author held an executive position in which he regularly witnessed this scenario firsthand. The CFOs with whom the author worked were typically brilliant individuals with MBAs from the top-ranked business schools in the world. Yet, it was not unusual to learn that the company had previously purchased such a financial contract and essentially had been cheated out of more than $10 million because the prior person/firm who sold it to them had pulled the wool over their eyes. How does a brilliant CFO get taken like that? How does she ensure she is taking a total systems perspective, including understanding a time horizon of over 20 years? How does she know what questions to ask about something even in her area (although on the periphery)?

d. A network engineer travels to Saudi Arabia to install the company's intranet at the Saudi site. He has read the cultural guidebook of do's and don'ts his company provided for that country. He encounters a situation that seems most unorthodox. What should he do? Many people need a deeper understanding of the differences in culture as opposed to bits of advice such as not showing the sole of one's shoe in the Middle East or being prepared to endure "chit chat" before getting down to business in South America. Rather than learning "dos and don'ts" from a guidebook, a person who understands a Colombian perspective of time, or a Japanese perspective of communitarianism, is better equipped to deal with a variety of situations that may arise.

Implications for Management Education

What conclusions can be drawn from rethinking the environment of management and its implications for management education? Several changes seem to be in order. First, doctoral students in management need to be prepared for a turbulent environment in which senior people undertake new initiatives without roadmaps that could be drawn from prior experience. Second, critical thinking skills need to be enhanced so that doctoral students are comfortable taking a systems perspective and know the kinds of questions to ask in order to learn about areas outside their specialties. Although validity demonstrated by statistical analysis is important, doctoral students will need to know how to determine what constitutes reasonable evidence of validity in fuzzy situations that do not lend themselves to easy mathematical formulation. Finally, it is imperative for managers to understand interactions, quality of interfaces, and relationships as units of analysis. Such a shift implies an emphasis on teaming and interdependence both in the learning process and in the nature of what is learned. These changes were among others in the design of the Doctor of Management Program at University of Maryland University College.

THE DOCTOR OF MANAGEMENT AT UNIVERSITY OF MARYLAND UNIVERSITY COLLEGE

University of Maryland University College (UMUC) is one of the 11 degree-granting institutions of the University System of Maryland. UMUC was founded in 1947 with a mission of providing degree coursework to working adults and is fully accredited by the Middle States Commission on Higher Education. In addition to fulfilling its mission in the state of Maryland, UMUC has been involved since shortly after its founding with providing such coursework in Europe and Asia, primarily to members of the military and their dependents (Hudgins, 2000). In 1978, UMUC instituted the Graduate School of Management, known today as the Graduate School since it now includes large programs in technology and education. In 2000, UMUC enrolled approximately 79,000 students, including 6,000 graduate students. The philosophy of the Doctor of Management (DM) program, established in 2000, is heavily influenced by the culture and history of UMUC, so the latter will be briefly profiled here.

The leadership of UMUC has established the goal of having the university become one of the five premier worldwide institutions of higher education. Although an ambitious goal for a school that does not yet have a national reputation, UMUC has developed a set of competencies that are aligned with the external environment of the early 21st century and consequently uniquely position the university to achieve this goal. Four competencies, in particular, will be highlighted here.

- UMUC fosters an interdisciplinary-minded faculty who approach curriculum development, for example, differently from discipline-specific faculty. UMUC's MBA program, for example, is an integrated set of courses that blurs disciplinary boundaries in the same way that the day-to-day business challenges of organizational are often fuzzy.
- UMUC has operated a large global, multi-campus operation since 1949, so its leadership and faculty do not have an American or Euro-centric perspective of higher education, students, or business operations.
- UMUC's mission has always focused on the working, adult learner.
- Although offering primarily face-to-face classes, UMUC has pioneered and created best practices in distance education.

Interdisciplinary Faculty

UMUC's faculty combine scholarly and practitioner expertise and accomplishments. Approximately 98 percent of the full-time Graduate School faculty have terminal degrees (nearly 90 percent including part-time faculty). At the same time, nearly all of the faculty have had substantial business experience. This blend means that the faculty have worked in environments without the traditional barriers between disciplines of strategy, technology, organizational behavior, and so forth. The managerial experience of the faculty allows them to see organizations and leadership more holistically. A faculty member at UMUC may have a Ph.D. in Finance, for example, yet her career may have evolved to the point that she had held a senior marketing position prior to academia. Consequently, she has developed not only appreciation for both disciplines, but also expertise in both.

Global Mindset

UMUC has had major international operations since 1949. Although it is true that most of the students have been Americans, thousands of students have attended from their respective home countries and all of the degree offerings have had to match the local cultures in certain respects. UMUC's major administrative offices have been in Heidelberg, Germany, and in Tokyo, Japan. From these locations senior academic officers have managed degree programs in over 50 countries. In fact, for much of its history, UMUC had more students in Europe than in the United States.

UMUC presidents have typically lived and worked overseas. Benjamin Massey, president from 1978-1998, taught for several years in the European Division and later held positions both as director of the European Division and director of the Far East Division. Ray Ehrensberger, who led UMUC for 23 years [1952-1975], lived in Russia and Turkey among other countries, and traveled extensively for UMUC, often departing from the main campus for months at a time (Hudgins, 2000). The same is true of several of the deans and other top officers. Of the three major divisions—Europe, Asia, and North America—many of the faculty have served in at least two.

This experience and university culture have prepared UMUC and its leaders to operate effectively worldwide. The surge of enrollment in web-based courses means that a typical course may include students from eight to ten different time zones. UMUC has developed the administrative structure and the faculty expertise to excel in such an environment.

Working Adult Students

From its inception, UMUC's sole focus has been the working adult. Consequently, the issues associated with working adult students are central, not secondary, to the mission of the school. The university has maintained a very high level of rigor and quality, yet found ways to provide flexibility and service. The entire tenor of an institution is different when all of its resources are devoted to a single audience, the adult learner.

Finally, adult learners want a different kind of faculty member. They want faculty to have all of the expertise of traditional universities with at least two additional features. First, adult learners care about the quality of character of the faculty (Vaill, 1998). They will not respect a brilliant faculty member who is also arrogant or a renowned scholar who is insensitive to the needs of women. Second, UMUC faculty are passionate in their belief that adult education is something quite special. The faculty are expert at understanding the specific needs of adult learners and tailoring courses and degree programs accordingly.

Distance Education

UMUC offered its first course in distance education in 1959. Today, the worldwide web has become the predominant distance course delivery method. UMUC has pioneered in this area with its proprietary software product, WebTycho. UMUC's excellence and quality in distance education have been identified as the best of the web by *Forbes* magazine (*Forbes*, 2000). Although not enough studies have been conducted to draw conclusions, early indications are that web-based courses are as effective, if not more effective, than classroom-based courses for certain subjects and populations in higher education (Navarro and Shoemaker, 2000).

Introduction of the Doctor of Management Degree

One might think that a program aspiring to be the benchmark of its kind would have one or more silver bullets—features that no one else has discovered. But, the UMUC DM program lays claim to no such find. The program does combine, though, several leading-edge features that, taken as a whole, do seem to create, in synergistic fashion, an emergent feature that makes this program stand apart from other programs. These features include:

- Interdisciplinary design
- Applied and scholarly focus
- Revised dissertation requirements
- Integration of the worldwide web
- Partnership with employers
- Processes to assist in student degree completion

Interdisciplinary Design

Nearly every critique of higher education for at least the past 40 years has decried the rigid disciplinary focus of academia. The idea of integration of disciplines is praised roundly by academics in high places, yet a number of structural and historical factors reduce this praise mostly to lip service. Hybrid fields have a difficult time achieving equal status in the eyes of the academic community (Argenti, 1996), respected journals tend to be discipline specific, and faculty promotion criteria often encourage a young faculty member to focus on a narrow specialty.

The traditional Ph.D. has been the quintessential discipline-specific academic pursuit. Golde and Dore (2001) found that only 27.1% of doctoral students reported being prepared by their programs for interdisciplinary study even when it was allowed by their doctoral programs. Although many less traditional doctorates have an interdisciplinary component, this feature is enhanced at UMUC because of the interdisciplinary nature of its faculty members. Developing a global mindset is also an important element of the UMUC education. This perspective is achieved by requiring interdisciplinary study in the area of international operations as well as in the doctoral core seminars required of all students. Moreover, all courses are designed to include an international perspective. This view is further strengthened in distance education courses, which typically involve students working in five or more different countries. Many courses require assignments in which students study local companies, so the class is enriched by examples from all over the world.

Thirty-six of the forty-eight minimum credit hours of coursework for the degree support an interdisciplinary foundation of learning. Eighteen credit hours are breadth courses ranging on topics from behavioral sciences to technology. An additional 18 hours are in the doctoral core seminars, which examine the philosophical underpinnings of topics such as inquiry, leadership, and social systems design. The comprehensive exam experience, then, is designed to evaluate the interdisciplinary rather than the discipline-specific portion of the degree program.

Applied and Scholarly Focus

The UMUC DM is avowedly an applied degree. Yet, it is possible for a degree program to be both practical and scholarly. In fact, it is apparent that epistemology is central to many of the actual scenarios provided earlier: how a senior executive knows which questions to ask, how validity of proposed change management programs is determined, how evidence of an effective technology is marshaled. An assumption and assertion of this program is that this form of learning will markedly increase the effectiveness of the mid-life (median age 47) professionals drawn to UMUC's program. This learning is primarily accomplished in the 18 credit hours of doctoral core seminars mentioned above.

Partnership with Employers

The applied nature of the DM program creates interesting opportunities for collaboration with employers. The partnership with employers manifests itself in several ways. An advisory panel of both academics and business leaders serves to guide the graduate school in the conduct of the program. A surprising note is how strongly the CEOs on the panel have emphasized the importance of the scholarly portion of the DM program. Various businesses have also created eponymous fellowships that support the students in their studies. These businesses are then open to having doctoral research performed within their organizations. Initial contacts with organizations have shown them to be very supportive of UMUC's DM program in these ways. UMUC's response has been similar to that of Thomas Leigh, director for the Coca-Cola Center for Marketing Studies at the University of Georgia: doctoral students do fascinating work, and companies are realizing this. These students are tuned in to what is relevant and what is not (James, 1999). Proctor & Gamble is considered a pioneer in directly supporting doctoral students, providing $10,000 every year to each of several doctoral students conducting research on topics relevant to P&G.

Dissertation committees in the DM program are encouraged to include a doctorally-qualified member from outside academia. Perhaps most novel, all dissertations are required to include, at an early stage, a concept paper and presentation, in lay person's terms, to a group of qualified practitioners. This group would then have an opportunity to provide input for the remaining design of the dissertation research.

Revised Dissertation Requirements

The dissertation requirements for the UMUC DM program represent an effort to streamline the dissertation process by removing tangential activity and focusing on the creation of pieces of research that can be widely disseminated. In this way, the student gets an audience for her work and the field gets a timely, accessible contribution. At all stages of the dissertation research process, DM students are encouraged to expand the boundaries of traditional thinking and scholarship, both in methodology and content. Therefore, specific dissertation approaches and formats for a doctoral student are not limited to the model presented here. In general, though, a dissertation will contain three stand-alone papers.

- *A Concept Paper.* The student writes, in lay person's terms, a general outline of the research proposal identifying the definition of the problem, a preliminary review of the literature, and a proposed methodology. The student also identifies a stakeholder group of practitioners who are interested in the outcome of this research. If the dissertation were an ethnographic case study of one organization, for example, the stakeholder group would be the organization's top management team. If the dissertation addresses a wider topic, such as the architecture of the Internet, the stakeholder group may be experts drawn from a number of different organizations. The student delivers the paper to the stakeholder group and also makes an oral presentation. The student then has an opportunity to get feedback from a group of practitioners about all aspects of the proposal including its fidelity to real world conditions.
- *A Knowledge Assessment Paper.* This interdisciplinary paper consists of an extensive literature review relevant to the dissertation. The student prepares a paper that must be accepted by an acknowledged conference through a refereed review process. Requiring dissertation work to be presented is unusual. Although it presents somewhat of a hurdle to the student, there are now enough reputable conferences, and the turnaround times are short enough, that this expectation is not unreasonable. This requirement also means that reviewers external to the university have validated the student's work.
- *A Publishable Journal Paper.* The next chapter of the dissertation is a stand-alone paper describing the outcome of the student's research. This paper must be of a quality that the dissertation committee members deem to be publishable. All students are encouraged to submit their papers for publication. However, the vagaries of the journal acceptance process and the extensive time lags between submission and publication are such that requiring acceptance of the paper could unduly delay awarding the degree.

Integration of the Worldwide Web

Although all coursework can be taken in face-to-face classrooms, doctoral students who desire experience with web-based coursework can take as much as a third of the coursework online. UMUC's online courses are designed to mirror the interactions of a workplace where people who may be working on the same project are not co-located. All face-to-face courses are also web-enhanced, using the WebTycho system. This allows classroom faculty to take advantage of some of the learning experiences only available in a virtual environment.

Processes to Assist in Student Degree Completion

Factors that have inhibited students from degree completion include their relationship with their advisor (Green, 1991) and their connectedness with other students (Kluever, 1997). The UMUC DM program has established a number of practices that work to connect the students with each other, with the faculty, and with the institution. Following Boyatzis and Kram (1999) the program includes relational learning by intentionally developing interdependencies among the students in the 18 credit hours of core doctoral seminars. Effective teaming is taught and employed in many of the other courses, including virtual teaming of students who may mostly or completely work on a project without meeting in person. Faculty working with doctoral students are all oriented to the importance of the student-faculty relationship in degree completion. In addition to the common interactions, UMUC offers well-attended brown bag lunches for faculty and students to discuss mutual interests. Dissertation committees are also required to meet collectively with the student three times per year so that the students can deal with the committee as a whole rather than getting individual advice that may conflict or at least not easily integrate with other advice.

CURRENT TRENDS AND EXISTING DEGREE PROGRAMS

For several reasons, it is exceedingly difficult to know how many doctoral programs there are in management and how many doctorates they award. Some are offered in traditional business schools that do not separately report a sub-field. Some DBAs have become primarily management degrees but some emphasize other subjects, such as finance. Some are offered as leadership degrees in schools of education (George Washington University). Some are organizational change degrees in schools of education (Pepperdine University). Some are doctorates in professional studies (Pace University). Many others have different degree designations such as Doctor of Management (University of Hertfordshire), Doctor of Science in

Health Services Management (Tulane University), or Doctor of Strategic Leadership (Regent University).

The British system appears to have standardized around the DBA as the applied management doctoral degree. A wide variety of more practical doctorates are now in place that attempt to address the business challenges and the criticisms identified in this chapter. In a study of the content of 16 DBA programs in the U.K., Bareham, Bourner, and Stevens (2000) discovered the following intended audiences for these programs, in decreasing order of frequency: the management practitioner, those in or aspiring to senior management positions, and management consultants and educators.

The same study found the following stated intended learning outcomes: to appreciate the contribution of research to the work of senior managers, to develop research skills, to make an original contribution of knowledge in the field of management, to apply research findings to management practice within an organization, to increase skill in managing research and researchers, and to further personal development.

A few programs with this type of mission will now be briefly described. This review of existing programs is not intended to be either comprehen-

TABLE 1
Design Elements of Selected Doctoral Programs in Management

	George Washington University, School of Business and Public Managemen, Ph.D.	Case Western Reserve Univ., Weatherhead School of Management, Executive D.M.	Cranfield University, Cranfield School of Management, D.B.A.	Union Institute, Graduate School of Arts and Sciences, Ph.D.
Interdisciplinary Design	no	yes	no	yes
Applied and Scholarly Focus	mostly	yes	yes	yes
Parnership with Employers	no	no	yes	no
Revised Dissertation Requirements	no	yes	yes	yes
Integration of the Worldwide Web	no	no	no	no
Processes to Assist Students	no	some	no	yes

sive or representative. Rather, four programs are profiled which are attempting to achieve objectives similar to that of UMUC's DM program. Moreover, the programs described here are all primarily part-time, designed for practitioner-oriented students, attracting mid-career professionals (average age at least 35), and attempting to break at least somewhat free of the traditional Ph.D. design criticisms. These programs also represent a range and variety in how they are rethinking objectives for doctoral programs in management. Table 1 provides a summary of these programs on the dimensions described above: interdisciplinary design, applied and scholarly focus, partnership with employers, revised dissertation requirements, integration of the worldwide web, and processes to assist students. In providing data about these dimensions, there is no assertion that a program is better for having or not having these qualities. The data are shown only as a basis of comparison for the primary case study of this chapter.

The George Washington University

The George Washington University has one of the largest management doctoral programs of AACSB-accredited schools, as well as offering the Executive Leadership Program in Human Resources Development (Ed.D.) alluded to above. The School of Business and Public Management offers a Ph.D. degree but with several non-traditional elements. For example, students develop their own individually customized plans of study, which may minimize coursework and heavily emphasize other efforts. Their marketing materials suggest that students are encouraged to be imaginative and innovative in their study plans and *not to confine planned activities to the classroom*. The school has attempted to defuse the tension surrounding dissertation defenses by creating a colloquium option. If the full committee, including external reviewers, deems the student's final dissertation draft to be exemplary, a student is essentially pre-approved and is allowed to schedule a colloquium. In such situations, the student structures the final presentation more as a learning session for all in the room rather than a traditional defense.

Case Western Reserve University

Case describes its Executive DM program as the first doctoral program in the world to integrate concept and practice within the context of today's emerging and pressing global issues. Although the program is offered by the Weatherhead School of Management, faculty are drawn from throughout the university including the law school and the university ethics center as well as the political science, anthropology, and psychology departments to provide a strong interdisciplinary emphasis to the program. The faculty all have an interest in the philosophy of science and a broad perspective on applied knowledge and inquiry, or practitioner-scholar research. Although the program only began in 1995, they have already modified their dissertation requirements in response to their experience thus far. The crux of the dissertation consists of three separate publishable-quality articles each written using a different research methodology (participant observation and ethnographic methods, qualitative research methods, and quantitative methods and survey research) and each written during a different year in the program.

Cranfield University

Cranfield created a DBA program in 1999 and differentiated it from its Ph.D. by designing a research-based degree driven by a management issue or problem rather than an academic question. In addition to contributing to the body of knowledge, the outcome of the research is designed to provide valuable insights to the sponsoring organization because students use ongoing work roles as a basis for their research. Consistent with other doctoral programs in the British system, the program provides for very few structured courses. The bulk of the degree work consists of three research projects conducted under the supervision of three professors. The program takes four years to complete and the projects have fixed, eight-month timelines.

The Union Institute

The less traditional Union Institute Graduate College claims over 1,300 Ph.D. students in its School of Interdisciplinary Arts and Sciences. Many of these students pursue management studies. The Project Demonstrating Excellence (PDE) is the Union Institute's equivalent of a doctoral dissertation. Students are referred to as *learners* and the students and their work seem to be the centerpiece of the program (as opposed to the faculty, for example). The name PDE is used to encourage learners to achieve a broader perspective regarding the possibilities for demonstrating the development of new knowledge in a field. The PDE may take a traditional form or it may include an artistic or social action project accompanied by a contextual piece that firmly anchors the project in the scholarly issues and works relevant to the study and its related fields. Also unusual is the makeup of the dissertation committee, which includes two Union faculty, two doctorally-qualified people representing the greater academic and professional community, and two peers who are either other learners in the program or graduates. Learners also play a large role in the governance of the program by electing members of The Learner Council that oversees the program.

Rethinking the Dissertation

This section will conclude with a brief overview of the different types of dissertation formats. As discussed above, the traditional dissertation format and process has been heavily criticized. Also, as mentioned, many faculties have run into gridlock when attempting to change such requirements. At the same time, some schools have altered their dissertation requirements. A Council of Graduate Schools (1991) study of arts and sciences programs found that 19 percent had officially approved other options for the dissertation. In the management field, several programs have encouraged, at least informally, dissertation work that begins fairly early in the doctoral program. This way, elements of the dissertation are built in throughout the program, rather than having the student wait for the completion of comprehensive examinations before the bulk of the dissertation work commences. Other formats for the dissertation include: three major applied research projects, which are expected to be submitted for publication in appropriate professional journals; a Doctoral Project completed in four courses (designing project, appropriate research projects, doctoral writing, and creating the doctoral project) culminating in a publishable book-length manuscript that adds new thinking to the literature; a 50,000 word thesis (programs in the British system frequently specify the number of required words), which must produce at least one high quality journal article about innovations in management practice; a more practical dissertation consisting of designing, building, and implementing a new organization or a major change initiative in an existing organization; or, creating a dissertation portfolio. Such a portfolio might include a number of items, such as:

- a research study written in publishable form
- a research presentation to at least one professional meeting
- at least one literature review, suitable for publication in a review journal
- a detailed outline for a graduate course in the student's specialization area
- a review of current advanced textbooks at a publishable level
- the design, implementation, and evaluation of a curriculum unit or module.

FINAL CONSIDERATIONS

This chapter suggests a number of ideas for educators to consider as they strive to modify and improve doctoral programs. Spriestersbach and Henry (1978) were certainly not the first to observe nearly 25 years ago that the standards of Ph.D. education remain unexamined and the appropriateness of existing practices in Ph.D. education remain largely undemonstrated. It seems both clear and ironic that substantial research opportunities abound in the area of doctoral education. What exactly happens in the process of the acquisition of this education? What is learned and to what end? Most doctoral programs would benefit greatly from a wholesale introspection and rethinking of the goals and strategies of their programs. One response might be: whatever we are doing must be working because we receive a huge number of applications for our program every year. It may be that adequate student flow has, to date, undermined such an inquiry. Nonetheless, no researcher or educator would be satisfied with this answer in his field of study, so it should not be a satisfactory justification for failure to evaluate the design of doctoral programs.

Should doctoral programs be more standardized? The Association of Business Schools of the U.K. has made this suggestion for DBA curriculum. At the same time, the entrepreneurial nature of degree programs seems to be one of the sources of renewal in American higher education, so a standardized design may not be the answer. On the other hand, it does seem desirable to be able to determine the different forms in which management education is offered and the number of students to which it is offered. It would also be beneficial to have data about attrition rates, for example.

Should doctoral programs continue to be discipline specific? If people got together today to create higher education from scratch, would they, in today's environment create departments by discipline? Would they reestablish an ivory tower that essentially sits apart from other organizations? Are there forms of university/employer partnership that enhance the learning process (and, of course, help employers too)? Perhaps a general question in this area is, what is the interaction of scholarship and practice that academia should foster (David, 1997)?

A final area of inquiry deals more with the specifics of the programs. Paradoxically, although the Doctor of Philosophy is seen as the pinnacle of education, it has been argued that it is primarily a training degree (Heiss, 1970). Should the degree be focused mostly on quantitative research skills? Given that doctoral graduates infrequently enter jobs with this focus, should doctoral programs have other tracks that emphasize teaching or applied curricula? In any of these scenarios, what should constitute a dissertation? Or, is the notion of a dissertation an antiquated idea? A central challenge in this area is to ensure that management scholarship is germane to the managerial world yet systematic in its rigor.

At the dawn of the 21st century, educators have an opportunity to refashion doctoral education to meet the needs of the New Economy. A mid-level manager (or higher) in the 1960s would likely have held a baccalaureate degree. By the 1980s, such a manager increasingly would have had an MBA or other type of masters degree. Education has historically been a differentiator for career progression in society (David, 1997). It would behoove academia to consider a scenario of unprecedented growth in interest in doctoral education by, say, 2020. Corporate universities are already positioning themselves to provide a level of education beyond the masters' level. Yet, academic universities possess a degree of intellectual capital for educating at the doctoral level far beyond that which is currently available through corporations. The wise, intentional deployment of this intellectual capital will allow universities to stay at the forefront of doctoral education.

REFERENCES

Argenti, P. (1996). Corporate communication as a discipline: Toward a definition. *Management Communication Quarterly, 10*(1), 73-98.

Atwell, R. H. (1996). Doctoral Education must match the nation's needs and the realities of the marketplace. *Chronicle of Higher Education,* (Nov. 29), B4-5.

Bareham, J., Bourner, T., & Stevens, G. R. (2000). "The DBA: What is it for?"*Career Development International, 5,* 7.

Bowen, W. G., & Rudenstine, N. L. (1992). *In pursuit of the Ph.D.* Princeton University Press.

Boyatzis, R. E., & Kram, K. E. (1999). Reconstructing management education as lifelong learning. *Selections.* (Autumn 1999/ Winter 2000).

Council of Graduate Schools in the U.S. (1991). *The role and nature of the doctoral dissertation.* Washington, DC: Council of Graduate Schools in the U.S. ERIC Document Reproduction Service No. ED 331 422.

David, P. (1997). Inside the knowledge factory. *The Economist, 345,* 8037, (October 4), 3-21.

Dent, E. B. (1999). Technology clients and psychology: The case of smart cards.*OD Practitioner, 31*(1), 20-26.

Duke, N. L., & Beck, S. W. (1999). Education should consider alternative formats for the dissertation. *Educational Researcher, 28*(3), 31-36.

Forbes. (2000). Best of the Web in Education, *166*(7) (September 11), 305-316.

Goodchild, L. F., & Miller, M. M. (1997). The American doctorate and dissertation: Six developmental stages. *New Directions for Higher Education, 99*(Fall), 17-32.

Golde, C. M. & Dore, T. M. (2001). *At cross purposes: What the experiences of today's doctoral students reveal about doctoral education.* Pew Charitable Trusts.

Green, S. G. (1991). Professional entry and the adviser relationship: Socialization, commitment, and productivity. *Group and Organization Studies, 16*(4), 387-407.

Heiss, A. M. (1970). *Challenges to graduate schools.* San Francisco: Jossey-Bass.

Hudgins, S. (2000). *Never an ivory tower: University of Maryland University College the first 50 years.* Adelphi, MD: University of Maryland University College.

James, D. (1999). Corporate, academic worlds meld for Ph.D. students.*Marketing News, 33*(21), 4, 7.

Johnston, S. (1997). Examining the examiners: An analysis of examiners reports on doctoral theses. *Society for Research into Higher Education, 22*(3), 333-347.

Kluever, R. (1997). Students' attitudes toward the responsibilities and barriers in doctoral study, *New Directions for Higher Education, 99*(Fall), 47-58.

LaPidus, J. B. (1997). *Doctoral Education: Preparing for the Future.* Council of Graduate Schools.

McCall, Jr., M. W., Lombardo, M. M., & Morrison, A. R. (1988).*The lessons of experience: How successful executives develop on the job.* Lexington, MA: Lexington Books.

Miles, R. E. (1985). The future of business education.*California Management Review, 27*(3), 63-73.

Navarro, P. & Shoemaker, J. (2000). Performance and perceptions of distance learners in cyberspace. *American Journal of Distance Education, 14*(2), 15-35.

Spriestersbach, D. C. & Henry, L. D., Jr. 1978. The Ph.D. Dissertation: Servant or Master? Improving *College and University Teaching, 26*(1), 52-5, 60.

Syverson, P. D. (2001). Data sources. Council of Graduate Schools*Communicator, 34*(2), 6-7.

Vaill, P. B. (1991). *Managing as a performing art: New ideas for a world of chaotic change.* San Francisco: Jossey-Bass.

Vaill, P. B. (1998). *Spirited leading and learning: Process wisdom for a new age.* San Francisco: Jossey-Bass.

Walshok, M. L. (1995). *Knowledge without boundaries: What America's research universities can do for the economy, the workplace, and the community.* San Francisco: Jossey-Bass.

Weick, K. E. (1995). *Sensemaking in organizations.* Thousand Oaks, CA: Sage Publications

Winter, R., Griffiths, M., & Green, K. (2000). The academic qualities of practice: What are the criteria for a practice-based Ph.D.? *Studies in Higher Education, 25*(1), 25-37.

CHAPTER 7

EMERGING COMPETITORS IN EXECUTIVE EDUCATION

Thomas E. Moore

In the past, three types of competitors have dominated the high end of the executive education market: universities, consulting firms, and corporate universities. Each of these three competitors has at least one key attribute demanded by executive education users. Universities have been considered the "thought leaders;" consulting firms have had the advantage of scalability and global reach, and corporate universities have had the ability to align executive education with the strategic goals of the organization. During the last three years, however, a fourth set of competitors has entered the field of executive education. These new competitors are the for-profit entities created by universities and business schools. To understand why the new business entities were created, we interviewed many of the founding directors and university administrators who initiated the new ventures.

In this chapter, we will examine why these for-profit entities were created. We will also take a look at their different organizational structures, business models, potential partnerships with technology firms and value propositions to customers. Finally, we will examine how these new entities will compete in the executive education marketplace with the traditional

Rethinking Management Education for the 21st Century
A Volume in: Research in Management Education and Development, pages 157–182.
Copyright © 2002 by Information Age Publishing, Inc.
All rights of reproduction in any form reserved.
ISBN: 1-930608-21-7 (cloth), 1-930608-20-9 (paper)

business schools, consulting firms, and corporate universities along the dimensions outlined in Moore (2000) "The Shifting Landscape of Executive Education."

CATALYST FOR THE CREATION OF THE NEW ENTITIES

Beyond a doubt, the chief catalyst for creating the new entities has been the explosion of interest in e-learning solutions. Only five or six years ago, e-learning—often called distance learning or distributed learning or even computer-based instruction– was offered in unsophisticated forms and was principally relegated to the area of software and product training. These products were sold either as CD-ROM or intranet company solutions to train people in the area of sales, computer literacy or organizational orientation. The organizations that talked about shifting their cost from traditional training to distributed or distance learning were often companies spending large sums on training entry-level employees for specific skills. Very little of the e-learning material was used at the management level, not even for entry-level management, and virtually no distance learning products were being used in traditional executive development programs.

Distance learning began to play a more visible role the graduate level, rather than in executive education. On a generic level, the University of Phoenix was touting its on-line education as a major new competitor in the MBA marketplace. In reality, a very small percentage of the University of Phoenix's enrollment was actually online. More than 90% of its students were completing courses at convenient sites in shopping malls. The Fuqua School at Duke University entered the market early with a global MBA program. This expensive program—aimed at global managers and carrying an MBA brand of a top-10 business school—captivated the attention of top business schools around the world. During the early days of the global management program, most business schools watched Duke's progress carefully. Duke was able to capture the high ground through its pioneering efforts, delivering a program that included both face-to-face intensive seminars as well as a distance-learning component.

Around 1998, the environment began to shift dramatically. A variety of high-visibility, new competitors began to emerge. UNext, a for-profit company founded by Mike Milken and Andrew Rosenfield, grabbed headlines with its major funding and the contracts it signed with Columbia, Chicago, Stanford, and the London School of Economics. UNext promised these universities large equity opportunities to fund their endowment. In return, the schools would allow their faculty to design courses that could be delivered through UNext's Cardean University. At the same time, a variety of other top-50 business schools began to announce distance learning programs, some of which were completely on-line, and others that were in a hybrid format (i.e., blending face-to-face instruction with e-learning). The

University of Florida announced such a program; the University of Georgia announced a customized program with PricewaterhouseCoopers Consulting; and the University of North Carolina announced a hybrid model MBA powered by Quisic, an e-learning developer, designed for teams from various corporations.

Beginning in 1999, a series of investment reports began to forecast the huge market potential for e-learning solutions, both in the degree program and in the executive education markets. What follows are a few quotes from those research surveys.

A U.S. Department of Education study showed that nearly half of 3,800 institutions of higher education were providing some type of distance education, and by the year 2002 that number would reach 85%. The same report quoted 12 distance learning universities around the world with more than 100,000 learners enrolled in each university, creating almost three million enrolled learners. None of them were in the United States. The study also quoted IDC as saying the market for web-based training was expected to generate $5.5 billion in revenue by 2002.

WR Hambrecht Company Equity Research Report claimed that the on-line training market was expected to nearly double in size every year, reaching approximately $11.5 billion by 2001. The Hambrecht report identified the following key trends:

- Branding is the key strategy element on which e-learning providers should focus, because low market transparency and limited knowledge of e-learning products will drive companies to make the safe choice by choosing branded products.
- Companies will look for one-stop shopping. Namely, they will seek a series of products and services, including assessment, custom curriculum design, on-line monitoring of performance, reporting and tracking, from a single vendor rather than a series of stand-alone training courses.
- Consolidation activity should accelerate because highly-fragmented, long development cycles will cause inefficiencies in the e-learning space, and merger and acquisition activity should intensify.
- Technical barriers for e-learning will begin to diminish; bandwidth will continue to increase, and the interactivity of various products will become more and more standardized.
- The winners in this new space will be those who move first and build brand names quickly.

  The Merrill Lynch Analyst Report dated May 23, 2000, "The Knowledge Web," stated that the global corporate and government learning market was huge, measuring approximately $300 billion in 2000, and projected to grow to $365 billion by 2003. Web-based corporate learning was expected to enjoy explosive growth, measuring $11.4 billion by 2003, up from $550 million in 1998, representing a CAGR of 83%.

TABLE 1
Corporate Learning Market Estimates

	U.S. Online Market Size			
Market Segment	2000E Addresable Global Market	1999E	2000E	CAGR: 1999E-2003E
Content		$0.7 billion	$6.2 billion	73%
Learning Services		$0.2 billion	$4.1 billion	113%
Delivery Solutions		$0.2 billion	$1.1 billion	53%
Total Corporate Learning	$300 billion*	$1.1 billion	$11.4 billion	79%

Notes: *Figure includes government learning market

Source: IDC, "The U.S. Corporate e-Learning market Forecast, 1998-2003" January 2000. Marrill Lynch Global Growth Group. Merrill Lynch Analyst Report, "The Knowledge Web" May 23, 2000.

As universities and business schools began to understand the huge upside potential in the e-learning marketplace, they began to explore ways of entering this market. Their reasons for market entry were:

- To diversify their offerings beyond traditional face-to-face delivery.
- To take advantage of a paradigm shift in the way learning is taking place around the world.
- To create entities which could grow in value as quickly as e-learning companies (such as Saba, Docent, and the Apollo Group).
- To get out from under the traditional university governance process, which is slow and cumbersome and requires a certain degree of egalitarianism across colleges and departments. By creating separate entities, they could be more nimble and respond more aggressively to the marketplace. They could pick the hot areas that the market was demanding, rather than investing across the board based on university politics.

By creating separate entities, they could contract directly with faculty to secure key subject matter experts and provide them royalties and equity options that are not available through the university process.

They could develop a series of relationships—outsourcing some activities and partnering for others—thereby creating a value chain as a full solution provider for the customer. These kinds of relationships would be enormously difficult through the traditional university processes.

The University Response

As each of the colleges and universities moved to create separate entities to compete in the e-learning marketplace, they wrestled with what form these new entities should take. Almost all of the universities chose a for-profit entity of one design or another. Some chose the traditional corporate models, others chose S corporations, and still others chose LLCs (limited liability corporations). Each of these legal forms was weighed in light of tax considerations and how it might aid in attracting additional funding in the future. For example, one compelling feature of a for-profit entity was the opportunity to award equity to staff (who were being hired to run these entities) and to key faculty (whose intellectual capital would become critical assets). Schools were finding that in order to recruit the kind of talent necessary to run the for-profit entities, they had to compete with dot-com companies that offered significant stock incentives along with aggressive salaries and bonuses.

The e-learning marketplace is segmented into several sub-markets. The schools creating these entities have chosen to focus on different markets. In addition to focusing on different markets, the new entities had to decide where they were going to direct their investment and attention. . Each of these entities made decisions about where they would concentrate their efforts along the value chain and where they would form relationships with others. The focus on the e-learning industry value chain and ultimate customer market segment is becoming increasingly critical in establishing a business model that can actually become profitable at some point in the future.

Let us take a look at some of the entities that were created by universities to learn who were the catalysts for their creation, within which markets each competed, and where in the value chain they chose to focus their efforts.

TEMPLE UNIVERSITY

The Catalyst

At Temple University, the Board of Trustees was the primary catalyst in the formation of Virtual Temple, a for-profit entity established to deliver online education programs and to generate additional revenue for Temple. The primary rationale was to protect and expand the university's revenue base.

"Virtual Temple marks the University's entry into a burgeoning field of online education that can potentially reach one billion students worldwide, instead of the traditional student population of about 14 million in the United States," said Kyriakos M. Kontopoulos, chair of the Ad Hoc Committee on Virtual Temple and professor of social administration at the university. His remarks at a meeting of the Temple Faculty Senate in November 1999 captured the feeling of urgency generated by the new elearning climate: "If we lock ourselves into these traditional markets, are we going to lose out? We need to get a piece of the action." (Rauch, 1999)

The Structure

Temple University voted to establish a for-profit corporation in which the University would be the sole member. The new corporation would operate independently of the University. In outlining the new entity's mission, university officials said that the mission would include, but not be limited to: (1) extending the delivery of on-line educational programs via the Internet and other modalities in regional and international markets, and (2) generating additional revenues for the benefit of Temple University. Virtual Temple would not have the authority to confer Temple degrees without the prior direct approval by the Temple University Board of Trustees.

Temple chose to create the for-profit entity because of the flexibility that model afforded. The university felt that a for-profit structure could respond to new opportunities more quickly and encourage innovation. Most important, the model provided a vehicle for new sources of capital to finance these efforts. According to the Proposal,

> "Virtual Temple," as a "for-profit" entity, will be in a position to seek and obtain capital investment from a variety of external sources not available to the University itself. As an independently managed "for-profit" entity, "Virtual Temple" will also have flexibility in designing compensation systems and incentives for its employees and those with whom it contracts. (Temple University, 1999)

In a document outlining Virtual Temple, university officials noted that "entry into this market is highly competitive, uncertain and risky" (Temple University, 2000). But Martin Dorph, CFO of Temple, said the move will protect the university from any economic failure, while giving the new entity flexibility to make corporate alliances and tap into sources of investment capital.

eCORNELL

The Catayst

At Cornell, faculty at several of the university's schools were the catalyst for the creation of eCornell. Various faculty members were designing distance learning courses, and the university feared losing these professors if it did not act. "Cornell has to decide whether it is going to play in this arena or let faculty leak out to other marketing opportunities," said Prof. Deborah H. Streeter, who taught a distance-education course in entrepreneurship and was a strong supporter of eCornell. (Carr, 2000)

By creating an entity that could later go public, the university hoped to gain additional capital to retain talent.

> There's a need to recruit high-level staff, talented staff, and you're competing with private enterprise on that front. You have to be in a position to be profitable, and to be able to pay your people, so that you can compete with the private sector Internet and technology companies. It appeared that a for-profit version made more sense, and that's the way the university went

said David Lipsky, professor of industrial and labor relations, who chaired the university committee on distance learning. (Lipsky, 2000)

Extending the Cornell brand was another catalyst for creating eCornell. Commenting on the Executive Committee's action on Sept. 7, 2000, Cornell President Hunter Rawlings observed:

> This is a very important step for the future of the university. The creation of eCornell presents an extraordinary opportunity to extend the high-quality educational programs of Cornell to organizations and individuals far beyond the confines of our physical campus. (Cornell University, 2000)

Mary Sansalone, former vice provost, described the value that the Cornell brand would bring:

> eCornell will protect the Cornell name while the university adapts to an educational world increasingly shaped by information technology. And it will ensure that Cornell and its colleges and faculty gain the greatest possible return on distance-learning programs. (Powers, 2000)

The Structure

In October 1999, the Board of Trustees at Cornell voted to form eCornell, a legally separate, but Cornell-controlled, for-profit company. eCornell would create and market distance-learning programs. eCornell would be the commercial entity that will be authorized to use the Cornell University name for the production of distance-learning programs.

The initial strategy for eCornell is to offer continuing education programs from Cornell's professional schools where Cornell has either the top brand name or sufficient strength in a niche market to be competitive in the marketplace.

Within this business model, eCornell would rely on Cornell faculty for content. Its primary customer base would be professional education and continuing education. On Sept. 7, 2000, the Executive Committee of the Cornell Board of Trustees approved an initial capital funding allocation for eCornell of $12 million from the university's endowment for the period beginning July 1, 2000, and ending June 30, 2001. (Cornell Chronicle, 2000) According to the Proposal for eCornell, revenues coming in to Cornell University, specifically the portion going to the provost's office, would be targeted for on-campus IT needs.

To summarize, Provost Don Randel said that as a for-profit corporation, eCornell can promote the following opportunities (Powers, 2000):

- operate in a complex and dynamic market environment
- generate significant revenues that can be used for faculty compensation, support of faculty lines, programs and laboratories
- attract the capital needed to launch new programs
- partner with third parties and commercial partners when needed for capital and greater name recognition in the marketplace
- partner with other universities and entities that may want to sell their content through eCornell
- provide opportunities for transfer of technological advances made by eCornell to the university with the goal of enhancing the not-for-profit instruction by Cornell faculty for Cornell students.

UMUC

The Catalyst

At the University of Maryland University College, Dr. Gerald A. Heeger, president of the university, said the growing market for online education and the school's existing position in this market were the primary reasons for starting a company. The move was necessary because the institution was seeking to compete globally with online education programs.

> The on-line piece of it has expanded the possibilities so that the markets became bigger, and the potentiality became bigger. But the risks became bigger as well. You have to make bigger investments. Instead of being concerned about a local market, you're now thinking national and international. That drives up cost of infrastructure. It drives up cost of marketing,

Heeger said (Heeger, 1999). The need to be competitive and receive funding was the catalyst for the creation of UMUC Online, Inc.

In addition to gaining access to capital, the for-profit entity would break the traditional thought-mold of the university. "The development of this company will enable us to break the traditional 'thought-mold' for the way educational providers compete in a commercial setting," Heeger said. "Colleges and universities that want to participate in this competitive online market must think and act differently in order to succeed. We are doing just that."

Finally, the for-profit entity would help the university market its offerings to the business community in a manner that resonates with corporate leaders. As UMUC's David Freeman explained, "A lot of time, companies find it difficult to work with universities. They can't figure out who is in charge, or where the accountability is. Our goal here is to create a playing field where UMUC can interact with these corporations in the language and the methodology that they understand" (Katz-Stone 2000).

The Structure

In December 1999, university president Gerald Heeger launched UMUC Online.com Inc. as a for-profit corporation founded with $1 million in UMUC funds. The new entity would provide worldwide distribution and marketing services for the university's portfolio of online degree programs. (UMUC already had 13 undergraduate and 10 graduate programs online.) The primary customers would be undergraduate and graduate students, especially military personnel.

UMUC selected a for-profit structure because of its ability to gain access to capital, which would be used to build infrastructure, fund marketing, and attract new talent.

"Online education, developed and delivered properly, is exceptionally expensive, demanding a complete institutional commitment and a deep infrastructure to be successful in the long term," Heeger said.

> Given the competition and given the goal of addressing a national and international marketplace, you need capital. It's expensive to build the infrastructure to support these kinds of institutions. It's expensive to pay for the production of new kinds of courses. It's expensive to market these kinds of courses. You can't always expect that a university, within the range of its budget, can afford to take on some kind of new challenge. (Heeger, 1999)

DUKE

The Catalyst

At Duke, Blair Sheppard was the entrepreneurial catalyst for the creation of Duke's for-profit entity, Duke Corporate Education (DCE). Sheppard had pioneered the concept of custom executive education at the Fuqua School of Business, and he had proven his abilities in the graduate degree arena by developing GEMBA, a hybrid, global executive MBA program. His success with GEMBA earned him the respect and trust of both the Duke administration and the faculty, who saw e-learning paired with traditional face-to-face teaching as a novel means by which to distribute their ideas and gain additional income. Sheppard's threat to leave Duke to head UNext seemed to be the final "straw" to get the University and Fuqua faculty to approve the new entity.

John Gallagher, director of computing at Duke, summarized Sheppard's role in DCE:

> Blair is the entrepreneur who has developed this idea, who has pushed this idea, and who has made this happen. You need to have somebody who has not only the vision but also the willingness to convince people, the willingness to be the guy who is going to absorb the bulk of the risk by identifying himself with it and absolutely tirelessly push it forward. Blair has been that. In the next few years, there will be a lot of people trying to claim credit for Duke Corporate Education, but there is no question that this was Blair's. (Bleak, 2000)

The Structure

Duke sees the optimal structure of its for-profit entity, Duke Corporate Education, Inc. (DCE) to be a separate entity with equity held entirely by Duke University. Early attempts by Duke to have key customers, partners and VCs take equity positions did not come to fruition. Originally, Duke wanted VCs involved as a way to bring market discipline and appropriate valuations to the new entity. However, the complications of a payment to Duke (equivalent to the fee being generated as profit in corporate programs) made the value proposition untenable for venture capitalists who had considered early investment in DCE. The DCE venture was launched based on support from Duke University, without any significant investment from partners or VCs.

DCE is a private corporation that was created to house and expand the university's Fuqua Business School tailored executive education programs. The goal of DCE is to provide a one-stop shop for corporations. DCE will deliver products from the top of the organization to the bottom, and it will leverage Duke's brand, faculty and existing corporate relationships.

As a for-profit entity, DCE could provide many benefits to Duke University. For example, through DCE, Duke faculty would be able to significantly supplement their income while enriching their professional experience. At the same time, Duke would enjoy greater revenue potential, because DCE could take better advantage of scale than does traditional university delivery.

BABSON

The Catalyst

In February 2000 at a Babson Board of Trustees Retreat, the senior administrators at Babson made a presentation to the board on the threats and opportunities facing Babson for the next 3-5 years. One of the central themes was the emergence of e-learning and its impact on management education. The board wrestled with concerns about protecting existing programs, such as the large evening MBA program, from e-learning competitors while considering new markets that e-learning might open.

An underlying theme was Babson's position in the management marketplace as an innovator and entrepreneur. Through extensive curriculum development during the early 1990's, Babson unfolded a unique, integrated curriculum in the graduate school, eliminating all functional courses and building an integrated set of modules around entrepreneurial thinking. The undergraduate program initiated a similar massive curriculum restructuring immediately following implementation of the new MBA. The trustees' concern was that Babson play a prominent role in e-learning as a way to consolidate its reputation as an innovator and to enrich existing programs by developing e-learning tools which could be embedded in existing residency programs. The trustees requested that the administration develop plans for the creation of a separate entity. The entity would develop distance learning curricula which could be used by both the graduate school and the school of executive education to expand their markets, protect Babson's existing programs, and embed the new distance learning curricula into existing campus-based programs. Craig Benson, a new trustee and one of the founders of Computervision, pushed the college to think about this investment not as a business opportunity that would break even early and bring large financial returns, but rather as an investment in Babson's market position as a leading innovator in management education.

The Structure

The Babson trustees agreed to establish Babson Interactive as a for-profit, limited liability corporation. This decision was made after significant discussion on the virtues of a limited liability corporation in terms of tax benefits, stock options, and the flexibility it provided as the market evolved. The early decision was to focus on the part of the value chain that included needs assessment, content, expertise, branding, and program design. Babson Interactive decided that it did not want to create an infrastructure to do actual production, nor did it want to invest in designing and supporting the platform for distance learning products. The for-profit entity decided to identify partners that would work with Babson Interactive on a series of specific projects which would create products to expand market opportunities. At the same time, the entity would develop e-learning solutions that could be embedded into existing programs such as the evening MBA program. The strategy for the new entity was clearly a combination of offensive activity to develop new markets and defensive activity to protect its existing franchise with evening students and to extend its brand position as an innovator.

Two other schools that have created new entities but have been less willing to share their motivation or specific structure are NYU and Harvard.

NYU

In 1998, New York University became the first major American university to establish a for-profit arm to sell online courses. NYU opted to create its own company rather than deal with outsiders. One reason, CEO Gordon Macomber said, is that the university is more comfortable controlling the venture itself. The new venture is called NYU Online, and it is tasked with translating NYU's education content into online education classes (Walsh, 2000). NYU Online's customers include corporations, individuals, and other organizations, such as corporate universities and educational institutions.

NYU Online's first program, the Certificate in Management Techniques, was introduced in February 2000. Initial education products are both for-credit degree programs and non-credit certificates programs targeted to three markets: corporate universities and other corporate training programs, individuals interested in continuing professional education, and educational institutions that do not have the capacity to offer online education.

NYU is focusing on a business model that takes the university's expertise and delivers it directly to corporations. NYU does not appear to be interested in traditional executive education.

HARVARD

In contrast with the above examples, Harvard University formed a non-profit entity, Harvard Business School Interactive (HBSi). HBSi is a wholly owned, nonprofit operation controlled by the Harvard Business School.

Announced on November 28, 2000, HBSi will offer products that complement classroom executive education programs at HBS or the client company. The products will range from individualized online offerings to comprehensive "suites" of courses that utilize a variety of media. HBSi will combine face-to-face executive education with state-of-the-art e-learning technology. According to Dean Kim B. Clark, "HBSi is the magic that melds the classroom teaching that is a hallmark of the Harvard Business School experience with the creative use of the latest e-learning tools—combining and customizing them to offer a total solution for client organizations." The offerings would include participation from HBS faculty and live interactive activities.

For a summary table of the early development activities of the new entities, see Table 2.

PARTNERSHIP EXPERIENCES

Almost all of the new entities began to form partnerships very early on in their corporate lives. Some formed alliances or partnerships with endusers, such as Duke working with Deutsche Bank to offer a cross-continent MBA and a series of executive programs. Others formed relationships with organizations that offer a series of services including product design and development, hosting and distribution. These companies were organizations like UNext, who works directly with university faculty after creating an agreement with the university, or companies like Pensare, Quisic, Cenquest, and FT Knowledge, who act as partners or vendors with schools such as Duke, Stern, Harvard, Babson, Northwestern. In these cases, the business school entities have a variety of different relationships with the companies. The schools who entered the game early often took equity in their partners. They also received very favorable agreements in which the technology partner would take a piece of the revenue stream rather than charging the college for design and production. Latecomers are finding that the relationships are less attractive with these companies, who now expect schools or the new entities to pay for design and development time as well as share revenues once the product gets to market.

PENSARE

Duke Corporate Education formed a strategic alliance with Pensare to provide corporate clients with tailored business education and e-learning consulting services. Duke sold its e-learning platform to Pensare for a 16% stake in Pensare. Pensare will maintain and support the internet-based platform, tools and content to support DCE programs. The content will be delivered to multiple layers of management.

TABLE 2
Summary of Early Development of the New Entities

School	Catalyst	Legal Form	Principal Market	Funding Source	Total Funding	Partners
Cornell	Faculty	For-profit corporation (eCornell)	Executives	Cornell	$12 million for July 1, 2000–June 30, 2001	Will seek as needed to gain capital, expertise or market position
NYU	Was the first major univeristy to establish a for-profit arm (1998)	For-profit corporation (NYU Online)	Individuals, Corporations, Other educational institutions	NYU	$21.5 million	Interwise Click2learn McGraw-Hill
Temple	Board of Trustees	For-profit corporation (Virtual Temple)	Adult learners	Will seek outside funding	(not known)	Will seek partners
Babson	Board of Trustees	For-profit limited liability corporation (LLC)	Corporate executive education	Babson	$2.5 million	Canquest PLT (Accenture carve-out) Pensare
UMUC	President Gerald Heeger	For-profit corporation (UMUC Online)	Individuals, Corporations	UMUC	$1 million initially (hopes for $35-50 million over 3 years from outside sources)	Will seek partners
Duke	Blair Sheppard, senior associate dean for academic affairs at Fuqua	For-profit corporation (Duke Corporate Education)	Corporate executive education	Guaranteed line of credit	$15 million	Pensare

Duke selected Pensare on the basis of its platform and online learning tools. Also, prior to the strategic alliance, Duke had worked with Pensare for nearly a year, which meant that Duke had an understanding of Pensare's technology and strengths. Duke's Fuqua School of Business had also partnered with Pensare to co-produce and deliver a new program call the Duke Cross-Continent MBA. The program is an accredited program offered for sale to corporate customers and other business schools. Pensare will provide the Internet MBA program and will have exclusive rights to the technology platform, which was created jointly by the two companies. Pensare will also provide ongoing support for the program.

In evaluating a potential partnership, Duke looked at the business goals of Pensare and found that Pensare's goals were compatible with Duke's strategy. Pensare wants to be in the business of producing courses and support software for the provision of high-quality, internet-mediated business education in companies and universities. Given the large scale of this goal, Pensare does not have time to tailor courses to individual clients and thus looks to universities for this expertise. In addition to its partnership with Duke, Pensare is partnering with Stanford, Harvard, Wharton, UCLA and Berkeley.

QUISIC

Quisic has partnered with the Kenan-Flagler Business School at the University of North Carolina at Chapel Hill to offer a hybrid MBA program aimed at executives from larger, multinational companies. The students will learn and interact both over the Web and on-site (two and a half weeks at Chapel Hill, plus three ten-day residencies at international locations).

CALIPER LEARNING NETWORK, INC.

The Wharton School of Business partnered with Caliper Learning Network, Inc. to develop a program, "Building a Business Case." The program was designed to be delivered via Caliper's platform. Wharton faculty teach the program at a Caliper studio, and the program is broadcast live to students in other Caliper classrooms nationwide. Over 700 students have taken the program since it was offered in 1998.

UNext

UNext.com has partnerships with Columbia University, Stanford, Carnegie-Mellon, the University of Chicago and the London School of Economics. It offers these schools options in UNext (which is still a private company) in exchange for their intellectual contributions. UNext.com offers courses and degrees through its Cardean University. It doesn't offer the entire course catalog from its partner universities. Rather, it has aggregated relevant classes from each university into its own online program, which was launched in August 2000. As of March 2001, Cardean had 2000 students enrolled in its MBA program and hopes to double that number by summer 2001 (Lewis, 2001).

Another type of partner is the companies who have created learning management systems (LMS). The two leading companies providing this type of service are Saba and Docent. An LMS is a software platform that helps manage and deliver training over the Internet. The platform helps companies to capture, store, catalog, and disseminate learning online. For example, Docent is working with European business school INSEAD to power its new e-learning program, INSEAD Online. Docent will provide the platform that helps students plan and select learning programs, register for classes, and assess and certify their knowledge and performance. Both Saba and Docent want to become one-stop shops for corporations in need of e-learning assistance and are collaborating with content providers to broaden their content offerings. Both companies also have partnerships with the Big Five consulting firms.

HOW WILL THESE FOR-PROFITS COMPETE?

In 1999, a study of a group of executive education managers, consultants, and corporate university directors examined the competitive capabilities of executive education providers (Moore, 2000). Interviews with these managers revealed eight dimensions that underpin the competition among the three types of executive education providers (business schools, consulting firms, and corporate universities). These dimensions group into three broad categories of capabilities: Talent, Process, and Impact. Specifically, the eight dimensions of competitive capabilities for executive education providers are:

- Talent
  - Thought Leadership: the provider offers top-quality talent
  - Honest Broker of Talent: the provider connects executives with the best talent
  - Coaching and Mentoring: the provider offers intensive, individualized, interactive education
- Process
  - Global Reach: the provider meets the needs of a globally-distributed executive workforce

- Technology: the provider leverages technology to improve executive education
- Cycle Time: the provider quickly responds to the changing needs of executives and businesses
• Impact
- Alignment with Strategy: the provider's offerings align with the business' strategy
- Business Results: the provider ties executive education to business results

We can now extend the 1999 study to include a fourth type of provider, the for-profit university entities that offer some form of distance or online education for executives. The question is: how do these new university entities improve the competitiveness of traditional business schools? Table 3 summarizes the results of the 1999 study and extends those results—adding a column for the fourth type of provider (for-profit entities established by business schools). This table presents the perceived competitive capabilities for the four types of providers. Following the table is a discussion of

TABLE 3
Current Perception of Provider Group Capabilities

	Provider Groups			
	Colleges and Universities			
Dimensions of Competitive Capabilities	*Traditional B-Schools*	*e-Learning Subsidiaries*	*Consulting Firms*	*Corporate Universities*
Talent				
Thought Leadership	H	H	M	L
Honest Broker of Talent	M	M+	M	M
Coaching and Mentoring	L	L+/-	L	M
Process				
Global Reach	M	H	H	M
Technology	M	H	M	M
Cycle Time	M	M-H	H	M
Impact				
Alignment with Strtegy	L	M	M	H
Business Results	M	M+	M	H

Notes: H = High level of capability
M = Moderate level of capability
L = Low level of capability

each competitive dimension and how the new university entities augment the competitiveness of the university.

TALENT

Under the broad category of Talent, corporations looked for three capabilities from an executive education provider: (1) access to thought leadership, (2) being an honest broker of talent, and (3) coaching and mentoring (i.e., assigning a process or content coach to individual managers to help them improve performance). When we examine the impact that the creation of for-profit entities by universities has on these three dimensions of Talent, we see that the entities provide a means by which business schools can retain their leadership position over consulting firms and corporate universities.

THOUGHT LEADERSHIP

When business schools create for-profit entities, their focus is not on improving the thought leadership capabilities of the university. The 1999 study found that business schools have consistently been rated as having significantly higher thought leadership than consulting firms or corporate universities. As a result, most business schools will not be measurably enhanced by the for-profit entities. Rather, it is the for-profit entities that leverage the massive base of thought-leadership of their parent universities. These entities will be using existing faculty from the business school as their primary sources of information in the short term. Later, they will be adding other faculty, authors, and consultants, but this is not a key reason for creating these new entities.

Although e-learning solutions may not improve business schools' ratings in thought leadership compared with that of consulting firms and corporate universities, they do impact this crucial competitive dimension. The e-learning offerings of business schools may hinder the attempts of consulting firms and corporate universities to gain on this dimension. Currently, consulting firms and corporate universities boost their thought leadership by hiring "stars," namely, well-known gurus like Gary Hamel or other recognizable names in management education. Sizable honorariums or fees attract top professors. But if the for-profit subsidiary of a university can offer competitive compensation to its university's thought leaders, then these thought leaders may be less likely to offer their talents to other providers. This benefit, combined with the prestige of the university, may make it more likely that professors will form exclusive relationships with the business school.

HONEST BROKER OF TALENT

In the short term, the for-profit entities will not increase the university's standing as an honest broker of talent (i.e., having the willingness to identify and use the best talent from other organizations rather than insisting on incumbent talent). In the beginning, the universities will simply use their own incumbent faculty to create distance learning products. However, in the not too distant future, colleges and universities could recruit the best talent that might reside in other colleges and universities, consulting firms, or in non-academic environments.

The university subsidiaries can eventually improve brokerage of talent by assembling "Dream Teams" that include both incumbent university faculty and respected non-academics (authors, consultants, and business executives). University subsidiaries could even create custom programs for particular companies that include respected executives from within the customer organization. The inclusion of internal corporate managers who have strong company cultural appeal could lead to learning solutions that have greater impact than most universities can deliver today.

Universities do face a threat because there are relatively few barriers to entry in online education. Consulting firms or corporate universities with enough forethought and financial backing could procure the same top talent as the new entities created by universities. In early remarks about the emerging market for online education, Hambecht described how first mover advantage and branding are critical components for success. Colleges and universities could build on their existing brand name and talent pool to create very strong offerings in online education. Moreover, colleges and universities could establish significant market advantage if they can aggressively recruit and lock up the full spectrum of academic and non-academic top talent.

COACHING AND MENTORING

Historically, business schools have done a poor job in providing coaches and mentors—focusing, instead, on one-to-many, classroom-based education. University for-profit entities will not change this one-to-many focus, so the entities will not improve business schools' ability to deliver coaching and mentoring. As a matter of fact, most university subsidiaries offer less coaching and mentoring than the traditional business school. Rather than providing more capability for high-touch executive education with one-on-one coaching and mentoring, the distance learning activities are focused on a one-to-many approach.

In defense of online education, some argue that online tools and simulations can provide some of the feedback that managers might get from a coach or mentor. Although automated feedback is not as good as personal attention by a competent mentor, automated feedback is better than the lack of feedback in lecture-oriented, book-learning educational settings. Online education can also support valuable peer-to-peer interactions (between globally dispersed coworkers or between mutually non-competing classmates). Online communities could compensate for an overall lack of professor-to-student mentoring.

PROCESS

The next category of capabilities that customers of executive education look for is in the broad area of Process. The Process area has three dimensions: the ability to provide global reach, the ability to respond to rapid cycle times, and the ability to bring technology to bear on executive education.

GLOBAL REACH

For-profit university entities will improve business schools' global reach. Currently, business schools have only moderate capability to deliver executive education programs around the world. E-solutions expand their reach significantly and allow them to deliver complete e-learning solutions and hybrid solutions including face-to-face delivery and e-learning to managers worldwide. For-profit university entities can also expand their reach if the schools partner with third-party content distributors who are good at disseminating information. As Andrew Rosenfield, CEO of UNext, put it,

> Most faculty are great at creating knowledge, but universities are not very good at disseminating it. We can help knowledge creators effectively package and disseminate knowledge in ways that meet the demands of today's fast-moving companies. And we can do it far better than the traditional providers, who still rely on live delivery.

TECHNOLOGY

University subsidiaries will clearly boost the technological capabilities of universities to provide greater value for executive education customers. As recently as one year ago, business schools, consulting firms, and corporate universities had only dabbled with distance learning and e-business solutions. At that time, none of them had distinguished themselves as offering high-quality executive development products. Rather, they offered simple products focused on skill training, sales training, or company orientations. The new for-profit entities created by business schools will, in fact, give business schools key leverage on this dimension. The new technologies, whether they be business simulations or interactive platforms, could very well give business schools a key edge over their consulting firm and corporate university competitors.

CYCLE TIME

The for-profit entities may help business schools to improve their cycle times (i.e., the ability to uncover customer needs, and to design and deliver executive programs in a short amount of time). Currently, business schools are only moderately capable in cycle time. By contrast, consulting firms are often more responsive and quicker to react to business customers. In the future, the financial motivations of the for-profit university entities will help them accelerate cycle times.

However, e-learning does not uniformly accelerate cycle times. Developing new online content (especially top-quality content based on thought leadership) is not easy. Content development cycle times will continue to be long. However, once these for-profit university subsidiaries develop a portfolio or a library of learning objects, they will be able to respond much more quickly to corporate needs, giving them an advantage in cycle times.

Impact

The third category of capabilities sought by customers of executive education is Impact; namely, the ability to integrate executive education with other executive development activities and to have an impact on business results.

ALIGNMENT WITH STRATEGY

Distance learning subsidiaries will significantly boost the competitiveness of business schools in terms of the ability to align executive education with business strategy. University entities will assemble e-learning solutions from a library of learning objects in a way that aligns the program with the strategic intent of the customer firm. Then the entity can quickly cascade the learning solution throughout the customer organization.

Most sustained executive education programs are built around change models within corporations. These change models require a number of actions, such as a single lexicon and a unified set of business perspectives. E-learning solutions help a business school's executive education programs to define and present a consistent lexicon and set of perspectives. At the very top of the organization traditional face-to-face executive development can be followed by hybrid models that combine face-to-face learning with e-learning solutions. Finally, moving deeper into the organization, a university subsidiary can roll out e-learning solutions that align new management objectives with the business' strategic intent.

BUSINESS RESULTS

Corporate universities continue to have a real edge in developing executive education that drives business results because they enjoy better proximity to the business and its executives. Corporate universities have daily access to senior management, to the information infrastructure of the firm, and to the proprietary data that records the business performance of the firm. This helps corporate universities design programs that create results.

E-learning solutions can help level the playing field, giving universities daily contact with executives through online channels. Moreover, e-learning solutions, as part of a comprehensive executive development program, may very well aid business schools in demonstrating business results.

At the very least, e-learning solutions can do a far better job of insuring specific competency mastery by managers, guaranteeing that individual skill sets are truly implemented. Although there remains a gap between individual competencies and organizational results, e-learning may provide at least some answers for this difficult problem. Corporate universities will maintain their edge, but e-learning solutions will help strengthen the contribution of business school's executive education programs to business results.

CONCLUSION

The success of e-learning subsidiaries at colleges and universities is unclear at this time—interim results alternatively suggest doom and euphoria. On the one hand, none of the e-learning entities are an unbridled success, and the end of the dot-com bubble has dampened the irrational exuberance for e-anything. On the other hand, the value proposition of leveraging top thought leaders and creating new revenue streams in education remains compelling. Furthermore, global competition and the rise of knowledge-based work put a premium on executive education. Finally, the increasing ubiquity of computer networks, computer-savvy workers, and busy 24x7 lifestyles suggest that online learning is both feasible and desirable. Nonetheless, e-learning is too embryonic to reach any conclusions, as Al Vicere, a leader in executive education at Penn State University, stated in a recent study (Vicere, 2000).

The financial side of the overall e-learning market is especially gloomy. The drop in the NASDAQ has dashed some of the hopes of both e-learning software companies and of the new entities created by colleges and universities—the IPO gravy train is over. Companies such as Docent and Saba, who were riding high back in 2000, have seen their stock plummet to less than one-fifth of its peak value. Many of the software/service companies that universities are dealing with were start-ups that now desperately need their next round of strategic investing. For example, companies such as Quisic, Cenquest and UNext are scrambling for funding while Pensare, an early leader in this space has gone bankrupt. Clearly, financing an e-learning venture will be harder in the years to come.

Most agree that e-learning is a fragmented market and that consolidation has already begun. The future will see a wave of mergers and acquisitions as some of the large publishing companies roll up boutique e-learning players into their portfolios. For example, Pearson plc, publisher of the Financial Times, established FT Knowledge, an education and management development provider. It then acquired consulting firm Forum Corp. and educational services firm NCS. FT Knowledge also aligned with Cambridge University to build an MBA program and now offers online application services and online courses for MBA programs worldwide.

Like the dot-coms, colleges and universities are also struggling with their e-learning business models. Nascent e-learning subsidiaries have not yet significantly contributed to the bottom lines of universities and colleges, as the article "Is Anyone Making Money on Distance Education?" concluded (Chronicle of Higher Education, February 2001). Worse, Fathom, the creation of Columbia University, recently announced that their $18.9 million investment has failed to generate a sustainable business model. Fathom has laid off or reassigned staff, cut advertising, and asked Columbia University for an additional $10 million investment to retool the subsidiary.

Virtual Temple, the for-profit distance learning company started two years ago shut down in July of 2001 with little fanfare. The current president of Temple, David Adamany was quoted in the Chronicle of Higher Education as saying, "I didn't see any profit potential here." When asked about other University for-profit subsidiaries he replied, "good luck to them...when they make money, tell them to call me."

But other e-learning subsidiaries of universities believe that their programs are moving toward success through growing online student bodies, growing revenues, and the potential for a near-term breakeven point. Unfortunately, these subsidiaries' costs are so embedded in the normal processes and procedures of the parent that the true costs of these programs are not known. In short, the e-learning marketplace is in its infancy. Fragmentation is giving way to consolidation; valuations of e-learning firms have reached extremely low levels. Colleges and universities are still in the early ascent of the e-learning curve.

In the past, some colleges and universities thought that the e-learning space promised incredible potential for creating value for their endowments and for developing new markets with large cash flows. This euphoria is fading, leading to more realistic expectations. Those organizations now realize that branding and first-mover advantage do provide some strategic leverage, even though early investments failed to create quick profits. Colleges and universities need a long-term perspective as they create their futures in the evolving e-learning marketplace.

More and more analysts point to the corporate market as a source of real opportunity. Corporations tend to pay an order of magnitude more per contact hour than would an individual undergraduate or graduate student. Although large corporations are slow to embrace e-learning for their middle management executive training programs, a market for online executive education is developing. Companies such as Siemens, Cisco, Lucent, and others, are beginning to demand e-learning solutions that augment traditional face-to-face executive education. Hybrid models, combining face-to-face and e-learning, could improve the impact of corporate training while reducing costs.

The e-learning market will evolve as the new for-profit subsidiaries create realistic business models, and as they partner with the new e-learning software/service companies with broader production capabilities and technologies. As client corporations embrace distance learning as a valuable component of executive education, the market will broaden and deepen. Increasing acceptance of online executive education will lead to new revenues and profits for those colleges and universities that had the time, money, and patience to pursue this growth opportunity.

The colleges and universities that created for-profit subsidiaries stand to improve their market position when competing in the corporate executive education market against consulting firms, corporate universities, and other colleges and universities. E-learning subsidiaries help colleges and universities boost competitiveness on some dimensions and retain competitiveness on others. For example, we know that e-learning allows universities to maintain their edge in thought leadership. Forward-thinking universities have the opportunity to access thought leaders outside their universities. They can reach into the consulting community, the corporate community, and, in fact, into other universities to develop a portfolio of stars. These university subsidiaries can then leverage their incumbent and newly-recruited portfolio of talent to create high-impact e-learning solutions. Although this will not give universities a substantive new advantage, it may sustain their advantage in thought leadership. By contrast, more conservative universities may suffer brain drain as other organizations (including consulting companies and corporate universities) capture top talent using lucrative e-learning content contracts.

E-learning technologies and for-profit subsidiaries will help universities and colleges improve their global reach, technology, and cycle time. This helps educational institutions compete against consulting firms and corporate universities. With the right e-learning tools and methodologies, colleges and universities can leverage their competitive advantage in talent by creating e-learning solutions that are stand-alone or that augment traditional face-to-face learning. Business schools could develop an arsenal of e-learning tools that address the organizational needs of their clients—deploying a global, 24x7 e-learning solution on the client's intranet. New tools and methodologies help colleges and universities launch executive development programs rapidly, competing with more nimble consulting firms.

E-learning tools and business-focused subsidiaries also help colleges and universities create executive education programs that have measurable impact on client corporations. A general lack of demonstrated, measurable business performance improvement is one of the dirty secrets of executive education over the last decade. Although corporate universities, consulting firms, and business schools all talk about delivering education that creates measurable business results, most have failed to quantify the impact of executive education. Efforts to measure the business impact, in terms of real learning and real change in behavior, are too costly for most organizations, so the impact remains unproven.

Fortunately, the addition of emerging e-learning technologies to the portfolio of traditional face-to-face learning could help the problem of unproven impact. Some new e-learning technologies offer corporations a way to systematically measure educational outcomes and perhaps even behavioral changes. These advanced tools and techniques remain in early development. The good news (for universities) is that new off-the-shelf learning management systems (such as those from Docent and Saba) help address the measurement problem. These tools begin to offer organizations the ability to capture knowledge and to measure impact in a much more systematic way than ever before. As a result, e-learning technologies may help universities and colleges to compete in delivering executive education with measurable business impact. The bad news is that consulting firms and corporate universities can also buy these same off-the-shelf tools. The ability of university subsidiaries to aggressively capture the power of these new tools before others do remains suspect.

Although the beginning of the new millennium was not friendly to the e-learning industry, the long-term potential for e-learning applications remains phenomenal. Those colleges and universities that created new e-learning entities are well positioned to lead as the industry evolves. But, these same colleges and universities must be patient and be prepared to make investments for long-term advantage rather than short term profits. The next few years will be tumultuous for executive education, character-ized by wild fluctuations in demand for various products, exciting new technologies, and important revelations about what works. E-learning sub-sidiaries will revise business models constantly, and corporations will exper-iment with new tools and techniques.

REFERENCES

Bleak, J. (2000). *Duke Corporate Education, Inc.* Cambridge, MA: Harvard Graduate School of Education.

Carr, S. (2000). Faculty members are wary of distance-education ventures. *Chronicle of Higher Education. 46*(40), A41.

Cornell Chronicle. (2000). Trustees' executive committee authorizes the creation of 'eCornell.' (September 14), 1.

Cornell University. (2000). Cornell trustees authorize creation of 'eCornell.' (September 7),1.

IDC. (2000). *The U.S. corporate e-learning market forecast, 1998-2003.* Boston: IDC.

Heeger, G. (1999). Logging in. *Chronicle of Higher Education.* December 1: 1. http://www.chronicle.com/free/99/12/99120101u.htm

Katz-Stone, A. (2000). Online learning. *Washington Business Journal,* (January 21), 35.

Lewis, J. (2001). Learning on the Job. *Red Herring,* (February 12), 64.

Lipsky, D. (2000). Personal communication.

Merrill Lynch Global Growth Group. (2000) *The knowledge web.* New York: Merrill Lynch.

Moore, T. (2000). The shifting landscape of executive education. *efmd FORUM.* (January), 4-13.

Powers, J. (2000). Cornell board of trustees approves resolution to create e-Cornell. *Cornell Chronicle,* (March 16), 1.

Rauch, J. (1999). Temple ventures into realm of virtual teaching. *Philadelphia Inquirer,* November 11. http://www.temple.edu/temple_times/11-11-99/virtual.html

Temple University. (2000). *Proposal for Virtual Temple.* http://www.temple.edu/EOP/news/proposal.html

Vicere. A. (2000). *Ten observations on e-learning and leadership development.* Paper pre-sented at International Consortium for Executive Development Research meeting, October.

Walsh, M. (2000). NYU: Private university in public market. *Crain's New York Business,* (January 24), 18.

SECTION IV

CRITICAL REFLECTIONS ON MANAGEMENT EDUCATION FOR THE 21st CENTURY

CHAPTER 8

CORPORATE UNIVERSITIES
The Domestication of
Management Education

Elena Antonacopoulou

There is little doubt that education has become a big business in our times. This is nowhere reflected better than the growth and importance university business schools have enjoyed in recent history. In a business context where uncertainty and unpredictability prevail graduate schools have been seen as the marketplace for developing future executives. This picture, however, is one that is much less so today, as increasingly the provision of education (management/executive education specifically) has become a very competitive market with many new players, including corporations that once relied on business schools to provide their future executives.

As earlier chapters in this volume have already highlighted, the growing investment in e-learning and distance learning initiatives, globalization and changing student demographics, as well as the overall trend towards intellectual property are transforming both the way learning is supported and the meanings that education is acquiring. Corporate universities have

Rethinking Management Education for the 21st Century
A Volume in: Research in Management Education and Development, pages 185–000.
Copyright © 2002 by Information Age Publishing, Inc.
All rights of reproduction in any form reserved.
ISBN: 1-930608-21-7 (cloth), 1-930608-20-9 (paper)

become the new fad in management education stimulating several changes both in the way education is conceptualized, management learning is supported and power and political dynamics in individual development are renegotiated. Corporate universities have instilled a new paradigm in management education, which is fast shaping a new ideology emphasizing corporatization and commercialisation. It is this new dominant ideology, which in turn has generated a new set of pressures and measures of quality in management education. The emphasis on consumption, relevance, performativity and short-terminism are manifestations of this new ideology. The 'McDonald University'[1] model of assembly line education may lack academic gravitas but in a 'McDonalidized Society' (Ritzer, 1996) that measures and values speed and immediate results, such a model of education is yet another approach for systematically 'producing' the learning that is readily employed as a means to an end—profitability. Such ideology in management education, characteristically removes reflection from action, encourages a tendency to 'bank' (Freire, 1972) on qualifications instead of continuous learning and promotes an instrumental approach to addressing knowledge and skills gaps.

This new ideology in management education operates in direct contradiction to the principles of life-long learning and education so central in many organisational and societal debates promoting images of learning organisations within learning societies (Antonacopoulou, 1999a). The commercialisation of management education does not only force a redefinition of the focus and orientation of education. It essentially challenges the identity, practice, and survival of (management) educators, perhaps not because it challenges the legitimacy of their position, but because it undermines the underlying principles of their practice as educators.

It is therefore, of paramount importance to carefully consider the implications of the current ideologies and assumptions in management education, not forgetting that defining moments in education's history as far back as the ancient Greeks pronounced education as a pedagogy for freedom, not oppression and certainly not one of careless mass production and consumption.

It is these issues that this chapter seeks to address as we critically reflect on management learning and carefully rethink management education. The discussion begins with an overview of the main drivers and characteristics of the new ideology in management education. The notions of commercialization, digitization and corporatization of management education are discussed in relation to the main issues underpinning them. The discussion then focuses on the role of corporate universities in management education and, in particular, it draws attention to their approach in relation to management learning. The analysis seeks to question whether the emphasis on organizational knowledge, which is seen as one of the main aspects of the domestication of education, supports genuine organizational and individual learning, a central principle underpinning the development of corporate universities as management education providers. The chapter concludes with some reflections on the essence of education and revisits the notion of *paideia* to retrace the centrality of education in supporting individual development and social progress.

COMMERCIALIZATION, DIGITIZATION, AND CORPORATIZATION: NEW TRENDS IN MANAGEMENT EDUCATION

The emphasis on 'quality' in higher education has been gaining momentum world-wide in recent years and has been a central cause for many of the changes observed both in the way higher education institutions are organised, as well as the redefinition of what essentially education should be all about (Warner & Palfreyman, 1996; Harvey & Knight, 1996; Brennan, et al., 1997). The difficulty of reaching an agreed definition of what 'quality' is and what it should entail, however, has made more obvious the competing priorities that need to be managed within higher education and perhaps more significantly. It has highlighted the differing perspectives of the various stakeholders within and outside the education system.

The obsession with quality in the context of higher education is reflected in the introduction of the various national bodies intended to monitor the performance of higher education institutions (in the United Kingdom, e.g., the QAA, HEFC, and Universities UK). The monitoring of performance has resulted in the introduction of standards and an emphasis on outcomes as mechanisms for quality assurance (Burke, 1995; Harvey & Knight, 1996; Brennan et al., 1997, Hyland, 1997). 'Competencies' have thus become the new measure of superior performance (Burke, 1989; Boam & Sparrow, 1992; Barnett, 1994; Hyland, 1994; Boulter et al., 1996; Antonacopoulou & FitzGerald, 1996). Therefore, managing quality in higher education is not purely a matter of dealing with the competing and often contradicting interpretations of the term 'quality' as referred to by different people (Harvey & Knight, 1996). Instead, it is also about what Brennan et al., (1997: 2-6) describe as the controversies of 'language' (e.g., students as customers), 'power' (i.e., level of autonomy and ownership) and 'change' (i.e., the appropriateness of existing practices to changing circumstances).

Clearly, these developments help explain the new trends in management education and the shift in emphasis on profitability, investment in technology, and company specificity in the production of knowledge. These trends reflect respectively the notion of commercialisation, digitization and corporatization in management education. This new terminology/language captures the competing discourses as education has come to mean different things to different people and its quality is measured by new standards (contribution to profits, use of technology and corporations as new management education providers). Moreover, this new language is also reflective of the approach and techniques employed in teaching and learning that are shaping the business curriculum. More importantly, terms like commercialisation and digitization are transforming the identity of university education, which is a cause of concern as some commentators point out (Werry, 2001; Noble, 1998; Feenberg, 1999). Some of these concerns are perhaps more evident in university business schools where the emphasis on transferability of skills and bridging the gap between theory and practice are key measures of quality (Bridges, 1994; Barnett, 1990). The pressure to provide programmes, which reflect the 'practicalities' of the business world, partly explains the traditionally functionally-based focus of the MBA curriculum. In some respects this reflects the confusion of in management education as to what we think we are trying to produce as an MBA (Antonacopoulou, 1999b). This is a critical question to raise in the light of the zeal by many business schools to jump on the bandwagon of dot-coms, e-learning and corporate learning as the new mass education offerings. It comes therefore, as no surprise that increasingly headline news include announcements such as:

"Wharton Goes Global" (*Daily Pennsylvanian*, June, 2001)

"At Darden, Executive Education means better business" (*Business Wire*, June, 2001)

"Thunderbird Executive Education offers Strategic Finance and Accounting Program for the Oil and Gas Leader (*Business Wire*, June, 2001)

"Peterson's and Western Governors University Partner to Bring Greater Distance Learning Choices to Students Worldwide" (*PR Newswire*, September, 1999)

"National Technological U. Forms For-Profit Company to Market Courses" (*Chronicle of Higher Education*, July, 1998)

"Graduate Education Programs with International Vision: How Graduate Business Schools are Transcending Borders" (*World Trade*, July, 1999)

"Who owns On-line Courses? Colleges and Professors Start to Sort it Out" (*Chronicle of Higher Education*, December, 1999)

"Babson College and Cenquest Selected by Intel to Develop Custom MBA Program for Employees. Deal Redefines Corporate Role in Curriculum Development with Program that Combines Online and ONSITE Instruction" (*Business Wire*, December, 2000)

"Joining Stanford, Harvard focuses on e-learning –(Harvard U.)" (*AACSB Management Education News*, December, 2000)

What is increasingly common to all the initiatives emerging as a result of these recent trends is the tendency to treat education as a commodity. It is the commodification of education in turn which supports the trends that are much in evidence. Institutions of higher education are no longer seen as just institutions of intellectual development but as sites of capital accumulation and intellectual property which can be bought and sold in an increasingly competitive market (Noble, 1998). The notion of education as a commodity is increasingly raising concerns and criticisms with the implications of education as a commodity. Some of the most criticised implications include the intensification of academic labour, the increasing power and control that administrators gain, with the associated pressures exerted on those who have to perform in line with the new standards and requirements, and in general a return to Tayloristic principles of mass production and consumption of education offerings (see Clarke, 2001; Noble, 1998).

Moreover, another set of implications is the nature of the knowledge that underpins the new education trends. In particular, the extent to which this knowledge facilitates learning at the individual, organisational, as well as, wider social level. This issue is much less discussed in the existing literature, yet it could be a defining distinction between the education provided in public universities in comparison to the education provided by corporate universities. It is this latter set of issues that the remainder of the discussion in this chapter seeks to address. A review of the recent trend of 'corporate universities' as reflective of the corporatization of education is useful in confronting more directly the relationship between knowledge and learning within education and the language and meanings that education acquires. First, a review of the nature and purpose of corporate universities is necessary.

CORPORATE UNIVERSITIES: THE DOMESTICATION OF EDUCATION?

The trend towards the commercialization of education is not only reflected in the initiatives of institutions of higher education but in the initiatives of management consultancies and corporations as well. The latter have had probably the most significant impact in management education in recent years with the massive growth of what is now being referred to as 'corporate universities.' As Meister (1998: 213) points out:

> Because life-long learning has become so crucial, corporations are increasingly shouldering the responsibility for servicing the educational needs of working adults. Education, once the purview of the church, then the government, is now rapidly falling to corporations. The rapid growth of corporate universities, from 400 in 1988 to over 1,000 today, underscores the fact that the private sector is entering the business of education in order to remain competitive in the global marketplace[2].

Apart from dissatisfaction with post-secondary education and the recognition of the role of life-long learning on competitiveness, corporate universities are also intended to instill a learning culture that can support better knowledge management and the development of a 'Learning Organization,' which is expected to have an impact on company profitability (Senge, 1990). Moreover, corporate universities are seen as centers of excellence, instilling new common cultures. What Meister (1997: 5) refers to as the "cultural DNA of the organization," so that strategic goals are achieved. For example, educating the supply chain and not just employees is expected to act as a strategic tool to address turbulence in an industry. As Bailey (1997: 7) of Harley Davidson University has pointed out, the challenge is to: "Integrate, corporate goals and functional or department expectations into training programs that ensure positive dealer behavior and customer response, while considering ROI".

Probably one of the most significant objectives of corporate universities is reflected in the re-organization of the training function and Human Resource Development more generally to embrace more fully the importance of learning. As Turner & Hammon, (1997: 5-6) of the TVA (Tennessee Valley Authority) University put it:

"The mission of TVA University is:

- To provide TVA employees with continuous learning opportunities so they can maintain high individual performance and be full partners in achieving TVA business goals;
- To offer TVA customers the same continuous learning opportunities and related services we provide our employees."

Meister (1997) goes one step further and exemplifies what she sees as the main differences between traditional training and a corporate university, arguing that the former is reactive, decentralized and fragmented, intended for wider audiences, while being limited in depth and operating as a staff function. A corporate university on the other hand, is proactive, centralized and based on a learning philosophy. It provides customized curricula for key jobs and is increasingly run as a business which can add value (e.g., Motorola University Inc.).

Despite the fact that the purpose of corporate universities is relatively clearly spelled out, a clear definition of what a corporate university entails is still lacking (Donkin, 1999; Lester, 1999). As Mottl (1999: 23) pointed out: "The phrase is a catchall for any kind of educational commitment that extends beyond the standard tuition reimbursement and the new hires training companies typically offer employees." Others like Thomas (1999, cited in Blass, 2001: 157) argue that "a corporate university is not a geographical place, a corporate training department (except in the United States), or a real university....The corporate university is a good brand, and Americans are good at brands."

The emphasis on brands and branding is reflective of the commodification of education and the drive towards mass production and consumption. As Bradshaw (2000) argues, if one uses the analogy of a supermarket, when a brand does not sell it is removed off the shelves and an alternative brand is sought to replace the original. If this is applied to the current state of management education it is possible to explain why branding is encouraging greater specialization in the educational offerings of public universities[3], as well as in the way corporate intranets are replacing traditional training programs in brick-and-mortar corporate universities.

The lack of clarity as to what is a corporate university is further reflected in the various features it entails. For example, in some cases a corporate university is a dedicated teaching center with dedicated teaching staff, Deans and several accredited degrees and certificates. Typical of this arrangement are Crotonville of General Electric and Motorola University Inc. The latter is currently a $100 million world-wide business with 400 dedicated professional staff and another 700 program developers, writers, translators, and instructors responsible for developing courses and facilitating the knowledge sharing within the organization. According to Densford (1999) at least 40 hours of training are offered to each Motorola employee each year.

In other instances, a corporate university is a staff college where a range of courses is offered either by the company using internal trainers or in collaboration with other education providers. For example, the Cable & Wireless (C &W) College offers some C & W programs for senior and high potential managers, as well as short courses in Engineering, Management and Sales, and qualification programs e.g. HND, MSc MBA in collaboration with local universities (Ashton, 1997). Another example is A.D. Little, which has been offering formal accredited educational programs since 1989 (Moore, 1997).

Another feature of a corporate university is that it can be a purely virtual arrangement (Rowley et al. 1998). For example BAe Virtual University offers professional qualifications and degrees at master's level, through partnerships with other education providers. The university acts as an umbrella for coordinating various educational alliances and tailoring educational offerings to the needs of the company (BAe, 1999, cited in Blass, 2001). Even academic universities are launching virtual universities. The Open University is the oldest of its kind. More recently, New York University has launched New York University Virtual College, making all instructional materials digital and interactively accessible through one common user interface (Chisholm, 1997; Vigilante, 1997).

Finally, the notion of corporate universities encapsulates educational partnerships between a consortium of organizations and universities[4]. This model is reflected in the approach adopted by Petróleos de Venezuela, S.A., (PDVSA, the third largest oil producing company in the world). The Petroleum Industry Learning Center (CIED - Centro Internacional de Educación y Desarrollo) is defined as a corporate university, because it operates as an institute for management development, professional and technical development, and industrial training. Its scope is to provide educational offerings for PDVSA and its subsidiaries and affiliates, as well as to other oil companies, service and supply companies and even other industries (Rios & Cohen, 1997). To support this objective PDVSA has entered into an alliance with a range of organizations and universities including Babson College, the American Welding Society, the University of Tulsa, Wharton, the University of Pennsylvania, the Center for Creative Leadership, as well as Professors from different schools of Harvard University. The written agreement, for example, that underpins the alliance between Babson College and PDVSA includes the following activities:

> membership in the consortium for executive development, patronage of open enrollment programs, custom programming delivered in the US and in Venezuela, membership in Babson's International Advisory Board, International Management Internship program, joint educational research and development, application of distance learning technologies and co-sponsorship of management development for other companies." (Rios & Cohen, 1997)

It is important to note that a common characteristic of the various modes of corporate universities discussed in the preceding paragraphs is that they are supported predominantly by a common set of teaching and learning methods. Traditional classroom instruction is giving way to a massive investment in technology (intranet, internet, groupware, on-line interactive courses, web-based training etc.). The use of technology as the main driver supporting learning is based on the principle of forming learning communities and supporting knowledge sharing across a range of constituencies within and outside the organization and increasingly across organizations, industries and world-wide. What is evident in the technology-based mode of education is that the language of learning is changing significantly. Many companies no longer just talk about computer-based training, which was perceived in the 1980s as a significant departure from "sitting next to Nellie" (watching skilled workers on the job) and talk and chalk approaches. Now reference is made to distributed learning technology, collaborative learning, electronic storefront, network technologies, and distance learning.

The language of learning within organizations may have changed but has management learning been enhanced as such?[5] This is a question that the current initiatives do not seem to address, particularly when one notes the persistent use of training to describe learning. Failure to acknowledge the difference between training and learning runs the danger of reinventing the wheel in management learning (Antonacopoulou, 2001). It should not be forgotten that there is already a large body of literature reporting on empirical studies regarding the way individuals within organizations learn (Burgoyne & Stuart, 1977; Thomas, & Al-Maskati, 1997; Antonacopoulou, 1998). With regard to managerial learning in relation to training in particular, it should be noted that from the individual's point of view training does not always imply learning, because the expectations of the individual from training are often subordinated by the expectations of the organisation. As long as training does not develop the individual as a person (by providing the confidence, self-insight, and freedom to initiate new actions) it is unlikely that individuals will learn (see Antonacopoulou, 1999c).

Therefore, although the initiatives of corporate universities may have tried to incorporate the new language of learning and continuous development, essentially they do remain predominantly focused on training activity[6]. They are more concerned with the development of job specific skills, which can be applied directly to specific jobs. For example, Unipart U. offers 180 courses, which are designed to be practical so that attendees train for work and can apply a morning's learning to the afternoon's job (Unipart, 2002). Recognizing that knowledge is a perishable commodity is one of the reasons for investing in corporate universities. However, it is also evident that the underpinning drive is to develop knowledge, which is applicable and relevant to the needs of the business now. The drive towards organizationally relevant knowledge and skills, therefore, is also reflective of an attitude, which emphasizes short-terminism. Motorola University for example adopts the slogan "right knowledge, right now" (Staunton, 1999, cited in Blass, 2001).

From all of the above it appears that the drive behind the investment in corporate universities is not education for its own sake but education for the organization's sake, often not even for the development of the individual, given that the curriculum of corporate universities is defined by business goals and the perceived relevance of knowledge for the organization. This point returns to the long standing debate of the imbalance between individual and organizational development and the tendency for organizational objectives to supercede and determine individuals' learning, even under best efforts to develop learning organizations (Antonacopoulou, 2000a). This argument is also reflected in the proposed purpose of corporate universities to assimilate employees into a common organizational culture. As Norman Friberg (1997) of Volvo University, Volvo Cars of North America Inc. pointed out, the mission of Volvo University is:

- "To provide for a superior workforce, capable of meeting Volvo's strategic goals, through a comprehensive program of employee development and training
- To provide for the professional growth and development of our employees and business partners
- To provide a seamless organization sharing a common culture."

In terms of the later point a Culture of Excellence program has been initiated at Volvo since 1996, which sought a transformation of the retailer culture to ensure that there is "improved customer satisfaction, improved profitability, increased employee involvement, and reduced turnover" (Friberg, 1997). This 'School of Leadership' initiative at Volvo is reflective of the emphasis placed on the support of top management. As Meister (1997: 2) points out, the Chief Executive Officer becomes "Chief Learning Officer." The results of her study in 1996 revealed that in 15% of the companies surveyed the CEO spent three or more days per month facilitating learning. The infamous 'pit' sessions that Jack Welch of General Electric initiated at Crotonville (see Bower & Dial, 1993) is reflective of the best practices that Meister's study identified, among which she lists the following:

- The CEO invests personal time in facilitating learning and promoting a "culture of learning."
- The CEO identifies learning goals for the organization.
- The CEO enlists external learning partners to sustain continuous learning.
- The CEO encourages experimenting with new learning methods.
- The CEO publicly acknowledges the importance of continuous learning in achieving marketplace success. (Meister, 1997: 2-3)

It is evident from the overview of the principles on which the development of corporate universities rests that it is distinctly based on a business ideology. The language of leadership, cultural uniformity, performance, and profitability reflect a central assumption upon which recent changes in education and training policy are being built: namely the belief that training and development are linked to economic performance[7]. This is a long standing assumption in the HRD field and one that has been dismissed by studies (e.g., Hayes et al., 1984; Mangham & Silvers, 1986) which show no direct connection between the two and emphasise the complexity and multiplicity of variables influencing (financial) performance (Keep & Mayhew, 1996).

It is, therefore, problematic when such ideology is enforced in relation to management learning and education. Even in the organizational context, education, and learning as terms often carry a much broader meaning by comparison to training, which is often seen as narrow and specific (see Antonacopoulou, 2000b). Further still when one carefully examines the meaning of the word education—from the root *e* from *ex*, out, and *duco*, I lead, means leading out—it becomes even clearer that the business ideology of *domesticating* knowledge for organisational ends hardly approves of questioning, experimenting and critical thinking, all of which reflect more aptly the meaning of education. If one is only expected to attend learning events with the intention of acquiring job-specific and organisationally focused knowledge and skills, then could this be called education? As one of Muriel Spark's (in her book *The Prime of Miss Jean Brodie,* quoted in More, 1974: 42) characters confirms:

> To me education is a leading out of what is already there....a putting in of something that is not there...is not what I call education. I call it intrusion, from the Latin prefix *in* and meaning in the stem *trudo,* I trust...to trust a lot of information into the pupil's head.

Essentially therefore, education is intended to encourage freedom; education *is* freedom if one takes the view of educators such as Socrates, Newman (1853), Freire (1972) and more recently Barnett (1990). The fundamental principle of education as 'leading out' is that of inquiry and critique, which drives the search for truth. It is the constant search for truth that emphasizes the significance of knowledge for its own sake. The domestication of knowledge production, however, which is what one could describe the organisation-specific knowledge that corporate universities seek to support, could hardly be perceived to be educational. Blass (2001: 167) offers a useful comparative analysis of corporate and public universities on this issue pointing out that:

> public universities endeavour to allow students to discover their own 'truth' through knowledge while corporate universities offer the organization's view of 'truth.'" Both also offer opportunities with regard to developing critically, but in the corporate university it is focused around problem solving and gaining competitive advantage.

This is a view supported by Carlos Cavallé, Dean of IESE, a Graduate Business School in Spain. He points out that:

> Universities are about research, teaching and learning carried out in a humanistic spirit of intellectual freedom, multidisciplinary inquiry and methodological rigor...business school facilities are able to propel executive clients beyond their highly focused, if vital, concerns. They are uniquely able to give a comparative perspective across industries, sectors and disciplines. Whereas corporate universities are engaged mainly in the transmission of knowledge, business schools are much more adept at generating it... Whereas the former aim for quick solutions to current problems, the latter take the time to ask why and seek to elaborate general principles of wide applicability, taking into account the impact of business decision on people and society—something companies ignore to their peril. (Cavallé, 2000: II)

The comparative analysis provided by Blass (2001) highlights several other differences between a public and corporate university. The main difference identified are summarised in Table 1.

The wide ranging differences between a public and a corporate university leave little room for any similarities other than the fact that they share

TABLE 1
Comparative Analysis of Two Different Models of 'University'

	Public University Sector	*Corporate University*
Title	Originated from scholarly community, development into corporation numbed *Universitas.*	Title conveys culture & community of learning developed in-house
Historical account	Medieval/classical roots. Development of old uni. sector 17-19th century, new uni. sector 20th century, mass expansion	Developed from in-house training and education departments, offering new services, Creating research & development
Aims	To provide liberal and/or professional education at a 'higher' level to the public.	Expand the knowledge base of their companies, adding to competitiveness, acting as catalyst for change.
Outcomes	Qualifications (degrees, professional qualifications) & research.	Raised horizons on what can be achieved, conveys the ethics, values, & history of company.
Level of education	Undergraduate, postgraduate, and doctoral.	Any, from low-level functional training to postgraduate study from partnerships.
Size & diversity of student body	Any member of the global public who fulfills the entry requirements.	Every employee in the organization, some guarantee a minimum amount of training per year.
Knowledge generation	Mode 1 production of knowledge. Some mode 2 through industry partnership arrangements. Published for public consumption, peer reviewed.	Mode 2 production of knowledge. Research shared with partner organizations, in-house publication. Not publicly published.
Ownership & control	"Owned" by the state in terms of funding. Reports publicly & is accountable to state organizations. "Control" is loose due to concept of academic freedom.	Owned by the company, control varies according to the decentralized nature of in-house buying. Always has to be some business justification.
Links with public universities	Primarily collaboration exists in research projects.	Links regarding delivery of accredited courses and come research.

Source: Blass (2001: 168)

the same name, 'university.' In posing the question, however, 'What is it in a name?' Blass concludes that the term 'university' is inappropriately used when reference is made to corporate universities. The latter, he argues, reduce the significance of the term and undermine the importance of the services of universities.

The critique of the assumptions that underpin some of the practices of corporate universities is not intended to undermine their role or contribution to management education. The very fact that there is such difference in what a corporate and a public university is provides little scope for challenging the legitimacy of one over the other. There are several examples of successful partnerships between corporate universities and higher education institutions that would suggest that there is scope for complimentarity and opportunities for mutual learning (Cavallé, 2000).

The overview of the characteristics of corporate universities and their approach towards management learning and knowledge production highlights more vividly the ideology that underpins current trends in management education. It is an ideology focused on commodification and commercialization of education that forms the core of this analysis and the basis for rethinking management education. Acknowledging that such an ideology may be detracting from the essence of what education is provides the necessary foundation for considering ways in which all those involved in education need to reflect on their contribution to the current state and the future that they can help create. It is critical when we think about the future of management education that we focus our efforts not to justify the value of management education because of its consequences but because of its principles. It is the latter that the current emphasis on commodification is undermining. The last part of this discussion briefly revisits the core principles of education in the process of rethinking how management education could respond to the challenges that confronts it.

RETHINKING MANAGEMENT EDUCATION— REDISCOVERING THE ESSENCE OF *PAIDEIA*

Recently, our metaphors of business schools have become indistinguishable from metaphors of markets. The problems of business schools are pictured as problems of creating educational programs (or public relations activities) that satisfy the wishes of customers and patrons rich enough to sustain them....A university is only incidentally a market. It is more essentially a temple—a temple dedicated to knowledge and a human spirit of inquiry. It is a place where learning and scholarship are revered, not primarily for what they contribute to personal or social well-being but for the vision of humanity that they symbolize, sustain, and pass on..... Higher education is a vision, not a calculation. It is a commitment, not a choice. Students are not customers;

they are acolytes. Teaching is not a job; it is a sacrament. Research is not an investment; it is a testament (March, 1996).

James March's comments during a faculty seminar at his retirement reflect a scholar's deep reflections from his quest for scholarship. March's comments essentially reflect an entirely different ideology toward education and higher education institutions. The non-consequentialist ideology which March advocates speaks volumes about the value of education and learning for its own sake rather than any set of expected or predefined consequences. For March there is no room for profitability as a drive shaping the purpose of education. Profitability becomes insignificant when compared to the richness of the lessons one constantly learns when one pursues scholarship with passion. March's comments encourage us to step back and carefully rethink our approach and role as educators. We cannot just criticize current trends in management education without also reflecting on our own contributions in creating these trends in the first place.

Peter McLaren (2001: 117) drawing on a Freirian pedagogy quotes Cohen's (1993) forceful comments about the duplicitous role that university intellectuals have assumed in relation to the sociality of capital and their failure to challenge the perils of capitalism:

> University discourse and practices are condemned as mobilizing the academicization and domestication of meaning through a modernist process of historicization—a process that, in effect, amounts to creating various self-serving theologies of the social that enable professors to speculate on the future in order to justify their social function as intellectuals.... Universities and their gentry operate as a discursive assemblage directed at creating a regime of truth, a process that fails to undertake the important task of "inventing systems independent of the system of capital.

Taking stock of Cohen's critique and March's example, we need to be conscientized (from Freire's (1973) concept of *conscientization*, i.e., a critical reading of commonsense reality) and ask ourselves and others what have we learned from the history of management education to-date and what can we learn from the trends that we are experiencing? Why does education continue to fail so many learners? And, what can we as educators do about it? These critical questions deserve a much more extensive analysis than space in this chapter permits. Perhaps a start can be made in appreciating that any form of reflection as to what lessons our experiences hold calls for a more careful rethink of how and whether we actually learn from the experiences we encounter. Placing learning in the context of our experiences as educators invites us to retrace education through the notion of *paideia*.

What the ancient Greeks viewed as paideia was the cultivation of each individual's natural, in-born potential in every domain of social activity, which cannot be achieved through fixed programmes. As the Jungian theorist Luigi Zoja (1997) has argued, paideia was a major innovation of the Ancient Greek *polis*, representing an institutionalised form of the psychological process of individuation. Indeed, what makes paideia so significant as a concept and so central in education is that it is a psychological, as well as a social process of shaping the person as a member of a social entity to which the person contributes and in turn is shaped. In other words, paideia is a much broader concept for describing the social and psychological contribution of education influencing the development of individuals as an undivided part of the wider social whole. It is due to the reciprocal interaction between the development of the person and the social whole that the quality of life of the person and the society at large are being constantly transformed. Therefore, paideia is a much broader notion than education. Education is one of the products of paideia. Paideia lies at the core of education. From the Greek word education—εκπαιδευση— (ekpedevsi—ek)—*pedeco* (παιδευω)—meaning I nurture from young age. I guide one's development. I provide opportunities for learning. I contribute to the development of the person as a social being. (See Maratheutis, 1986; 1995). Paideia does not draw boundaries to childhood from adulthood (pedagogy and andragogy see Knowles, 1980) when it comes to development and learning. What is central to paideia is the whole person as a free spirit in search of its own self-fulfilment. This search for self-fulfilment and self-actualisation is not restricted by time or space. Self-fulfilment is to a large extent a matter of mutual-development.

The latter signals the commitment that March is referring to, and draws on the principle that the nurturing aspect of education can only take place when there is mutual development between the educator and those being educated. The mutual development of educator and educated suggests fundamentally a relationship based on trust and respect that every individual has the capacity to think critically, to be responsible for the decisions they make and to be accountable for their actions. This is why paideia advocates mutual learning and not teaching. The former is taken to be one of the most fundamental human qualities, the latter is seen as dogmatic, which paideia categorically dismisses as anti-educational. The relationship between learning and teaching, therefore, becomes central to the nurturing approach that teachers and learners are invited to jointly adopt. On this issue Martin Heidegger had to say the following:

> Teaching is more difficult than learning because what teaching calls for is this: to let learn. The real teacher, in fact, lets nothing else be learned than learning. His conduct, therefore, often produces the impression that we properly learn nothing from him, if by "learning" we now suddenly understand merely the procurement of useful information. The teacher is ahead of his apprentices in this alone, that he has still far more to learn than they—he has to learn to let them learn. (Heidegger, 1968: 15)

In the Greek language, paideia also means struggling, exerting great effort to achieve something. The struggle that paideia implies is when one strives for something with passion—it is *a labour of love*. This reflects what Heidegger had in mind when he argued that teaching is more difficult than learning. Learning, as the Greeks realized, is ultimately a labour of love, for one's teacher, for one's community, for oneself and for truth. Yet, love itself must be cultivated and developed through learning (Antonacopoulou & Gabriel, 2001). When it comes to supporting learning, therefore, distinctions such as pedagogy or andragogy become unnecessary.

What really matters is not whether we have a child or an adult learner but whether we care deeply enough to work with the individual needs of that person, which ultimately make him/her individual (unique). If we are prepared to embrace fully the challenge that learning and education present us as educators and educated, then we are more likely to invest in becoming more successful *pedagogos* (παιδαγωγός from the words—*paideia* [*pedi*—child] and *agogos*—[conduit/root]) a source and resource for learning[8]. This is perhaps where the ultimate of what being a scholar is all about—supporting learning by being prepared to learn, embracing existing experiences as foundations for existing and future learning, and fundamentally nurturing that unique human (child-like) quality of inquisitiveness and aporia towards that which is taken as reality and truth. As Freire reminds us, education is about the transformation of reality and for that consciousness is key. Consciousness however, is founded on our knowing and as Freire (1973: 88) argues:

> Knowing, whatever its level, is not the act by which a subject transformed into an object docilely and passively accepts the contents others give or impose on him or her. Knowledge, on the contrary, necessitates the curious presence of subjects confronted with the world. It requires their transforming action on reality. It demands a constant searching. It implies invention and reinvention.

The above reflections on rediscovering paideia as we rethink management education raise a number of important points about the way we see ourselves as educators (pedagogos), what we see as education (and management education more specifically) as seeking to achieve and in what way. Moreover, it calls for carefully rethinking both the impact we have and our responses to the current trends in management education, e.g., the development of corporate universities.

CONCLUSION

This chapter has reviewed the main trends in management education and has focused in particular on the nature and role of corporate universities in management education. The analysis revealed the assumptions and orientation of corporate universities towards management education and has questioned the appropriateness of organisational-specific (domesticated) knowledge for management learning. The discussion has also sought to retrace the core principles of education in an effort to draw attention to the powerfulness of key ideologies driving education against the current focus on the consequences of education (e.g., profitability).

Management education therefore, based on the principle of inquiry and the ideology of paideia could widen its scope beyond the education of managers and executives, not only as members of organisations but as members of the society at large. Its objective should not be to provide just knowledge and skills relevant to a specific organisational need but to provide an educational experience which sensitises them to the challenges and dilemmas of managing in different contexts (cultural, economic and political) and conditions. Management education therefore, should stand for the development/nurturing of managers who have the consciousness to be responsible for the decisions they make and accountable for the actions they take. Management education should not just seek to promote greater social responsibility but also greater responsibility for the active role managers play as educators (by bringing diverse practical perspectives, which enrich the educational experience) and not just as those to be educated.

Education is not a privilege of the few (either the elite or university intellectuals). Instead, education involves all in interchangeable roles of educators and educated. Management education therefore, should not encourage banking on the MBA qualification. Qualifications alone do not make a person educated. Qualifications could betray education if one is indifferent about the impact of one's actions. Management education could more powerfully stand for mutual education. Drawing on existing work on participatory research (Servaes, 2001), management education could be participatory education. In other words, based on the principle of paideia, participatory education would rest on the assumption that human beings have an innate ability to create knowledge. Therefore, knowledge production is not the monopoly of 'intellectuals', but it is a product of a joint effort by social actors who care about the consequences of their actions. Co-production of knowledge in management education would encourage a dialectic process of dialogue between educators and educated. Such dialogue would ensure that the learning is not only actionable (relevant and applicable) but that it enhances conscienticization of the implications of ones actions.

Adopting a pedagogical approach to management education calls for a careful rethink of our assumptions about adult learners. If we move beyond the stereotypical assumptions of how adults should learn and instead concentrate in our approach on supporting learning by nurturing the child-like qualities of inquisitiveness and curiosity, then we are more likely to be an effective *paidagogos*—a source and resource for learning. This latter point also signals that we can not be a source of learning unless and until we are prepared to be reflexive about our own learning and willing to embrace learning opportunities in a non-arrogant way. The enormity of the unknown should remind us that education requires humility as a foundation for our willingness to learn and our ability to teach.

Recent trends in management education, therefore, are a reminder that so long as we fail to reflect and acknowledge how we contribute to the current state of management education (e.g., by following single-mindedly and unquestionably the measures of our performance in teaching and research by chasing ranking lists) we will continue to undermine the principle that make us educators. If we fail to concentrate in rediscovering the ideology of what we stand for as educators we will but continue to suffer from our own superficiality towards our role as pedagogos, our social obligations as educated and our on-going contributions to paideia.

NOTES

1.   According to Jeanne Meister (2000: II) "in the last 37 years, more than 50,000 managers of McDonald's restaurants have graduated from Hamburger University located in a 130,000 square foot facility on the McDonald's corporate campus in Oak Brook, Illinois. It is an impressive operation that reflects McDonald's international scale—phalanx of translators allows the 30 resident instructors to teach in 22 different languages simultaneously."

2.   More recent accounts suggest that the number of corporate universities has risen to 1, 600 and it is also estimated that by 2003, 30% of all learning will be delivered over corporate intranets (Meister, 2000: II)

3.   In a recent article in the *Financial Times* (April 3, 2000: II). Jeanne Meister argues that universities must think of themselves as entities offering branded goods in this case course curricula. She offers the following examples to illustrate the point: "Imperial College in the UK is well known for its information technology curriculum while Wharton in the US is known for financial management and Carnegie Mellon is becoming 'the' university for a master of science in electronic commerce offered jointly by the schools of computer science and business." Branding of course extends beyond universities and their courses. A recent*Business Week* Survey of the Top 20 providers of management education listed The Centre for Creative Leadership, notably not even a university (see Reingold, 1999).

4.   Large American technology companies have entered into partnerships with top-tier universities. Bradshaw (2000: III) describes the case of UNext.com, based in Chicago is in partnership with Universities and Business Schools in Chicago, New York (Columbia), Pittsburgh (Carnegie-Mellon), California (Stanford) and London (London School of Economics). University Access on the other hand, is in partnership with the University of North Carolina, the University of Southern California and London Business School (see also Schneider, 1999).

5. As distance learning is becoming much more widespread in business education, so much so that the AACSB—The International Association for Management Education—recently issued a special report focused on the design and quality issues of such programs (AACSB, 1999). Even one of the founders of UNext.com, Andrew Rosenfield has been quoted in a recent *Financial Times* article as saying that: "on-line material is designed by people who think learning is like reading a textbook." How people learn online and what technologies can support this learning is increasingly being recognised as "one of the biggest problems facing companies and business schools which want to sell in to corporate universities." This is partly why commentators argue that some face-to-face interaction will always be necessary (see Bradshaw, 2000: III).

6. Carlos Cavallé in a recent *Financial Times* article (April 3, 2000: II) supports this observation saying that: "Some corporate universities are all too often the old training department with an exciting new mission statement." He quotes Kevin Wheeler an advocate of corporate universities as saying that corporate universities is: "the training department in sheep's clothing—it just changes its name but still does everything the old training department did. The best corporate universities offer initiative driven programmes designed to accomplish specific corporate goals—promote change, raise productivity, develop leadership potential and the like."

7. Cavallé (2000: II) argues that: "Motorola University says that for every dollar invested in training results in $30 of increased productivity over three years."

8. At the time of writing this chapter my 10 week old son Alexandros has been a major source of my learning, as much as I have tried in my new role as a mother to nurture and support his early steps in exploring life. For all the lessons that he is offering me I sincerely thank him. I also wish to acknowledge the valuable discussions with Educational Psychologist, Christina Paleologou who helped clarify my thinking on the notion of paideia.

REFERENCES

AACSB—The International Association for Management Education. (1999). *Quality issues in distance learning*, AACSB, July.

Antonacopoulou, E. P. & FitzGerald, L. (1996). 'Reframing competency in management development: A critique'. *Human Resource Management Journal*, 6(1), 27-48.

Antonacopoulou, E. P. (1998). Developing learning managers within learning organisations. In M. Easterby-Smith, L. Araujo & J. Burgoyne (Eds.), *Organisational learning and the learning organisation: Developments in theory and practice*, 214-242. London: Sage.

Antonacopoulou, E. P. (1999a). Learning structures and their social construction: A European perspective on management education. *Comportamento Organizacional e Gestao*, 5(2), 69-86.

Antonacopoulou, E. P. (1999b). Teaching critical thinking to MBAs. Paper presented at the 1st *International Critical Management Conference*, UMIST, Manchester. July.

Antonacopoulou, E. P. (1999c). Why training does not imply learning: The individuals' perspective. *International Journal of Training and Development,* 4(1), 14-33.

Antonacopoulou, E. P. (2000a). Employee development through self-development in three retail banks. *Personnel Review,* Special Issue on New Employee Development: Successful Innovations or Token Gestures? 29(4), 491-508.

Antonacopoulou, E. P. (2000b). Reconnecting education, training and development through learning: A holographic perspective. *Education + Training,* Special Issue on 'Vocational Education and Training in SMEs', 42(4/5), 255-263.

Antonacopoulou, E. P. (2001). The paradoxical nature of the relationship between training and learning. *Journal of Management Studies,* 38(3), 327-350

Antonacopoulou, E. P. & Gabriel, Y. (2001). Emotion, learning and organisational change: Towards an integration of psychoanalytic and other perspectives. *Journal of Organizational Change Management,* 14(5), 435-451.

Ashton, D. (1997). The design and launch of the cable and wireless college. Paper presented at the *Designing a Virtual Corporate University Conference,* 12-14 March, Cambridge, MA.

BAe (1999). *Achievement Through Knowledge,* Farnborough: BAe (in house Virtual University prospectus document).

Bailey, B. (1997). Transferring your corporate university overseas: Lessons from Harley-Davidson University. Paper presented at the *Designing a Virtual Corporate University Conference,* 12-14 March, Cambridge, MA.

Barnett, R. (1990). *The Idea of Higher education,* London: The Society for Research into Higher education and Open University Press.

Barnett, R. (1994). *The Limits of Competence,* London: Open University Press.

Blass, E. (2001). What's in a name? A comparative study of the traditional public university and the corporate university. *Human Resource Development International,* 4(2), 153-172.

Boam, R. & Sparrow, P. (1992). *Designing and achieving competency: A competency-based approach to developing people and organisations,* Maidenhead, UK: McGraw-Hill.

Boulter, N., Dalziel, M and Hill, J. (1996). *People and Competencies: The Route to competitive advantage.* London: Hay/McBer, Kogan Page.

Bower, J. L. & Dial, J. (1993). *Jack Welch: General Electric's Revolutionary.* Harvard Business School Case 9-394-065.

Bradshaw, D. (2000). Abandon hype, deliver the goodies. *Financial Times,* April 3: III.

Brennan, J. de Vries P. and Williams, R. (Eds.). (1997). *Standards and Quality in Higher education.* London: Jessica Kingsley.

Bridges, D. (1994). *Transferable skills in Higher education.* Norwich: ERTEC/UEA.

Burgoyne, J. & Stuart, R. (1977). Implicit Learning Theories as Determinants of the Effect of Management Development Programmes, *Personnel Review,* 6(2), 5-14.

Burke, J. (1989). *Competency Based Education and Training,* London: Falmer Press.

Burke, J. (Ed) (1995). *Outcomes, Learning and the Curriculum,* London: Falmer Press.

Business Wire. (2000). Babson College and Cenquest selected by Intel to develop custom MBA program for employees. Deal redefines corporate role in curriculum development with program that combines online and ONSITE Instruction. December.

Business Wire. (2001). At Darden, executive education means better business. June: 28.

Business Wire. (2001). Thunderbird executive education offers strategic finance and accounting program for the oil and gas leader. June: 12.

Carnevale, D. & Young, J. R. (1999). Who owns on-line courses? Colleges and professors start to sort it out, *Chronicle of Higher Education,* (December 17), A45.

Cavallé, C. (2000). Tempest in a tea pot, *Financial Times,* April 3: II

Celestino, M. L. (1999). Graduate education programs with international vision: How graduate business schools are transcending borders, *World Trade,* July.

Chisholm, K. (1997). Open University: The design, launch and evolution of a virtual university. Paper presented at the *Designing a Virtual Corporate University Conference.* 12-14 March, Cambridge, MA.

Clarke, L. (2001). Why do we need Coolclass? *The Coolclass Chronicle, 1*(1), online.

Cohen, S. (1993). *Academia and the luster of capital.* Minneapolis: University of Minnesota Press.

Daily Pennsylvanian. (2001). Wharton Goes Global. June, 7.

Densford, L. E. (1999). Motorola University: The next 20 years. *Corporate University Review,* (February 1).

Donkin, R. (1999). Learning curves for companies. *Financial Times,* (August 2), 12.

Feenberg, A. (1999). Distance learning: Promise or threat? *Crosstalk,* Winter (http://www-rohan.sdsu.edu/faculty/feeberg/TELE3.HTML)

Freire, P. (1972). *Pedagogy of the oppressed.* Harmondsworth, UK: Penguin.

Freire, P. (1973). *Education for critical consciousness.* New York: Seabury Press.

Friberg, N. (1997). Volvo University: Training the value chain. Paper presented at the *Designing a Virtual Corporate University Conference,* 12-14 March, Cambridge, MA.

Harvey, L. & Knight P.T. (1996). *Transforming higher education,* Buckingham, UK: The Society for Research into Higher education and Open University Press.

Hayes, R. H., Wheelwright, S.C. & Clarke, K.B. (1988). *Dynamic manufacturing: Creating the learning organisation.* Free Press, UK.

Heidegger, M. (1968). *What is called thinking?* J. Glenngray (Trans.). New York: Harper & Row.

Hyland, T. (1994). *Competence, education and NVQs: Dissenting perspectives.* London: Cassell.

Hyland, T. (1997). Work-Based experience and higher professional learning in British universities. In J.F. Forest (Ed.), *University teaching: International perspectives,* 101-117. New York: Garland.

Keep, E. & Mayhew, K. (1996). UK training policy: Assumptions and reality. In A. Booth & D.J. Snower (Eds.). *The skills gap and economic activity.* Cambridge: Cambridge University Press.

Knowles, M. S. (1980). *The modern practice of adult education: From pedagogy to andragogy,* (2nd ed.). New York: Cambridge Books.

Lester, T. (1999). Degree couture. *Human Resources,* (March), 74-78.

Mangham, I. & Silver, M. (1986). *Management training: Context and practice.* Bath, UK: School of Management, University of Bath.

Maratheutis, M. I. (1986). *Αγωγη του Προσωπου. Θ εωρια της Παιδειας,* Μιχαλακη Ι. Μαραθευτη, Λευκωσια. (ISBN: 9963-7558-2-8).

Maratheutis, Ì. É. (1995). *Μελετηματα Ελληνορθοδοξης Παιδειας.* Θεωπια της Παιδειας, Μιχαλακη Ι. Μαπαθευτη, Λευκωσια, (ISBN: 9963-7558-9-5).

March, J.G. (1996). A Scholar's Quest. *Stanford Business School Magazine,* June.

Marshall, S. (2000). Joining Stanford, Harvard focuses on e-learning—(Harvard U.). *AACSB Management Education News*, December 11.

McLaren, P. (2001). Freirean pedagogy and higher education: The challenge of postmodernism and the Politics of Race. In M. Richards, P.N. Thomas & Z. Nain (Eds.). *Communication and development: The Freirean connection*, 109-130. Cresskill, NJ: Hampton Press.

Meister, J. C. (2000). Savvy e-learners drive revolution in education.*Financial Times*, (April 3), II.

Meister, J. C. (1997). Corporate universities: An opportunity or threat to higher education. Paper presented at the *Designing a virtual corporate university conference*, 12-14 March, Cambridge, MA.

Meister, J. C. (1998). *Corporate universities: Lessons in building a world-class work force*. New York: McGraw-Hill.

Moore, T. E. (1997). The corporate university: Transforming management education, *Accounting Horizons*, (March).

More, W. S. (1974). *Emotions and adult learning*. London: Saxon House.

Motorola. (1999). *About Motorola University*, at http://mu.motorola.com.

Mottl, J. N. (1999). Corporate universities grow,*InternetWeek*, March 15: 23.

Newman, J. H. (1853) [1996 reprint]. The idea of a university. In F.M. Turner (ed.) *John Henry Newman: The idea of a university*. New Haven, CT: Yale University Press.

Noble, D. F. (1998). Digital diploma mills: The automation of higher education. *First Monday*, 3(1). Retrieved from http://www.firstmonday.dk/issues/issue3_1/noble/index.html on February 11, 2002.

PR Newswire. (1999). Peterson's and Western Governors University partner to bring greater distance learning choices to students worldwide. September.

Reingold, J. (1999). Learning to lead.*Business Week*, (October 18).

Rios, N. & Cohen, A. R. (1997). The inclusive alliance: Petroleos de Venezuela and Babson College partnership. Paper presented at the*Designing a Virtual Corporate University Conference*, 12-14 March, Cambridge, MA.

Ritzer, G. (1996). *The McDonaldization of Society*. Thousand Oaks, CA: Pine Forge Press.

Rowley, D. J., Herman, D.L. & Wechsler, H. (1998).*Strategy choices for the academy: How demand for lifelong learning will re-create higher education*. Jossey-Bass, New York.

Schneider, M. (1999). Turning B-School into e-school.*Business Week*, (October 18).

Senge, P. M. (1990). The leaders' new work: Building learning organisations.*Sloan Management Review*, (Fall), 7-23.

Servaes, J. (2001). Participatory communication research for democracy and social change. In M. Richards, P.N. Thomas & Z. Nain (Eds.). *Communication and Development: The Freirean Connection*, 13-32, Hampton Press: New Jersey.

Strosnider, K. (1998). National Technological U. Forms For-Profit Company to Market Courses. *Chronicle of Higher Education*, (July, 24), A30.

Thomas, A. B. & Al-Maskati, H. (1997). Contextual Influences on Thinking in Organisations: Learner and Tutor Orientations to Organisational Learning *Journal of Management Studies*, 34(6), 851-870.

Thomas, D. (1999). The corporate university as a model for organisational and individual learning. Paper given at the*IQPC Conference*, 22-23 June, London.

Turner, J. B. & Hammond, M. C. (1997). How to design and measure the effectiveness of your corporate university. Paper presented at the *Designing a Virtual Corporate University Conference*, 12-14 March, Cambridge, MA.

Unipart. (2002). *The faculty on the floor.* Retrieved from http://www.ugc.co.uk/learning/lea_0100.htm February 11.

Vigilante, R. (1997). Best practices in developing an on-line university: The launch of New York University's Virtual College. Paper presented at the *Designing a virtual corporate university conference*, 12-14 March, Cambridge, MA.

Warner, D. & Palfreyman, D. (Eds.). (1996). *Higher education management: The key elements*, Buckingham, UK: The Society for Research into Higher education & Open University Press.

Werry, C. (2001). The work of Education in the Age of E-College, *First Monday*, 6, 5, May: Retrieved from http://www.firstmonday.org/issues/issue6_5/werry/index.html February 12, 2002.

Zoja, L. (1997). Individuation and paideia, *Journal of Analytical Psychology*, 42, 481-505.

CHAPTER 9

MANAGEMENT EDUCATION IN AN AGE OF GLOBALIZATION
The Need for Critical Perspectives

Darryl Reed

Processes of economic globalization over the last few decades have not only dramatically altered the way business is done around the world, but have also greatly impacted political, social and cultural landscapes. The purpose of this paper is to examine how the analysis of these processes of globalization and their effects should be incorporated into management education. A basic premise underlying the argument developed in this paper is that management is a profession and that, as such, it has a responsibility to critically examine the effects of how it functions and investigate how its contributions to society may be improved. Such a responsibility implies that management education cannot have a narrow (instrumental) focus on training (potential) managers how to maximize profits. Rather, the profession must introduce students to the larger questions about the role of man-

Rethinking Management Education for the 21st Century
A Volume in: Research in Management Education and Development, pages 209–236.
Copyright © 2002 by Information Age Publishing, Inc.
All rights of reproduction in any form reserved.
ISBN: 1-930608-21-7 (cloth), 1-930608-20-9 (paper)

agement (and business more generally) in society and provide them with the conceptual skills to evaluate what it means for management and business to act responsibly. While these tasks are a challenge at the best of times, they are becoming increasingly more difficult as processes of globalization complicate the nature of corporate responsibilities and our ability to effect change. The basic argument of this paper is that in incorporating the analysis of globalization into management education, it is necessary to employ critical perspectives. The adoption of critical perspectives will be a key to enabling management education to meet the increased challenges of promoting responsible corporate behaviour in an age of globalization.

The paper proceeds in the following fashion. In the first section, an understanding of critical perspectives, in terms of Habermasian critical theory, is provided along with a brief discussion of the tension involved in employing critical theory analysis in management. As well, a distinction is introduced between three different forms of analysis—positive, normative and strategic. The second section then contrasts how mainstream and critical perspectives approach the positive analysis of globalization and suggests some implications for management education. The third and fourth sections follow a similar pattern, contrasting mainstream and critical approaches to normative and strategic analysis and drawing out the pedagogical implications for management education. In looking at the pedagogical implications, our focus is primarily at the level of curriculum content (including the need to incorporate more interdisciplinary perspectives), rather than pedagogical methods.

CRITICAL THEORY, GLOBALIZATION, AND RESPONSIBLE BUSINESS PRACTICES

In speaking of critical perspectives, our primary reference is critical theory. Critical theory has both a general and a specific referent. As a general term, critical theory refers to any form of social theory that is at the same time scientific, practical, normative, and self-reflective.[1] The scientific character of critical theory refers to rigor in its social science analysis. Its practical nature is comprised of the fact that its analysis of situations of oppression frees agents to address the sources of oppression. It is normative insofar as its analysis of oppression implies a normative critique of the existing situation. It is self-reflective to the extent that it provides an account of its own conditions of possibility and transformative effects. As such the term critical theory could be understood to apply to a range of thinkers and schools from Marx to the Frankfurt School and postmodernists.

The more specific referent of critical theory is the tradition of social theory frequently referred to as the Frankfurt School, the origins of which can be dated back to Max Horkheimer's assumption of the directorship of the

Institute for Social Research at the J. W. Goethe University in Frankfurt in 1930. The most prominent contemporary figure in this tradition is Jürgen Habermas. Habermas has developed the original project of the Frankfurt School in a variety of ways. *The Theory of Communicative Action* (1987), in which he reworks historical materialism on the basis of language, is his magnus opus and the foundation on which a variety of other works spin off. The most significant among the latter for our concerns are his theory of discourse ethics (1990; 1993) and his normative theory of law and politics (1996). In this chapter, I will primarily use the term critical perspectives to refer to the work of Habermas and other scholars whose perspectives are compatible with his general method and framework.

While critical theory, especially the work of Habermas, has been applied to management studies for at least a couple of decades (Mingers, 1992), there is some question as to whether there is a fundamental contradiction in undertaking such a project (Spaul, 1997). At issue is whether the tradition of critical theory, which historically has been hostile to capitalism, can be conjoined to a basic function (management), which is key to the perpetuation of that system. Elsewhere, I have argued that the more recent works of Habermas—including the theories of communicative action (1987), discourse ethics (1990, 1993), and law and politics (1996)—do allow for the *possibility* that a capitalist business system could be normatively justifiable (Reed, 1999a). This possibility for justification is based upon two basic conditions being met. The first is that a capitalist economy (with its hierarchical, non-participatory and inegalitarian structures) could somehow be viewed as representing a common good. The second is that capitalist business can be effectively brought under democratic control so that public policy decisions are determined on the basis of societal discourse (and not other forms of social power). While I have argued that these conditions can be met in principle, in practice there will always be a very strong tension. The basis of this tension lies in the fact that the normal workings of the capitalist system provide the economic (and political) elite with disproportional material and other resources. Access to such resources typically allows the economic (and political) elite to undermine the conditions mentioned above which provide for the legitimacy of the system. It is important to note here that this tension is structural in nature and inherent in the system. The actual degree of the tension at any one time reflects the nature of the actual historical structures in place, in particular the degree to which the structures are subject to "communicative" control or, alternatively, reflect influence exercised through other sources of social power (e.g., wealth, military, technological, kinship bonds, etc.).

Processes of globalization involve significant changes in the economic and political realms at both the national and international levels. Incorporating the analysis of these processes of change into management education is important insofar as they have altered the nature (and effects) of business practices, they have changed our understanding of what corporate responsibility entails and they have affected the prospects for promoting responsible business practices. Our understanding of how globalization may have effected such changes is largely determined by the types of analysis that we employ to investigate them. In what follows we will argue that mainstream analyses in different academic disciplines do not provide us with an adequate basis for understanding the full range of the causes and effects of globalization, the implications for corporate responsibility or what effective responses entail. The reasons for this include the tendencies of mainstream analyses to adopt forms of methodological individualism, to down play the role of power differentials in influencing public policy decisions, to assume the legitimacy of political and economic institutions, etc. Critical perspectives, by contrast, focus on the structural causes of change, highlight the role of power differentials in determining public policy, problematize the legitimacy of economic and political institutions, etc. Such characteristics better enable critical theory perspectives to understand, evaluate, and respond to processes of globalization as they relate to corporate responsibility.

In discussing the incorporation of the analysis of globalization into management education, there are a variety of approaches that one might take. Taking our cue from a Habermasian distinction between different forms of discourse, we have decided to organize our discussion around three basic forms of analysis, each of which tends to dominate different academic disciplines that are relevant to management education. These include positive analysis (social sciences), normative analysis (ethics, political philosophy) and strategic analysis (management, public policy). In examining each of these areas, we will contrast critical approaches with mainstream approaches and then draw the implications for management education.

GLOBALIZATION AND POSITIVE ANALYSIS

In using the term globalization in this paper, we are primarily concerned with processes of economic globalization (as opposed, for example, to the globalization of civil society) that involve the transnationalization of basic economic activities (viz., production, finance, marketing, etc.). Globalization, like all social science concepts, is open to contestation and may be conceptualized in different ways depending upon the intellectual traditions in which one is rooted. However, while a diversity of conceptualizations of "globalization" is possible, from the perspective of a (critical) socially responsible approach to management education, an adequate treatment of globalization must provide not only a description of the processes of globalization (with an eye to understanding how firms can maximize profits), but also some account of the causes of globalization and the full range of its effects. These latter aspects are essential for both an adequate normative evaluation of the acceptability of corporate practices and a better (strategic) understanding of how to promote more responsible business. In what follows, we will first indicate how globalization tends to receive a more circumscribed treatment in the business literature. We will then go on to show how some traditions of political economy tend to take a more critical approach to the analysis of globalization and discuss why such a perspective is important for management education.

Mainstream Approaches

The business literature (somewhat in contrast to the business ethics literature, discussed below) has long been interested in and influenced by processes of globalization (Dunning, 1993). In fact, one could easily argue that it has been processes of globalization that have determined the major conceptual shifts evident in business fields such as strategy over the last few decades. Grant (1995), for example, traces early shifts in this field—from "corporate planning" in the 1960s to "corporate strategy" in the 1970s—to those events commonly associated with the origins of "globalization" (viz., oil shocks, stagflation, increased competition from Japan, etc.). Subsequent shifts in the field (e.g., to the analysis of industry and competition and the quest for competitive advantage) can also be related back to processes of globalization, even if they were not always conceptualized as such when they were originally elaborated. Similar shifts in other fields such as marketing, finance can also be documented.

While the mainstream business literature is clearly interested in globalization, the nature of its analysis is informed by a positivist methodology, is generally limited to economics and managerial sciences, and includes the underlying normative assumption that the primary/exclusive concern of business is to maximize profits (with a correlative assumption that maximizing profits contributes to a larger societal good). As a result of these factors, most of the mainstream analysis tends only to problematize the response of firms to the changing global business environment. It does not problematize the effects of business decisions on stakeholder groups, either at the micro-level (e.g., how local communities are affected by the decisions of individual firms) or the macro-level (e.g., changes in unemployment levels, patterns of income distribution, etc.).

This is not to say that the business literature never addresses such issues as the role of the state, the potential social impact of business decisions, the environmental impact of business, etc. Clearly, many authors do address such issues (though some seem to abstract from them entirely). Porter (1990), for example, is well known as being a strong exponent on the notion that the state (and other extra-firm dynamics) can play a major role in promoting competitiveness in a global economy. Similarly, other leading figures in the field of strategy raise important questions about the traditional "imperialist" approach of business when entering developing markets (Prahalad and Lieberthal, 1998). The point, however, is that in raising these issues the focus of the authors is always on firms and how such stakeholder concerns impact profits. The emphasis is never on society, the state, the international order or the environment as objects worthy of consideration in themselves. The analysis only addresses the adverse effects of business on these entities to the degree that they can respond (or have an impact) in ways that affect the firm's bottom line.

The positivist assumptions and the underlying strategic concern with promoting profits also get reflected in the causal accounts that mainstream approaches provide of the emergence of "globalization." Typically, mainstream approaches do not concern themselves too much with such questions. To the extent that they do address them, it is argued that processes of transnationalization (in production, finance, marketing) have been largely induced by technological changes associated with the post-industrial revolution (e.g., in communications, transport, etc.) and innovations in organizational and financial theory and practice. The role of states is generally downplayed and/or viewed in a negative light—as overly bureaucratic (i.e., moving too slowly in response to objective conditions demanding change) and self-interested (e.g., engaging in "rent-seeking" behaviour). There is virtually no analysis of the role of business influence over public policy decisions (apart from their providing objective, technical advice). The (neo-liberal) form that globalization is taking is typically viewed as inevitable and irreversible.

Critical Approaches

In contrast to mainstream approaches, critical approaches to globalization, as exemplified in the international political economy (IPE) literature, are characterized by an interdisciplinary approach, attention to epistemological considerations and the incorporation of objectivist and subjectivist perspectives, including accounts of how structures shape and constrain the actions of individuals and organizations. From such critical perspectives economic globalization is understood as coming about as the result of a series of three interrelated structural changes that have occurred over the last few decades. These include a shift in production relations (from a Fordist to a post-Fordist model), changes in the form of state (from a Keynesian Welfare State to a Schumpeterian Workfare State) and changes in the international economy (from a Liberal International Order to a Neoliberal Global Order).

The *first* of the three areas of structural change can be conceptualized as a shift from a Fordist model to a post-Fordist model of accumulation (Lipietz, 1987). Cox (1994) explains this shift in accumulation strategy in terms of a distinction between core and peripheral aspects of the production process. Increasingly over the last couple of decades, large firms have been retaining only core aspects of the production process on a permanent basis (viz. research and development, finance, accounting, etc.), while contracting out other, more peripheral, aspects of the production process (e.g., production of component parts, maintenance, etc.). These changes in production relations are essentially designed to provide corporations with greater flexibility (which provides savings in terms of costs and advantages in capturing markets). While initially occurring within national boundaries (in Japan), the "outsourcing" of peripheral aspects of production has rapidly spread across borders. Accompanying the transnationalization of production has been a transnationalization of finance, marketing, etc. Firms can raise funds across borders with relative ease as international financial markets become increasingly integrated. Similarly, firms can develop global marketing plans based upon a standard set of products. While mainstream theorists incorporate the analysis of these changes, they do not link them to the other two processes of structural change. Nor do they adequately address the charges of critics (Korten, 1995; Mokhiber and Weisman, 1999) that (unregulated) processes of economic globalization have had a range of adverse social, political and economic effects.

The *second* area of structural change that helps to account for globalization involves the analysis of how states have been transformed in recent years. More specifically, countries around the globe have been "liberalizing" their economies and cutting back on social spending ever since the early 1980s and the Thatcher and Reagan "revolutions." These changes in the state, which were essential in facilitating the changes in production relations noted above, are conceptualized by Jessop (1994a) as a shift from a Keynesian Welfare State (KWS) to a Schumpeterian Workfare State (SWS). Jessop (1994b) argues that the KWS underwrote the social reproduction of Fordism through:

1. state management of aggregate demand;
2. competition policy, infrastructure development, transportation and housing policies;
3. the promotion of full employment and big business and;
4. the management of social problems and the promotion of mass consumption through welfare rights and social expenditures.

The key traits of the SWS, by contrast, include: 1) economic policy focused on the promotion of innovation driven structural competitiveness and; 2) social policy designed to enhance business flexibility and competitiveness in a global economy (rather than promote redistribution with the nation-state) (Jessop, 1993). Again, critical perspectives on globalization argue that these changes in the form of state have had adverse social and economic effects on significant sectors of society (especially the most vulnerable) as well as the democratic political process. Moreover, they argue, this shift in the form of state did not just happen as the logical result of public discourse and a commonly agreed upon objective analysis of the plight of the economy. Rather, it occurred as part of a conscious, well-financed and highly organized (and non-democratic) political strategy initiated by business leaders (and sympathetic politicians) in the largest, developed countries of the world (Cox, 1987; 1994).

Shifts in production relations and the changes in states that facilitated them are intimately tied up with a *third* area of change, viz., the international economy. Two aspects of the international economy are of particular importance for our concerns, viz., multilateral economic agreements and international financial institutions. Over the last two decades, as individual countries have liberalized their economies, a range of multilateral economic agreements (e.g., NAFTA, the Uruguay round of GATT, etc.) have been agreed to. These agreements not only allow for increased flows of capital and goods across borders, but also put in place provisions that severely limit the ability of subsequent governments to (re)impose restrictions. These agreements, of course, have been essential in promoting the transnationalization of post-Fordist production. They have also served as vehicles to encourage reluctant states in the developed world to introduce programs of economic liberalization. Again, the impetus for such agreements came primarily from big business in the dominant economic powers and operated through national governments as well as unofficial multilateral organizations (e.g., the Trilateral Commission, the Bilderberg Conferences, the Mont Pelerin Society, etc.) and official bodies (viz., the OECD, the G-7), etc. Critical perspectives argue that the dominant influence of business in these processes is reflected in the fact that non-business and non-trade agreements do not get institutionalized in the same ways. In the case of NAFTA, for example, environmental and labor issues were addressed through side deals that cannot be effectively enforced (Cox, 1987; 1994).

Pedagogical Implications

Critical approaches to globalization make important points with respect to both the causes and effects of globalization that are not addressed by mainstream theories. First, with respect to the causes of globalization, they note that the present form of economic globalization:

1. was not just the logical conclusion of a process of economic development based up technological advances, but;
2. came about as the result of concerted organizational efforts undertaken by large corporations to influence political policy on the basis of their material resources and political connections, and;

3. represents only one of different possible forms of what a global economy might look like.

Second, with respect to their effects, critical perspectives argue that processes of economic globalization:

1. have greatly reduced the policy autonomy of individual states around the globe,
2. have resulted in a dramatic shift in power between firms and states (with corporations in many instances virtually negotiating with states on an equal footing);
3. have resulted in a significant redistribution of wealth in favor of the rich within and across countries around the globe, and;
4. while inducing increased competition in some markets in the short run, may have laid the foundations for global oligopolies to dominant key markets around the world in the medium to long run.

These points of analysis have far ranging implications both for the normative analysis of management responsibilities and the understanding of how fulfilling such responsibilities can be effectively achieved (discussed below). A major pedagogical implication, therefore, is that critical analysis of processes of globalization (which highlight structural analysis) must be incorporated more systematically into management education. Without such a foundation, future managers will be ill-equipped to understand the context in which they are operating, unable to determine the nature of their responsibilities and incapable of effective response.

How such critical perspectives of globalization are to be incorporated in management education is an open question. A variety of possibilities exist, including inclusion in: 1) courses in individual management fields; 2) core management courses, and; 3) courses in other faculties/departments. Somewhat tellingly, however, processes of globalization are themselves undermining the prospects for incorporating critical perspectives into management studies.

Processes of globalization are extending the influence of business over universities and leading (post-secondary) education to be increasingly viewed as just another "commodity." One way increased business influence operates is through government cuts to education budgets (leading universities to turn to the private sector for funds) and the reapportioning of budgets to favour the sciences and professions over the liberal arts. Government also actively encourages universities to turn to the private sector by linking funding (e.g., for capital projects, research, etc.) to matching funds from the private sector. Moreover, in countries like Canada, governments are beginning to allow for-profit universities to operate which, as little more than glorified trade schools, focus on professional programs and do not have any liberal arts programs. The net effect of all these changes is to decrease societal perceptions of the importance of the liberal arts, to increasingly delink professional programs from the liberal arts and to eliminate critical perspectives, including any alternative (non-neoliberal) conceptions of what business and society might be (Slaughter and Leslie, 1997; Slaughter, 1998; Smith, 1999; Tudiver, 1999).

GLOBALIZATION AND NORMATIVE ANALYSIS

Globalization and associated processes of economic liberalization have created new opportunities for businesses literally around the world. Globalization also raises many questions about the obligations of business. An adequate understanding of the nature of corporate responsibilities in a global economy requires a critical perspective. Historically, the field of business ethics, including the newly emerging sub-field of international business ethics, has not been a particularly critical discipline. Nor has the field been quick to incorporate the analysis of globalization, or economic analysis generally (Enderle, 1996). Indeed, leading figures in the field are only just beginning to acknowledge that globalization is raising important theoretical and practical challenges (Boatright, 2000). In what follows, we will first discuss the non-critical nature of (international) business ethics, examine the challenges that globalization poses and indicate how mainstream approaches have not (yet) met these challenges. We will then go on to discuss the advantages of critical theory approach and some implications for management education.

Mainstream Approaches

Concern about how transnational corporations should operate has generated a lot of academic discussion over the past few decades across a range of academic disciplines, e.g., political science, theology, etc. The field of business ethics has also demonstrated some significant level of interest in the activities of transnational corporations. Most of this interest has (and continues) to take the form of case studies or the analysis of individual issues. There has been relatively little systematic attention focused on normative theoretic issues as they relate to international business or transnational corporations. There are, of course, obvious exceptions to this rather general statement. Two of the most notable are Donaldson's (1989) *The Ethics of International Business* and de George's (1993) *Competing with Integrity in International Business*. In what follows, I will draw upon these works to illustrate the non-critical nature of mainstream approaches to (international) business and their failure to address the challenges raised by processes of economic globalization. This critique will be organized around three basic tasks of ethics, viz., the delineation of norms, justification, and application.

Norms

One key task of any theory of ethics is to delineate the norms by which the various concerns of the field can be evaluated. A critically elaborated theory will provide a comprehensive list (at least in terms of the categories if not all the actual possible norms), which is grounded in some form of compelling logic (for why the norms listed are listed and others are not). In his work on international ethics, Donaldson proposes that international business ethics should revolve around respect for ten international human rights. His position is problematic in several ways. First, there is no clear reason why the rights that Donaldson chooses should be the ten basic rights to be respected. (Indeed, many would clearly object that the right to property is not a fundamental human right.) Second, and more anomalous for a theory of international *business* ethics, as Velasquez (1995) has pointed out, is the fact that in limiting his criteria to "human rights," Donaldson essentially abstracts from the analysis of business activities as business activities. He is, in effect, operating in the field of international human rights rather than international business ethics. While human rights are important and valid criteria for business ethics to employ, they clearly do not constitute the complete range of criteria that (international) business ethics needs. They tell us nothing, for example, about how we are to evaluate a range of questionable practices (e.g., the manipulation of transfer prices, tax evasion, etc.) that cannot be readily conceived as human rights violations. For his part, de George provides us with seven ethical principles. While most of these principles are relatively uncontroversial, there is no clear basis for the selection of these principles (and the exclusion of others). Also, the level of generality of these principles (e.g., produce more harm than good for the host country) leaves them open to a range of interpretations (and the obvious question of who determines, for example, what constitutes a balance of good over harm). While de George tries to further specify some of the implications of the general principles, we are given no compelling reasons why we should favour his interpretations over others.

One of the key normative theoretic challenges that globalization poses to the field of international business ethics, as Velasquez (2000) points out, is the tension between particular and universal norms. While there is no logical contradiction between the existence of particular norms and universal norms (though some theorists would clearly deny the existence of universal norms), conflicts do exist with respect to which norms can be considered universal and which merely particular. At issue is how we can provide a theoretical account and categorization of particular vis-à-vis universal norms. Neither Donaldson nor de George offers much guidance here. While Donaldson upholds universal norms,[2] the closest he comes to discussing the universal-particular divide is a distinction between minimal duties ("a duty of which the persistent failure to observe would deprive the corporation of its moral right to exist") and maximal duties ("whose fulfillment would be praiseworthy but not absolutely mandatory"). Instead of providing a theoretical account of this distinction, which does not really address the universal-particular divide, Donaldson offers only a few examples. For his part, de George accepts Donaldson's notion that firms may have responsibilities that go beyond moral minimums. He also believes that corporate responsibilities can change with circumstances (e.g., when operating in developing countries), especially due to a lack of background institutions. These are questions of application, however. He, like Donaldson, fails to really take up (let alone provide a theoretical account of) the distinction between universal and particular obligations.

Another key normative challenge that globalization confronts us with is the elaboration of criteria to evaluate the operation of international organizations, treaties, practices, etc., which enable and regulate transnational business practices. Again, our authors have little to say on this matter. While de George assigns great importance to (the lack of) background institutions, and strongly advocates that corporations assist governments in promoting them, he has little to say on the criteria for developing such institutions (apart from offering a lukewarm endorsement of the form of current arrangements on pragmatic grounds). A failure to address the nature of international political and economic institutions is problematic from the perspective of critical perspectives for the following reason. The regulation of international relations is primarily carried out on the basis of "international law." International law, however, has to a large extent been determined by historical power struggles in which political (and economic) elites in nation states have agreed to a *modus vivendi* based upon two basic principles, respect for sovereignty and non-interference in the domestic affairs of other states (McCleary, 1992). Historically, international law has served to provide a veneer of legitimacy to many clearly illegitimately regimes and enabled the larger powers in the world to dominate international relations on the basis of military and economic might. Because international law (and the regulation of international business) is not founded on the basis of democratic principles and institutions, this creates serious legitimacy problems for all international business (especially activities involving less than fully democratic governments). This is not a new problem, but it is one that is exacerbated by globalization in two basic ways. On the one hand, the sheer number of international transactions is increasing. On the other hand, the ability of citizens of nation states to determine their own future (and impose conditions on how corporations do business in their countries) is being undermined. This is happening because processes of globalization have served to increase the power of corporations vis-à-vis national governments and undercut the policy autonomy of national governments through international economic agreements, (structural adjustment) conditions imposed by international economic institutions, the perceived need to attract foreign capital, etc. Under these circumstances, it is incumbent on international business ethics to develop/employ norms (in the form of a normative political theory and a normative theory of international relations) for the evaluation of international economic and political organizations.

Justification

Any critical theory of ethics needs a justification program that provides a compelling explanation of why the norms advocated (and not others) should be accepted. Donaldson attempts to ground his international ethics in the tradition of contract theory. The basic problem that afflicts his approach (and contract theory generally) is that he does not provide a critical account of the conditions necessary for a contract to be valid (e.g., conditions than can ensure that coercion is not involved). For his part, de George provides no justification at all for the seven rules that he proposes (apart from a statement that "one can derive or defend them from a variety of high-level principles"). Again, the problem of justification is not new. The problem, however, takes on increased significance, as Hartman (2000) points out, in a globalized world. With increased intercultural interaction, the need for a firm meta-ethical foundation (especially for norms which we wish to uphold as universal) increases because it is less possible to rely on background assumptions that are relatively uncontroversial in given cultures (as cross-cultural interactions make them increasingly controversial). Similarly, the increased power of corporations in the global economy makes justification programs more important so that norms regulating international business do not reflect the increasing economic might and political influence of corporations.

Application

A general task of ethics is to determine how norms are to be applied in different contexts and under different circumstances. Again, while this task is not specific to the context of globalization, processes of globalization have made this task much more salient. Both Donaldson and de George take up the question of application, but not in critical ways. Donaldson, for example, in relationship to the question of whether corporations should be involved in countries that do not respect human rights, proposes a "condition of business" principle which states that firms are not required to abstain from doing business in countries that have violated human rights, but only those that are systematic violators of the most fundamental human rights. Even then it may be permissible to engage in business, provided one's business practices serve to discourage the violation of rights and do not benefit the government. What Donaldson fails to provide here are important indicators (e.g., what constitutes a lack of political participation, what constitutes helping an illegitimate government), a justification for such indicators and an indication of who is to determine whether the actual situation conforms to the indicators (e.g., the corporation, the corporation's home government or the people most directly affected). It is interesting (and perhaps telling) that Donaldson (and many people in the field of business ethics) took up the high-profile case of South Africa, but did not address, say, the situation of gulf states like Saudi Arabia (where the activities of corporations clearly do help non-legitimate governments that consistently violate fundamental human rights such as the right to political participation). For his part, de George examines the manner in which corporations operating in different fields (e.g., banking, resource extraction, manufacturing), should operate in developing countries especially in the light of inadequate background institutions. Like Donaldson, however, there is a failure to provide effective indicators (both of what effective background institutions are and how corporations should perform in their absence) or address the question of the role of the local population in decision-making processes affecting them. Neither Donaldson nor de George takes up the question of how processes of globalization are affecting the application of norms to particular contexts.

Critical Approaches

Critical management theorists have not paid as much attention to business ethics as they have to the more traditional management sciences. There is, however, an obvious basis for developing a systematic critical theory approach to business ethics that is compatible with the concerns of critical management studies. This obvious basis is Habermas' work on discourse ethics (1990; 1993) and law and politics (1996), both of which are firmly rooted in his theory of communicative action (1987). Habermas' theory of communicative action, in line with the linguistic turn in philosophy in the twentieth century, looks to language as a basis for investigating fundamental questions of epistemology. The particular approach that Habermas takes to the analysis of language is to focus on its performative aspect. In this context, Habermas views the "speech act" (in which we make contestable claims) as the fundamental unit of speech. Habermas distinguishes a range of different types of speech acts (e.g., aesthetic, pragmatic, ethical, moral, etc.) in which different types of claims are made (e.g., truth, beauty, effectiveness, goodness, correctness, etc.). His basic argument is that we can come to knowledge through a process (discourse) in which contestable claims are problematized. Meanwhile, his distinction between different forms of speech acts (and discourse) allows him to argue that there are different types of knowledge and that some of these types may be universal in nature while others are more limited.

Norms

One of the critical aspects of a critical theory approach to ethics is that it allows for a more systematic (less ad hoc) approach to the generation of norms. The key to this is the distinction between different types of practical discourses (ethical, moral, and pragmatic) and the distinction between what might be referred to as three realms of normativity (ethics, morality, and legitimacy). For Habermas, ethical norms relate to our (individual and communal) substantial conceptions of the good life, moral norms entail discursively agreed upon (universal) principles, while norms of legitimacy are constituted by the conditions necessary for the generation of legitimate law (the principles of the constitutional state and the system of rights). Corporate obligations in each of these three realms can be further specified. I have argued elsewhere that in the case of morality and ethics, this can be done through a slight adaptation to the use of immanent critique (Reed, 1999b). Immanent critique is a process through which theories are examined for internal consistency. In the case of morality, for example, we adapt this process by drawing upon standard economic theories (e.g., the neo-classical theory of general equilibrium) that develop arguments that the capitalist business system can represent a common good (i.e., everyone could agree to it) and then tease out normative criteria by which we can evaluate a full range of business practices. Such basic criteria would include whether or not firms generate profits on the basis of innovation (as opposed to limiting markets), whether firms discriminate against different groups of employees in hiring and promotion, whether hierarchical organization within firms contributes to efficiency, whether firms generate (negative) externalities, etc.

One of the problems that globalization poses, as we noted above, is the tension between universal and particular norms. Critical theory addresses this problem through its distinction between different types of discourse, most notably, between ethical and moral discourses. As we previously noted, ethical norms relate to our (individual and communal) substantial conceptions of the good life. Because such conceptions of goodness are inevitably related to the way that we have been socialized and the particular context(s) in which we have been raised, ethical norms are inevitably particular. Obligations relating to these norms are assumed by agents through their own actions and relationships to others. Critical theory then allows us to understand particular obligations as based upon specific (implied or explicit) conceptions of the good life and the particular relationships which corporation have developed with particular stakeholder groups. This is not to say that there cannot be rational discourse and agreement about them, but only that the scope of such agreements will be limited by the condition of common background or lifeworld (*Lebenswelt*) presuppositions. By contrast, Habermas argues that moral discourses, in which claims of procedural fairness are thematized, can result in universal norms. What allows for such universal norms is the fact that there is a universal logic inherent in language to which, as participants in discourse, we all have access. As such, then, moral norms necessarily reflect a (procedural) common good, for otherwise participants in the discourse would not agree to the norms. In this way, then, critical theory provides not only a clear distinction between universal and particular norms, but a theoretical account of the basis for the distinction and the conditions under which such norms can be upheld as valid.

A second problem that globalization raises is the need for norms to evaluate international economic and political institutions. Elsewhere we have argued how Habermas' normative theory of law and politics, which is again grounded in his theory of communicative action, can be directly incorporated into the analysis of business-state relations (Reed, 1999a). Characteristic of this theory is the emphasis on the importance of public discourse as the basis for the legitimacy of law. On this foundation, Habermas lays out the criteria under which citizens could be guaranteed the effective opportunity to actively engage in public discourse (viz., private autonomy rights, public autonomy rights and some minimal welfare rights) and the institutional criteria (viz., the principles of the constitutional state) under which such public discourses could effectively filter up through the formal political process and provide the basis for legitimate law. The practical implications of this theory for business-state relations would be a dramatic curtailing of the attempts of business to affect public policy through lobbying and other forms of influence. While Habermas has not expended as much energy in examining international space, he does argue that the same basic principles hold. Institutionally, Habermas (1999) would tend to see (a given conception of) the European Union and the European Parliament (rather than the Bretton Woods system and the UN) as the best model for understanding how international economic and political relations should be regulated.

Justification

As was mentioned above, the problem of justification is one that historically has not received much attention in business ethics. While the issue is beginning to be raised more in the context of globalization (Hartman, 2000; Velasquez, 2000), this has primarily been by way of allusion to the difficulty of the problem rather than providing constructive suggestions. The advantage of a critical theory approach is that it has a strong justification program that upholds the possibility of universal norms. Moreover, this justification program is not rooted in controversial (non-demonstrable or non-falsifiable) metaphysical premises, but rather in a theory of language that claims to admit of the possibility of falsifiability.

Application

As noted above, a general task of ethics is to determine how norms are to be applied in different contexts and under different circumstances. In the international realm, two basic sets of circumstances arise. On the one hand we have (as Donaldson and de George rightly acknowledge) different levels of development, which may influence what appropriate standards are (e.g., for wages). On the other hand, as de George highlights, there is also often a lack of background (political and economic) institutions. In principle, if there were appropriate (legitimate and capable) political institutions in place, they could determine (on the basis of societal discourse) appropriate standards for corporate activities. In the absence of such institutions, then corporations take on greater responsibilities, either for determining what appropriate standards are or (in the case of extremely illegitimate governments) determining whether they should operate in the country at all. A key question, however, is how corporations are to determine this. A critical perspective demands that this be done in a way that reflects the will of the local community for they alone can provide corporations with a sanction to operate in the absence of a legitimate government. Processes of economic globalization complicate this situation in a practical way, especially for corporations operating in developing countries, by encouraging a worldwide "race to the bottom." This means that even when apparently legitimate governments exist, they cannot establish appropriate standards. Under conditions of globalization, fair standards can only be effectively established through the generation of legitimate (discursively-determined) international standards. As a result, in a globalized economy without democratic controls virtually all official standards in developing countries must be treated with suspicion and corporations need to engage directly with local communities to determine appropriate standards.

Pedagogical Implications

Clearly one of the implications of a more critical approach is the need for courses and books in business ethics to move beyond what has become a standard model of presenting three approaches to normative theory (virtue theory, deontology and utilitarianism) and to incorporate more critical perspectives. While the literature in the field is beginning to move beyond this "holy trinity," very few of the pedagogical materials (at least in the English-speaking world) have. In addition, much greater attention clearly needs to be given to the question of how positions are justified (or not) so that students (and future managers) are able to critically evaluate which norms they should be applying in given situations. An important implication of globalization is that business ethics courses need to move beyond ethical theory (narrowly understood) and incorporate normative political theory (including issues of international relations). In a global economy it is not possible to address the fairness of international business practices without evaluating the legitimacy and fairness of the political and economic institutions and policies that determine the context in which business is conducted and regulated. In addition, in a global economy in which business as a whole is (arguably) the primary beneficiary of a lack of adequate background institutions, questions of application need to be expanded beyond the responsibilities of individual managers and firms to the possible collective responsibilities of business. This would include issues of whether industries should set standards for firms in their sector and/or make specific recommendations (e.g., not operating in non-democratic countries). It is, of course, extremely difficult to incorporate all of these suggestions into a standard, one semester course in business ethics, so a final implication of the need for more critical perspectives is that more time needs to be found in the curriculum for business ethics. Ideally, this should probably involve both more time for standard business ethics courses as well as an integrated approach in which normative issues are addressed in the various field of management education.

GLOBALIZATION AND STRATEGIC ANALYSIS

Globalization poses new challenges to promoting responsible corporate behaviour. Understanding what is involved in responding effectively to such challenges requires an investigation of two fields that are primarily concerned with strategic analysis, management and public policy. In what follows we will first give an account of the inadequacy of mainstream approaches to management and public policy for promoting responsible corporate behaviour. We will then go on to examine the possible contributions of critical management perspectives and how these need to be supplemented by a critical approach to public policy (broadly understood). We will then investigate the implications for management education.

Mainstream Approaches

In addressing the strategic question of how firms can be most effectively encouraged to be socially responsible, it is important to look at both the level of firms and industries and the level of public policy. At the firm level, there are a variety of methods and tools that have been developed over the last couple of decades by firms and industries, e.g., corporate codes, social and environmental accounting, etc. While such methods are generally highly publicized by corporations that adopt them, there is significant reason to question whether they are having any significant impact in effecting corporate behaviour (Frankental, 2001). A lack of significant impact could be due to either of two basic reasons. On the one hand, it might be argued that typically business does not take normative considerations into account (Ulrich and Thielemann, 1992) and that such methods are never intended to serve more than public relations functions. To the extent that this is the case, then the problem is largely one of moral formation and how one can inculcate more responsible attitudes, especially among senior management. Such an investigation is beyond the scope of our present concerns.

On the other hand, however, it could be the case that these initiatives clash with the broader environment of corporations, including their employment of mainstream approaches to management. Historically, up until the 1970s all of the management sciences were dominated by "hard" (or positivist) approaches. Typical of such hard approaches, in the area of systems thinking for example, was RAND system analysis and Jenkin's Systems Engineering. While such hard approaches have come under harsh critique (e.g., in terms of their positivist conception of enquiry and intervention, and realist epistemology), they still continue to operate. Such approaches do not readily allow for the inclusion of outside standards and goals. If these goals and standards are not effectively integrated into the incentive structures within the firm, however, then they are unlikely to be respected. What can typically happen then is that firms can formally adopt certain normative principles and values, but frustrate the prospects for their effective incorporation by employing traditional management practices.

If traditional management methodologies are incapable of effectively incorporating appropriate norms for the promotion of responsible corporate behaviour, then an alternative approach would be to incorporate incentives into the system through public policy, e.g., company law, regulatory agencies, etc. In principle, government regulation, properly enacted and enforced, allows society to uphold minimal standards while encouraging responsible action by well-motivated companies (by minimizing competitive disadvantages associated with being responsible) and discouraging irresponsible activities (through sanctions). It is sometimes argued that there is a price to pay for regulatory action—the two most common trade-offs cited being those between property rights of owners and socio-economic rights of other groups, on the one hand and those between growth and equity on the other. These trade-offs, however, can generally be justified from a normative perspective. Globalization processes, however, complicate the problem of regulating corporations to conform to justifiable standards. As discussed previously, processes of economic globalization involving programs of economic liberalization and deregulation have largely undermined the policy autonomy of states, including their ability to regulate corporate activities. Part of this lack of autonomy involves formal constraints in the form of international agreements (e.g., trade agreements), while part is based upon concerns about being globally competitive and the need to provide a favourable investment climate for business. In the US, this question has a previous life in the form of discussions around the Federal Corrupt Practices Act and the concern that such regulations put US firms at a competitive disadvantage vis-à-vis the firms of other nations.

In the face of impotent national governments, a public policy alternative to promoting more responsible corporate governance (and stemming an international "race to the bottom") might be international regulation through multilateral agreements. The potential of a multilateral approach however is undermined by the nature of the multilateral process. Multilateral agreements typically take the form of conventions or protocols (e.g., the Vienna convention, the Montreal Protocol). The general practice in developing such measures is that national governments come to agreement on a proposed pact, generally under the auspices of a multilateral body (e.g., UNCEP). This pact must then be ratified by a set number of national legislatures before it can come into effect. There are several obvious weaknesses in this system. First, the system is based upon norms of international law (and constitutes a bargaining process) rather than being rooted in a notion of political democracy (and involving processes of public discourse). As a result the interests that get represented in the bargaining processes are not necessarily those of a majority of the population (but rather the interests of a small elite—even in formally democratic countries). Second, individual countries cannot be forced to take part in negotiations concerning the pact or to ratify the pact (e.g., Norway and Japan have not ratified the international ban on whaling). Third, if they do not ratify agreements, countries are under no obligation to comply with its standards (e.g., Norway and Japan continue to whale). Fourth, even in instances when countries do ratify a pact, enforcement measures tend to be very weak or non-existent. (It has only been in the area of trade relations, where governments have agreed to strong enforcement measures, including the use of domestic courts to sue offending parties). As a result of these characteristics of the international state system, typically: 1) it takes a long time to reach agreements; 2) agreements are generally reactive rather than proactive; 3) tremendous (often irreparable) damage is done before agreements are reached; 4) agreements are reached only on issues where there is a consensus among the dominant economic countries (and the dominant business interests within them), and; 5) there is little or no effective enforcement. In an age of globalization, these characteristics of the international state system have not helped to limit an international race to the bottom, but rather have facilitated it in large part. NAFTA provides a prime example of the problem of multilateral regulation in an age of globalization in that it allows for enforcement of trade and investment related concerns, but not social, environmental and human rights concerns.

Critical Approaches

In the management sciences, there has been a growing movement, commonly known as critical management studies, that draws upon (Habermasian) critical theory. The first efforts to incorporate the work of Habermas into the field of management go back to the early 1980s (Mingers, 1992). The incorporation of critical theory perspectives was undertaken largely in response to methodological issues in the management sciences, in particular, issues of compatibility of different methodological approaches and the prospects for developing a complete managerial problem-solving framework. Particularly prominent among the proponents of critical thinking early on were theorists in the area of systems thinking. In early 1980s, for example, Jackson and Keys (1984) drew upon Habermas' (1978) earlier work, *Knowledge and Human Interest*, to try and address the problem of methodological pluralism. The result was the first metatheoretical framework—the system of system methodologies (SOSM). Flood and Jackson (1991) would later go on to develop another influential method to assist in the choice of methods for particular situations—total systems intervention (TSI). In the early 1990s efforts were undertaken to set out a comprehensive research plan for applying Habermasian critical theory across the entire range of management disciplines (Alvesson and Willmott, 1992a). Another significant development in the field related to developments in Habermas' own thought, most notably his theory of communicative action (1987) but also his normative theory (1990; 1993; 1996). This led to new understandings of how methodological pluralism was to be conceived, such as Mingers' "critical pluralism" (1997).

While critical theory was initially employed in management studies primarily as a response to methodological problems, its general critical orientation provides it with the potential to better incorporate concerns about corporate responsibility. Many critical management studies theorists initially expressed this potential in terms of Habermas' (1978) understanding of knowledge-constitutive interests, specifically an "emancipatory interest." The development in Habermas' thought noted above, however, called into question the adequacy of this approach. More recent work on multimethodology provides an alternative understanding for how critical approaches can better help the incorporation of normative concerns into management science. A case in point is Mingers' critical pluralism (1997).

Mingers conceptualizes his approach in terms of three interrelated notional systems. The first of these, the Problem Content System, draws upon Habermas' later work for:

1. an analytic distinction of different (social, personal, and material) worlds;
2. its basic categorization of normative theory and;
3. its epistemology (including an emphasis on the distorting effect that power relations play in the generation of knowledge).

The second notional system, the Intervention System, involves the analysis of agents and how they weave together different methods under different circumstances in order to intervene in particular problem situations. The third notional system, the Intellectual Resources System, provide a framework for integrating methodologies for intervention. Here Mingers combines the three different areas in which intervention can occur (i.e., personal, social and material) with four different phases of intervention to provide a conceptual framework for mapping interventions (see Table 1). While Mingers' primary concern is to explain how this conceptual framework can be employed to combine different methods (e.g., viable systems method, soft systems methodology, cognitive mapping, strategic choice, etc.), his problematization of the relationship between the three different notional systems, including his emphasis on questions of epistemology, agency and values (and the role of power relations in determining/ distorting these) provides an account of how appropriate norms can be critically generated and incorporated into the functional areas of management.

While critical management studies provide the prospect for more effective implementation of norms into the various functional areas of business,

TABLE 1
Linking Phases and Dimensions of an Intervention
(cf., Mingers, 1997)

	Appreciation of	Analysis of	Assessment of	Action to
Social	social practices, power relations	distortions, conflicts, interests	ways of altering existing structures	generate empowerment and enlightenment
Personal	individual beliefs, meanings, emotions	differing perceptions and personal rationality	alternative conceptualization and constructions	generate accommodation and consensus
Material	physical circumstances	underlying causal structure	alternative physical and structural arrangement	select and implement best alternatives

it is not without its limitations as a strategic approach. First, adoption of the approach does not guarantee successful implementation. It requires properly motivated and knowledgeable agents. Second, the successful operation of the system, when it does occur, involves "micro-emancipation" (Alvesson and Willmott, 1992b). Such micro-emancipatory benefits accrue primarily to those most closely associated with the firm (especially employees) and do relatively little to stem the questionable results of the system as a whole (especially the results emanating from processes of globalization including the international race to the bottom). Third, micro-emancipatory victories in organizations may not be unmixed blessings, for in addition to their positive micro-level benefits, they may also serve to reinforce, rather than oppose, larger (illegitimate) structures (Jackson, 1999). An example of this might be how the development of ethical codes by business is used to justify deregulation of business (and limits to their liability). Finally, there is the prospect that firms adopting critical management methods (especially to the degree that they seriously attempt to follow the implications laid out in Section III) may suffer from competitive disadvantages.

What all these limitations point to is the on-going need for regulation to promote responsible corporate activity. On the basis of our previous analysis, however, it would seem that the only viable (long-term) solution to regulation is some form of supranational regulation that is closely linked to democratic politics. The positive analysis above has indicated that with globalization there has been a tremendous shift in power between firms and states and with it an increasing lack of policy autonomy by nation states. The normative analysis has indicated the basic lack of legitimacy of the current interstate system (including international economic institutions and policies). The strategic analysis has argued that the national and international regulatory approaches to promoting more responsible corporate behavior are likely to be less effective than ever in a global economy. Under these circumstances, it would appear that the only possible way to effectively promote responsible corporate behavior in a global economy is to somehow develop institutions that allow for the globalization (and democratization) of the process of regulation (Habermas, 1999).

This suggestion, of course, will strike many as naïve at best and possibly even dangerous (not to mention morally repugnant). One argument that skeptics generally raise is the lack of precedence. In this case, they would be correct, but only partly. There clearly are no global organizations capable of regulating the global economy. There is, however, a set of institutions that is quasi-supranational in character that does to a large extent regulate a regional economy, viz., the European Union. The European Union is a unique and diverse organization that is rather difficult to categorize. Historically it has often functioned more like a multilateral organization insofar as individual countries have had effective veto-power of significant decisions. Recent changes, however, are moving the European

Union more in the direction of a supranational body by eliminating the veto power of individual countries. In addition, moves to increase the power and roles of the European Parliament are injecting a more direct (i.e., not mediated by national governments) form of democratic participation in the regulation of European affairs. The emergence of such developments in Europe indicates that the primary obstacles to developing supranational institutions are not organizational or technical. Rather, more critical perspectives would argue, they consist primarily of the vested interests of national political (and economic) elites around the world.

A second standard response by skeptics appeals to the concept of pragmatism. In this instance such an appeal can refer to at least two conceptually distinct claims. On the one hand, it may be asserting that attempts to develop such a supranational system are unlikely ever to be developed or work effectively. On the other hand, the claim could be that existing problems are so urgent (and resources so limited) that we need to focus our attention on existing approaches (viz., self-regulation, national regulation and multilateral regulation). Our role here is not to speculate on the probability of the emergence of a supranational regulatory system or to deny that there are urgent problems that need to be addressed in the short to medium run through the tools and institutions that we have at hand. However, if one starts from the goal of developing effective measures for promoting responsible corporate behavior, then in the long run the only likely prospect for success is the development of some form of democratic supranational control over corporations. Such a solution is not only pragmatic from the perspective of the global economy, it is also the only practical solution for addressing the situation of well-intentioned managers operating in a global economy. Only a democratically-grounded global system of regulation is capable of allowing managers to operate both effectively (with respect to their business goals) and in good conscience, for only such a system can ensure managers of the legitimacy of established norms while ensuring that they do not suffer significant competitive disadvantages by trying to be socially responsible.

Pedagogical Implications

Two basic implications arise from the analysis above. First, there is clearly a need to integrate more critical perspectives into management education. How critical perspectives can most effectively be introduced is an open question depending upon a wide variety of constraints. Ideally, one might hope that critical perspectives could be introduced across the full curriculum as part of a comparative approach to specific management fields (e.g., operations research, organizational behaviour, accounting, etc.). As there is an increasing body of critical literature in each of these fields, resources do not present a primary problem here, but clearly other factors might inhibit such a goal. A more limited approach might be the development of specific (core) courses that focus on critical perspectives. A recent example of this approach is a new course offered at Warwick (Mingers, 2000).

Second, there is a need for the incorporation of more public policy (broadly understood) into the curriculum. As government regulation largely determines the manner in which corporations compete, the promotion of responsible business cannot be separated from public policy. While managers are not the agents primarily responsible for public policy, they do need to understand how public policy enables or undermines the prospects for the promotion of responsible corporate behaviour. This is particularly true in a global economy where processes of globalization are undermining the prospects for effective government regulation. In such instances, managers, as managers, need to devise ways to enable corporations to compete in a socially responsible manner and, as citizens, need to contribute to the larger societal discourse of establishing effective regulatory systems.

CONCLUSION

Processes of economic globalization have had a tremendous impact over the last few decades not only on how business is conducted, but on virtually all aspects of our lives. They have also complicated the question of what corporate responsibility entails and how managers can most effectively respond. As a result, processes of globalization have also raised significant challenges for management education. If management education is to enable (future) managers to understand how to operate in a socially responsible way in a global economy, it must ensure that they have an adequate understanding of the full range of causes and effects of processes of economic globalization. This requires the incorporation of critical international political economy analysis into management education. The possibility of effective response also implies that managers know what corporate responsibility entails. Helping managers understanding corporate responsibilities in an age of globalization requires that management education incorporate critical approaches to international business ethics and normative political theory. Finally, effective response implies both a critical micro and macro level understanding of how to effect change in global economy. This means that management education needs to provide more critical management studies perspectives and integrate more public policy analysis. This is an ambitious agenda to set for management education. Nothing less, however, will adequately equip managers to confront the challenges they face in the 21st century.

NOTES

1. For the Frankfurt School, these four traits have more specific references. Their approach was "scientific" in terms of their commitment to undertaking a multidisciplinary research program which was directed at the formation of social theory which encompassed the social whole. The "self-reflexivity" of the tradition was rooted in its combining philosophical and social science analysis. It was most clearly expressed in its recognition of the social constitution of knowledge (especially as it is effected by the social relations of a capitalist society) and its use of immanent critique as a tool to address this problem. The "theory" of the Frankfurt School was "practical" in a particular sense that flowed from its self-reflexive stance. Horkheimer argued that, traditional theory, by failing to reflect upon its role in the process of social reproduction, contributed to the reproduction of oppressive structures. Critical theory, however, by engaging in immanent critique, was able to reveal rather than support structures of domination. Finally, critical theory was inherently normative in that its primary goal as theory was not the increase of knowledge for its own sake but rather the emancipation of society from oppressive structures (Horkheimer, 1972).

2. Donaldson, in his later work develops the notion of "hypernorms" to address the universal-particularist split. Again, this is not a critical approach as it relies on what is held to be an empirical consensus on norms, rather than a theoretical account of why these norms should apply to everyone.

REFERENCES

Alvesson, M., & and W., H., (Eds.). (1992a). *Critical management studies*. Newbury Park, CA: Sage Publications.

Alvesson, M., & W., H.. (1992b). On the Idea of Emancipation in Management and Organization Studies, *Academy of Management Review, 17*(3), 432-464.

Boatright, J. (2000). Globalization and the Ethics of Business, *Business Ethics Quarterly, 10*(1), 1-6.

Cox, R. (1987). *Production, power, and world order*. New York: Columbia University Press.

Cox, R. (1992). Multilateralism and world order, *Review of International Studies, 18*, 161-180.

Cox, R. (1994). Global Restructuring: Making Sense of the Changing International Political Economy. In R. Stubbs & G. R. D. Underhill (Eds.), *Political economy and the changing global order*. Toronto: McClelland & Steward.

DeGeorge, R. T. (1993). *Competing with integrity in international business*. New York: Oxford University Press.

Donaldson, T. (1989). *The ethics of international business*. New York: Oxford University Press.

Dunning, J. (1993). *The globalization of business*. NY: Routledge.

Enderle, G. (1995). Review of *Competing with Integrity in International Business*, by Richard de George, *Business Ethics Quarterly, 6*(1), 117-122.

Flood, R. L., and Jackson, M. C. (1991). *Creative problem solving: Total systems intervention.* Chichester: John Wiley & Sons.

Frankental, P. (2001). Corporate social responsibility—A PR invention? *Corporate Communications,* 6(1).

Grant, R. M, (1995). *Contemporary strategy analysis: Concepts, techniques, applications.* Cambridge, MA: Blackwell.

Habermas, J. (1987). *The theory of communicative action* (2 vols.). Boston: Beacon Hill

Habermas, J. (1990). *Moral consciousness and communicative action.* Cambridge: Polity Press.

Habermas, J. (1993). *Justification and application: Remarks on discourse ethics.* Cambridge, MA: MIT Press.

Habermas, J. (1996). *Between facts and norms: Contributions to a discourse theory of law and democracy.* Cambridge, MA: MIT Press.

Habermas, J. (1999). The European nation-state and the pressures of globalization, *New Left Review, 1/235*(May–June), 46–59.

Hartman, E. (2000). Socratic ethics and the challenge of globalization,*Business Ethics Quarterly, 10*(1), 211-220.

Jackson, M., & Keys, P. (1984). Towards a system of systems methodology,*Journal of the Operational Research Society, 35,* 473-486.

Jackson, N. (1999). Review of *Making sense of management,* by Mats Alvesson and Hugh Willmott, *Organization Studies, 20*(2), 347-351.

Jessop, B. (1993). Towards a Schumpetarian workfare state? Preliminary remarks on post-Fordist political economy, *Studies in Political Economy, 40,* 7-39.

Jessop, B. (1994a). The transition to post-Fordism and the Schumpeterian workfare state. In R, Burrows and B. Loader (Eds.), *Towards a post-Fordist welfare state.* London: Routledge.

Jessop, B. (1994b). Post-Fordism and the state. In A. Amin (Ed.),*Post-Fordism: A reader.* Oxford: Blackwell.

Korten, D. C. (1995). *When corporations rule the world.* San Francisco: Berrett-Koehler Publishers.

Lipietz, A. (1987). *Mirages and miracles : The crisis in global Fordism.* London: Verso.

McCleary, R. (1992). "Introduction." In R.McCleary (Ed.), *Seeking justice: Ethics and international affairs.* Boulder CO: Westview Press.

Mingers, J. (1992). "SSM and information systems: An overview,"*Systemist, 14,* 82-88.

Mingers, J. (1997). Towards critical pluralism. In J. Mingers and A. Gill (Eds.),*Multimethodology.* Chichester: Wiley.

Mingers, J. (2000). What is it to be critical? Teaching a critical approach to management undergraduates, *Management Learning, 31*(2), 219-238.

Mokhiber, R., & Weisman, R. (1999). *Corporate predators: The hunt for megaprofits and the attack on democracy.* Monroe, Maine: Common Courage Press.

Porter, M. E. (1990). *The competitive advantage of nations.* New York: Free Press.

Prahalad, C. K., & Lieberthal, K. (1998). The end of corporate imperialism,*Harvard Business Review, 76*(4, Jul/Aug), 68-77.

Reed, D. (1999a). Three Realms of Corporate responsibility: Distinguishing legitimacy, morality and ethics,*Journal of Business Ethics, 21*(1), 23-35.

Reed, D. (1999b). Stakeholder management theory: A critical theory perspective, *Business Ethics Quarterly, 9*(3), 453-484.

Slaughter, S. (1998). National higher education policies in a global economy. In J. Currie and J. Newson (Eds.), *Universities and globalization: Critical perspectives.* Thousand Oaks, CA: Sage Publications, 45-70.

Slaughter, S., & Leslie, L. L. (1997). *Academic capitalism: Politics, policies and the entrepreneurial university.* Baltimore: Johns Hopkins University Press.

Smith, D. G. (1999). Economic fundamentalism, globalization and the public remains of education, *Interchange, 30*(1), 93-117.

Spaul, M. (1997). Multimethodology and critical theory: an intersection of interests? In J. Mingers and A. Gill (Eds.), *Multimethodology.* Chichester: John Wiley & Sons.

Tudiver, N. (1999). *Universities for sale: Resisting corporate control over Canadian higher education.* Toronto: James Lorimer.

Ulrich, P., & Thielemann, U. (1992). *Wie denken Manager über Markt und Moral? Empirische Untersuchung unternehmensethischer Denkmuster von Führungskräften.* Berichte des Instituts für Wirtschaftsethik der Universität St. Gallen, Nr. 50.

Velasquez, M. (1995). International business ethics: The aluminum companies in Jamaica, *Business Ethics Quarterly, 5*(4), 865-882.

Velasquez, M. (2000). Globalization and the failure of ethics, *Business Ethics Quarterly, 10*(1), 343-352.